Shade Trees

[12—0]
Sugar Maple
(Acer saccharum)

[12—0a]
Thornless Honey Locust
(Gleditsia triacanthos inermis)

[12—0c]
Scarlet Oak
(Quercus coccinea)

[12—0b]
Chinese Pagoda Tree
(Sophora Japonica)

[12–1]
Spiraea Vanhouttei

NEW ILLUSTRATED ENCYCLOPEDIA OF GARDENING

UNABRIDGED

EDITED BY T. H. Everett

Assistant Director (Horticulture) and Curator of Education
The New York Botanical Garden

WITH CONTRIBUTIONS FROM

TWENTY HORTICULTURISTS AND AUTHORITIES IN THE UNITED STATES AND CANADA

Growers, Breeders, Exhibitors, Plantsmen, Writers, Lecturers, Professors, Editors and Superintendents of Famous Estates, who are Experts in all Fields of Horticulture, including Pests and Their Control.

VOLUME TWELVE—Sen-Ter

GREYSTONE PRESS • NEW YORK

Copyright © MCMLXIV By The GREYSTONE PRESS
100 Sixth Avenue
New York 13, New York
Library of Congress Catalog Card Number 60-7000
MANUFACTURED IN THE UNITED STATES OF AMERICA

In summer Senecio laxifolius bears large panicles of yellow, daisylike flowers.

A tender kind, of bold appearance, is S. Petasitis (Velvet Geranium, California Geranium). This native of southern Mexico has large, roundish, velvety, grayish-green leaves and bears great heads of bright yellow flowers atop 6-8-ft. stems. It grows well outdoors in climates such as that of southern California and may be grown in large, cool greenhouses elsewhere. This Senecio is propagated by cuttings which root readily in sand, vermiculite or other suitable medium. It should be pruned back after flowering.

Somewhat similar in appearance and requiring the same culture is the Mexican S. grandifolius. It differs from S. Petasitis in having much more flat-topped flower clusters and less rounded leaves.

A Choice Succulent. S. scaposus, a native of South Africa, is an interesting tender kind that is cultivated in greenhouse and window-garden collections of succulents. In mild, dry climates, such as that of southern California, it may be grown outdoors.

Senecio grandifolius, a tender shrubby kind from Mexico, forms flat-topped heads of yellow flowers.

S. scaposus is a low, shrubby plant that has regular rosettes of fleshy, rounded, linear leaves, 2-3 in. long, that are gray marbled with olive green. The young leaves are covered with a silvery cobweb of fine hairs. As the plants age they produce side branches. The flowers are carried 3-5 together at the tops of long stalks. They are daisylike and yellow, and each has about 12 ray florets.

This Senecio grows best in a very porous soil that contains some crushed limestone. A winter temperature of about 50 degrees suits it and at all times it should be exposed to full sun. It should be watered moderately from spring through fall, more sparingly in winter. Propagation is by means of seeds sown in porous sandy soil and by cuttings rooted in sand.

Two Tender Flowering Kinds. For blooming in the greenhouse (or outdoors in mild climates)

The Velvet Geranium, Senecio Petasitis, is a native of Mexico. Grown outdoors in California, it may also be cultivated in pots in greenhouses.

in spring, two rosy-purple-flowered kinds from South Africa are well worth growing. These are S. glastifolius and S. multibracteatus. The former is a perennial and may be propagated each year from cuttings; the latter is an annual and must be raised from seeds each year.

Except for the mode of increase, both require the same treatment and are rather similar in appearance. They are loosely branched and 2-3 ft. high. They have narrow, toothed leaves and large, loose, more or less flat-topped heads of bright magenta-purple, daisy-like flowers. These plants may be propagated from May to September.

Young specimens should be pinched when a few inches high to induce branching and again, occasionally, through their growing season for the same purpose. They thrive in any good potting soil and should be grown in full sun. When the plants have filled with roots the pots in which they are to bloom, they benefit greatly from weekly applications of dilute liquid fertilizer. Staking should be done carefully and the branches tied into place as the plants grow.

These Senecios thrive under the same conditions in the greenhouse that suit Chrysanthemums. A night temperature of 40-50 degrees is adequate.

Climbing Plants for Greenhouses. Senecio macroglossus (Cape Ivy) has evergreen, ivy-like leaves and lemon-yellow daisy-like flowers. S. mikanioides (German Ivy) has similar leaves, but bears clusters of small, rayless flowers. Both have twining stems and can be grown in a greenhouse with a minimum winter temperature of 45 degrees or in the window of a cool room. S. confusus, a Mexican climber, has thickish leaves and orange-red daisy-like flowers. It thrives best in a minimum temperature of 50-55 degrees.

These Senecios are planted in large, well-drained tubs or pots, and the shoots trained to wires or trellis fixed to the greenhouse wall or roof. A compost of loam and leaf mold is suitable. They should be shaded from the fierce rays of the sun in summer and freely ventilated on all favorable occasions. During the summer months they require abundance of water, but at other times it is only given when the soil is moderately dry.

The German Ivy, Senecio mikanioides, is a favorite window-garden plant.

S. tropaeolifolius is a climbing kind which has fleshy leaves, shaped like those of a Nasturtium (Tropaeolum), and yellow flowers. It grows from a tuber, needs exposure to full sun and should be watered with special care so that the soil is never excessively wet. A minimum winter temperature of 45-50 degrees suits it.

Climbing Senecios are propagated from cuttings in spring. Tips of the shoots, 2 in. in length, are taken off and inserted in small pots filled with sandy soil. The soil is moistened and the pots are covered with a bell jar until roots are formed. They are then potted singly in 3-in. pots. From these they are transferred to 5-in. pots when well rooted, and later on are set in large pots or tubs.

For Summer Bedding. S. Cineraria (Cineraria maritima) is a popular summer bedding plant. In mild climates this plant is hardy and forms a dense subshrub 1-2 ft. in height. It has large, lanceolate (lance-shaped), deeply divided silvery leaves and terminal clusters of cream or yellow daisy-like flowers. The flowers are not very important from a decorative point of view; the plant is grown primarily for the beauty of its foliage. A kind with even whiter leaves than this type is Senecio Cineraria variety Diamond. S. Cineraria is a native of the Mediterranean region. Both it and its variety are easily raised from seeds and cuttings. Both should be grown in full sun.

Somewhat similar in appearance to S. Cineraria, and often mistakenly named S. Cineraria variety candidissimus and Cineraria maritima variety candidissima, is the beautiful S. leucostachys, a native of the Argentine. It, too, is a tender, somewhat shrubby perennial, suitable for permanent outdoor cultivation in mild climates only, and excellent for summer bedding purposes elsewhere. S. leucostachys grows to a height of 1-2 ft., has whiter and more finely pinnate foliage than either S. Cineraria or its variety Diamond and loose heads of rayless, creamy yellow flowers. It is usually propagated by cuttings in the same manner as S. Cineraria but, like the latter, may also be increased by seeds. It should be grown in a sunny location.

When plants of these gray-leaved or white-leaved Senecios are raised from seeds it is necessary to sow them in well-drained pots or flats of sandy soil in February in order to have specimens big enough to set out in the flower beds or in porch or window boxes in May or June. The seedlings are transplanted 3 in. apart in well-drained flats containing rich, porous soil just as soon as they are big enough to handle easily. The young plants are kept growing in a warm, sunny greenhouse until 2-3 weeks before it is time to plant them outside, then the flats containing them are removed to a cold frame to give the plants a chance to harden off before they are transplanted outdoors.

When, for summer bedding, young plants are raised from cuttings shoots 4 in. in length are taken off in August or September, and inserted in a propagating bed of sand. They are set in a cold frame or greenhouse; they need careful attention, as they are very liable to decay at the sand surface level. Water should not be given until the sand is nearly dry, and the frame must be carefully ventilated to prevent too moist an atmosphere.

When rooted, they are potted separately in 4-in. pots, and sheltered in a frostproof greenhouse for the winter. At bedding time, in May or early June, they are planted as a ground cover, or an edging for taller plants, or used as

Senecio leucostachys is one of the most handsome of tender kinds. Here it is used effectively at the base of a rock wall.

Senecio Cineraria variety Diamond.

Senecio leucostachys is grown for its attractive gray-white foliage.

"dot" plants or set out in porch or window boxes.

As Foliage Pot Plants. Senecio Cineraria, its variety Diamond and S. leucostachys all are fine foliage plants for growing in pots in cool, sunny greenhouses and in sunny windows in cool rooms and sun porches. To have plants suitable for these purposes it is a good plan to dig up specimens of moderate size from the garden well before killing fall frosts and to pot them carefully in well-drained pots just large enough to hold the root balls without crowding. The soil used should be sandy and porous. After potting, the plants should be well watered and stood in a shaded coldframe or greenhouse.

Until the plants recover from the shock of being uprooted, which may take 3-4 weeks, the greenhouse or frame should be ventilated very sparingly and the atmosphere kept humid. Syringing the foliage lightly on sunny days is helpful during this period. When the plants have recovered and show signs of new growth, they may be gradually accustomed to exposure to sun and to free ventilation. They thrive in a minimum winter temperature of 40-50 degrees.

SENNA. Senna is obtained from the leaves and pods, and occasionally from the pulp of pods, of several kinds of Cassia.

SENNA, CAPE BLADDER. Sutherlandia frutescens, which see.

SENNA, SCORPION. Coronilla Emerus, which see.

SENSITIVE PLANT. A remarkable plant with fernlike leaves, of which the leaflets fold up at the slightest touch. It is dealt with under the heading of Mimosa.

SEPAL. The outer whorl of green or colored parts of a flower is called a calyx, and each segment of the calyx is a sepal.

SEQUOIA—*Redwood* (Sequo'ia). A magnificent evergreen, specimens of which are among the oldest and tallest known trees. Some Eucalyptus of Australia are said to rival it in height and its close relative Sequoiadendron attains greater age. Sequoia sempervirens is a native of the Pacific coast, where individual trees attain a very great height, sometimes upwards of 300 ft., one measurement of 364 ft. having been recorded. Trunk diameters, not girth, of 10-28 ft. have been recorded, and the age of these trees has been computed at 1,500-2,200 years, but whether this great age is correct it is difficult to say. On stumps of trees sawed down, 1,400-1,500 annual rings have been counted.

A thriving young tree of the Redwood, Sequoia sempervirens.

Sequoia belongs to the Taxodium family, Taxodiaceae, and the name is said to have been given in commemoration of Sequoyah, a renowned Cherokee half-breed who lived between 1770-1843, although other explanations of the derivation of the name have been given.

The Redwood or, as it is sometimes called, California Redwood, grows naturally over considerable acreage of humid coastal region in an area 450 miles long and 20 miles wide in northern California and southern Oregon. It does not grow far inland, nor out of the fog belt.

The bark of this noble conifer is thick, fibrous and reddish-brown; the branches even on old trees are comparatively small in diameter; the leaves are narrow and flattened, ¼-¾ in. long and about 1/10 in. wide, not scalelike as in the nearly related Sequoiadendron (Giant Sequoia or Big Tree). The cones are rounded and much smaller than those of Sequoiadendron, being from ¾ in. to rarely more than 1 in. long, ½-⅞ in. wide. They ripen during the second autumn after flowering. The seed wings are much narrower than in Sequoiadendron.

There are several varieties of S. sempervirens, of which the best is adpressa, sometimes called albo-spica. It makes a handsome tree, the tips of the shoots being cream-white. Other varieties are gracilis, glauca, pendula and taxifolia.

Propagation. Seeds form the best means of propagation, but these trees also grow well from cuttings. Cuttings are also commonly used to secure increase of the varieties, which, unlike the typical species, cannot be propagated from seeds.

Seeds can be sown in prepared beds out of doors in spring, in the same way as seeds of other conifers, but better results are obtained by sowing in a bed of sandy soil in a cold frame, or in flats of similar soil placed in a greenhouse or frame.

In a young state, plants of S. sempervirens are likely to be injured by cold winds, therefore some protection may be necessary. As soon as the seedlings are a few inches high they should be planted in an open border, and the main root may be cut through at that time to induce a greater number of fibrous roots.

Cuttings may be taken in summer of shoots starting from near the base of old trees, of shoots growing on the trunk, or even of side branches, although plants raised from the latter may need cutting back when well rooted, to induce an erect growth from the base. The cuttings may be 6-12 in. long; they should be inserted in a bed of sand or sand and peat moss in a warm propagating bed in a greenhouse or a cold frame. The former may take 2-3 months to root, the latter longer. The young plants must be kept in a cold frame over winter and planted out in spring.

In mild climates it is possible to root cuttings in a sheltered border out of doors; the cuttings should be 12-15 in. long and made of well-ripened wood. They may be inserted during winter or early spring and should be left undisturbed until the following autumn.

S. sempervirens is one of the few conifers that produce sprout shoots from trees that have been cut down; such shoots are of erect growth and excellent for cuttings. In a state of nature the tree often perpetuates itself by this means.

Sequoia is a tree for moist soil, humid atmosphere and sheltered places. It does not thrive in many places away from its native region, although small specimens may be found in Eastern gardens. The Sequoias give the best results where sheltered from wind, where there is considerable humus, and where the soil is deep and moist without being waterlogged. Moist climatic conditions are most suitable, and these trees do well in a mist-laden atmosphere. Atmospheric impurities are fatal to their well-being.

There is a critical time for S. sempervirens during its young days, for it is subject to injury from cold winds and the leading shoot may be killed. This may not only result in several new leaders being formed, but in a number of shoots appearing from about the base of the tree. This condition must be regulated by pruning.

As the trees advance in age they become hardier. They retain their branches to the ground line for many years, but large trees look far better when some of the lower branches are removed so as to expose the fine trunks covered with reddish-brown, fibrous bark; those branches should be removed gradually, the work being done during summer.

Economic Uses. The wood of S. sempervirens is light in weight, reddish in color and of very considerable importance for box-making, building purposes and other work. It lasts well when exposed to weather, withstanding atmospheric changes well. It is easy to work and can be obtained in very large boards free from knots. It is commonly called Coast Redwood and California Redwood. The bark is used as a medium in which to grow Orchids, as a mulch and for other purposes.

SEQUOIADENDRON—*Giant Sequoia, Big Tree* (Sequoiaden′dron). A close relative of Sequoia and by some botanists included in that genus. A member of the Taxodium family, Taxodiaceae. The name derives from Sequoia, and *dendron,* tree. There is only one species, Sequoiadendron giganteum. It perhaps attains the greatest maximum age of any known tree (see Taxodium mucronatum). Maximum age of some living specimens is estimated to be 3,500-4,000 years.

S. giganteum is the largest, but not the tallest (see Sequoia) evergreen tree known. It is a native of California and is found wild on the western slope of the Sierra Nevada, from Placer County to Tulare County, in groups or groves over an area of about 250 miles at altitudes of 4,300-8,000 ft. The most celebrated is the Calaveras Grove, which contains about 100 old and very fine trees, many of which are named after famous men. The tree was first discovered in 1833 and was rediscovered in 1852.

In a natural state the tree grows 150-320 ft. high, with a trunk 10-37 ft. in diameter.

Young trees are of formal pyramidal outline, and even those 70-80 years old are distinctly stiff in habit. The bark is reddish-brown and on old trees it may be 1-2 ft. thick. The thick bark has probably helped the trees in attaining their very great age, for it is not easily seriously damaged by forest fires. The branches are more or less pendulous, making the trees difficult to climb. Old trees may be without branches for two thirds of their height.

The leaves are small and scalelike, and are spirally arranged around the shoot. The male and female flowers appear on the same tree and the cones, which are 2-3½ in. long and 1½-2 in. wide, ripen during the second year. The seeds are very small and thin.

Varieties with Colored Leaves. Several well-marked varieties have been given descriptive names—argentea, with silver-variegated shoots and leaves; aurea, with golden leaves; glauca, with blue-green leaves; pendula, with curious weeping branches pressed close to the trunk; and pygmaea, of dwarf habit. All are more curious than beautiful.

In cultivation S. giganteum has proved hardier than Sequoia (Redwood) but, like its relative, it does not take kindly to conditions in the East. A 50-ft.-tall specimen grew at Rochester, New York, where the climate is moderated and humidified by the presence of a large nearby body of water, and smaller specimens are sometimes seen in eastern gardens. It requires the same general culture as Sequoia. S. giganteum does not renew itself by sucker growths from the stumps of cut-down trees as does the Redwood.

SERAPIAS—*Helleborine* (Serap'ias). A small group of terrestrial Orchids found wild in Europe, chiefly in the countries bordering the Mediterranean. The flowers are moderately large and few in number, on erect spikes. The sepals assume a somewhat tubular shape, often concealing the smaller petals, but allowing the large lip to project. The flowers are brownish or brownish-red, and usually appear about May. The name Serapias is derived from the Egyptian deity Serapis.

In very favored positions the plants will withstand winters where they are not excessively severe. These Orchids should have a sheltered position with a southwest aspect, and be planted in a well-drained mixture of loam, leaf mold and sand. They must be kept rather moist in summer and given a little protection in winter; or they may be potted and kept in a cold frame which is protected in severe weather in winter. The principal kinds are S. cordigera and S. Lingua.

SERENOA REPENS—*Saw Palmetto, Scrub Palmetto* (Sereno'a). A small and usually apparently stemless, fan-leaved Palm that occurs natively from South Carolina to Florida and Texas. It grows in great colonies, with the stems usually creeping but sometimes erect and several feet tall. A member of the Palm family, Palmaceae, this plant is of small horticultural importance and is only occasionally cultivated. Its name commemorates Sereno Watson, a distinguished American botanist of the last century.

The Saw Palmetto withstands more frost than most Palms but is not generally hardy north of Charleston, South Carolina. It thrives in any ordinary soil and may be propagated by seeds and division.

This plant takes readily to pot cultivation and may be grown in cool or temperate greenhouses and as a sunroom or porch plant. It thrives in patial shade, and is of slow growth.

SERISSA FOETIDA (Seris'sa). A shrub that grows about 2 ft. tall and is freely branched. It bears little evergreen leaves and attractive, small white flowers that are solitary or arranged in clusters. The plant is a native of southeastern Asia; its name is of Indian derivation. It belongs in the Madder family, Rubiaceae, and is the only member of its genus.

This attractive shrub may be grown outdoors in frost-free or nearly frost-free climates and is planted in gardens in the far South, where it succeeds under a variety of conditions and soils.

As a greenhouse plant and as a subject for growing in a cool sunroom or similar location, this shrub has much to commend it. It thrives in a well-drained, sandy peaty soil which should be kept always fairly moist but not waterlogged. A winter night temperature of 45-50 degrees is satisfactory with a 5-15 degree rise in the daytime permitted on favorable days. Full sun at all seasons is desirable.

Repotting, when needed, should receive attention in early spring, but, as Serissa foetida is a rather slow grower, this care will not ordinarily be required every year.

Little pruning is normally desirable; any that is needed to keep the plants shapely may be done as soon as the flowers have faded.

Applications of dilute liquid fertilizer to specimens that have filled their pots with roots may, with advantage, be given from spring through fall.

Cuttings form the readiest means of propagation. These, taken in summer or fall, root with great ease in a propagating bed filled with firmly packed sand, vermiculite, or sand and peat moss. As soon as the cuttings have formed roots an inch long, they should be potted individually in small pots in a mixture of two parts of sand, two parts of peat moss and one part of soil or loam. To induce a desirable branching habit, the young plants may be pinched when they have made an inch or so of new growth.

In addition to the plain green-leaved, single-flowered Serissa foetida there is a variety named variegata which has its leaves margined with yellow, and also a double-flowered variety, florepleno. The specific term foetida refers to the fact that the bark, when bruised, is ill-smelling.

SERPYLLIFOLIUS. A botanical term used to describe plants with thymelike foliage.

SERRATE. A botanical term describing leaves and other plant parts which have sharp, marginal teeth pointing upwards.

SERVICEBERRY. Amelanchier, which see.
SERVICE TREE. See Sorbus domestica.
SESBANIA GRANDIFLORA. See Agati grandiflora.
SESSILE. A botanical term used in describing leaves and some other plant parts which have no stalks, but arise directly on the stem of the plant.
SET. This word is generally used in describing tubers, or other similar propagative parts of plants, which are used for planting. Onion sets, for example, are small bulbs raised from seeds in summer and used for planting out of doors the following spring.

The word "set" is also used to describe the result of the successful fertilization of flowers in such phrases as "a good set of fruit," "a poor set of seed."

Set is also used as a verb meaning to plant, as in the phrase "to set out."

SETARIA (Setar'ia). A group of annual and perennial grasses, family Gramineae, that are mostly natives of the warmer parts of the world. The name is derived from *seta,* a bristle. One of these, S. italica, the Foxtail Millet, is of agricultural importance.

In gardens these plants are often known by the name Panicum. They differ from true Panicums in technical characters. (See also Panicum.)

Setaria palmifolia, Palm Grass, is planted as an ornament in gardens in the far South and is also grown as a decorative greenhouse plant. It is perennial, attains a height of about 6 ft. and has broad, grasslike leaves. The flower panicles are 2 ft. or so long but are interrupted rather than continuous. A variety with variegated, striped leaves occurs.

The Palm Grass grows well in any average soil. It needs a sunny position and may be propagated by seeds and by division.

A related kind, S. plicata, is often confused in gardens with S. palmifolia. It differs in having leaves about 8 in. long (those of S. palmifolia are 2 ft. long) and it has narrower flower panicles. It attains a height of 2-5 ft., and has broad leaves. It, too, is grown outdoors in the South.

When grown in greenhouses, S. palmifolia and S. plicata need a minimum winter temperature of 45 degrees. The preferred compost consists of equal parts of loam and leaf mold. Repotting is done in March, when the plants are taken out of their pots and divided into smaller portions. These are potted separately in smaller pots, and, when well rooted, are transferred to larger pots. They are watered carefully at first, but when they are well rooted the soil must be kept moist. During the winter, water is only given when the soil becomes quite dry.

SETCREASEA (Setcreas'ea). A group of tender, trailing or somewhat erect perennials that are natives of Mexico and the southwestern United States and closely resemble Tradescantia and Zebrina, to which they are closely related. They belong in the Spiderwort family, Commelinaceae. The name is of undisclosed origin.

Setcreasea purpurea.

Several kinds of Setcreasea are grown in greenhouses and as house plants but their identities are not always correctly determined and some of the plants so cultivated belong to the nearly related genus Callisia. Some have leaves prettily striped with silvery-white. In one named S. purpurea the foliage is a beautiful purple color. The three-petaled flowers, which are white, pink or purplish, last a short time only but open in succession over a long period.

The culture of Setcreasea is similar to that recommended for the tender kinds of Tradescantia and for Zebrina, which see.

Kinds. S. pallida, leaves waxy bright green, flowers lavender; S. purpurea (Purple Heart), foliage purple, flowers lavender-pink; S. striata, leaves green striped with white, flowers white. Following recent botanical investigation S. striata is now correctly named Callisia elegans.

SEVEN STARS. See Ariocarpus.

SEVERINIA BUXIFOLIA (Severin'ia). The only member of the genus Severinia. It belongs to the Rue family, Rutaceae, and is a native of southern China and Formosa. It was named in honor of M. A. Severino, an Italian professor.

This plant forms a shrub or small tree and may be used effectively as a hedge plant. It is grown in the far South and succeeds in any average garden soil. It may be propagated by seeds and by cuttings.

This shrub has evergreen, leathery foliage which somewhat resembles that of the common Boxwood. Its flowers are small and white and are borne singly or in small clusters.

SEVILLE ORANGE. The fruit of Citrus Aurantium, which see.

SEXUAL REPRODUCTION. The propagation or reproduction of plants as a result of the fertilization of a female element by a male element. Seeds and spores afford means of reproducing plants sexually. Sexual reproduction is in contrast to asexual or vegetative reproduction, which refers to the propagation of plants by means not involving two parents or the process of fertilization. Division, Cuttings, Grafting and Layering are methods of asexual reproduction.

SHADBLOW. Amelanchier, which see.
SHADBUSH. Amelanchier, which see.
SHADDOCK. See Citrus.

SHADE TREES

How to Select and Care for Them

Trees for shade should be planted only after thoughtful selection, for those that may be very suitable in June may be less so in August. The Linden and the Mulberry are delightful trees when they come into leaf, but in July and August the former may make everything near by

The trees spread their welcome shade over this fine expansive lawn.

dirty with dripping honeydew, and in August and September falling Mulberries stain almost everything with which they come in contact.

Moreover, on a hot day in summer, people may not question the kind of tree that gives them shade, but when shade is unnecessary they become critical if some common and uninteresting subject is standing in a conspicuous position on a lawn.

Old Apple trees such as this fine specimen serve splendidly as shade trees of moderate size. They have the special merit of blossoming beautifully each spring.

The Ginkgo is a tall tree that grows fairly rapidly and is seldom attacked by disease or pest.

Trees growing on lawns are not the only ones that have to be considered; the whole subject of trees for the sides of roads and streets

Tall Oaks here shade both front lawn and sidewalk.

must be taken into account, also field trees where shade and shelter are necessary for stock. Further, the trees that may be desirable for some locations and for some regions are undesirable for others.

Shade trees are also necessary for the successful cultivation of some kinds of plants. Many of the Rhododendrons, particularly those with large leaves, succeed better under the partial shade of Oak or Pine trees than when exposed to full sun. Ferns can also be more easily grown in moist ground beneath trees than in full sun, as well as certain kinds of Primulas, Liliums and other plants.

Selecting Shade Trees

Shade Trees for Planting on Lawns. When a garden is not large enough to allow of the inclusion of a number of trees, the selection of one or two is of great importance. When making a choice, the planter should try to visualize the trees at maturity. A particular tree may be excellent when half-grown, but be quite out of place when full size.

Thus trees of the largest size should not be planted in places where, at maturity, they are likely to endanger the safety of a house or other building, or to exclude light and air from rooms. Trees of the largest size should not be closer to buildings than their own average height at

The Moraine Honey Locust, a thornless and seedless variety of Gleditsia triacanthos, is a fine shade tree.

maturity. It is not wise to plant trees in places where they are likely to cause damage by falling branches when they have grown to a large size.

The Best Kind of Tree to Choose. A shade tree on a lawn should have many virtues. It should be a safe tree, or as safe a tree as it is possible to choose; that is to say, one that is not likely to shed heavy branches either on a calm day or during a storm. It should not be a kind that is likely to be struck by lightning, and should be capable of producing a distinct length of clean trunk 8-10 ft. high. The branches should be fairly wide spreading and droop to within a few feet or so of the ground, or, in the case of weeping trees, be just clear of the ground.

The great value of shade trees is that full advantage may be taken of the shady leaf surface without the inconvenience of low inside branches. Careful pruning during the early life of the tree will do much to assure the development of a tree of this type.

The shade the tree gives should not be so dense as to kill the grass beneath the branches. Conspicuously placed trees should be of good appearance from the time they come into leaf until autumn, or, in the case of evergreens, throughout the year; they must be hardy enough to withstand the greatest cold experienced in the place where they are planted. Moreover, they should not be unduly subject to insect attacks or to serious diseases.

The fastest-growing trees are not the best shade trees and only under very special circumstances should they be considered at all. Generally they have soft, brittle wood and weak crotches and are excessively liable to damage by storms; often they are extremely susceptible to diseases and pests. Some, notably Poplars and Willows, have far-reaching roots that are very likely to enter drains even at considerable distances from the tree, stop them up and cause serious damage. They may even harm foundation walls if these are not well constructed.

Among fast-growing trees to be generally avoided as shade trees are Box Elder, Catalpa, Poplars, Siberian Elm, Silver Maple, Tree of Heaven (Ailanthus) and Willows. Under very special circumstances some of these may be used,

The Tree of Heaven, Ailanthus altissima, grows very fast but is not considered to be a good shade tree, except for city gardens where other kinds cannot be expected to thrive.

but not if better trees can be expected to grow in the chosen location.

There are some situations where these fast-growing shade trees might be chosen. For example, in city gardens where growing conditions are extremely difficult, a Tree of Heaven is most likely to survive and thrive. In certain parts of the West where the choice of trees that will grow is extremely limited, a Box Elder may well be the best selection.

While very fast-growing trees are usually undesirable, there are many trees that make a good medium growth each year and are excellent for shade purposes, and there are a number of slower growth that are worth considering.

Not Good Risks. Several kinds of trees that have been used extensively in the past as shade trees are no longer considered good risks because of their susceptibility to diseases or pests which in recent years have become prevalent and for which, at present, there is no satisfactory control or none that is relatively easy to apply at a reasonable cost.

The American Elm is perhaps the best-known tree in this group. The spread of the devastating Dutch Elm disease and the great damage done to the Elm by the Elm Leaf Beetle are so serious that, fine tree though the American Elm is, it can no longer be recommended for general planting.

Certain Oaks are seriously affected by a Wilt disease that makes their planting hazardous in localities where this disease exists, or near places where this disease occurs. Before planting a new shade tree it is always wise to inquire of your State Agricultural Experiment Station whether there is any disease or pest prevalent in your section, or likely soon to spread to your locality, that may be extremely serious.

When selecting kinds of shade trees, consideration must be given to soil as well as to location. Acid-soil trees such as most Oaks will not thrive on alkaline soils, such as are found in many parts of the West, even though climatic factors may be favorable. Trees that grow naturally on moist soils usually will not grow well on dry soils, and trees that need porous, sandy or gravelly soils may resent a heavy clay soil.

Before deciding on the kind of shade tree to plant, it is wise to tour the neighborhood to determine which kinds are already thriving. It is wise, too, to consult a reliable nurseryman or informed gardener who knows trees and understands local conditions. Your State Agricultural Experiment Station will also be glad to help you in making your choice.

Nursery-grown trees are much easier to transplant than trees taken from the wild. This is because such trees have been transplanted frequently, which treatment results in the

Professional tree movers can transplant large trees such as this Plane tree.

Before a large tree is moved, it should be pruned to compensate for the unavoidable loss of some of the roots.

SHADE TREES

development of a compact mass of fibrous roots rather than the longer, more rambling roots of trees that have grown in one place without disturbance.

The size of tree to plant depends upon how quickly you require shade and what price you are prepared to pay. With the aid of modern equipment and techniques it is possible for experts to transplant successfully trees of huge size,

The tightly laced root ball is cut underneath to sever anchor roots.

The diameter of the root ball taken with a large tree should be ten or twelve times that of the trunk measured about 1 ft. above the soil surface.

Large trees may be moved short distances on stout platforms and skids.

After the ball is dug it is securely wrapped in stout burlap and laced with rope.

A row of Plane trees, transplanted the previous fall, break into full leaf in the spring.

60 ft. tall and higher, but the cost is great and the operation is not a practical one for most home gardeners to have done.

Trees 20-25 ft. tall and of nearly the same spread can be moved by capable nurserymen without special equipment beyond that ordinarily available in a nursery, and such trees will usually be the largest that the average gardener will have planted. The cost of such a tree and its planting in the selected location will amount to a fairly substantial sum, but when one considers what the money buys, the years and care the tree has taken to develop, and the waiting that will be necessary if a smaller specimen is planted, it may be very worth while. There is no doubt that well-selected and well-located shade trees add substantially to the actual cash value of a house.

Smaller and younger trees are more frequently planted. Specimens 10-12 ft. tall are comparatively inexpensive, are easily handled and in 10-20 years develop into sizable specimens. They give little or no shade at first.

Choosing the particular tree follows the decision of the kind of tree to plant. It is wise to visit the nursery personally for this purpose.

The tree selected should be symmetrical and straight. It is important that its leader (central shoot) be undamaged and intact. A divided trunk or bad crotches between limbs that may tear apart later when the branches become heavier are bad faults.

It is important that the tree be vigorous and that it should have been making a reasonable amount of growth in recent years. Needless to say, it should not have any serious infection or be damaged by borers or other serious insect pests. The bark should be intact, not damaged by frost cracks (these longitudinal splits occur on the south side of the tree as it has been growing) or by accident. Any old pruning cuts present should have healed over or should be in the process of healing rapidly.

Planting

The time to plant shade trees varies somewhat according to local conditions but in nearly all situations the most favorable times for leaf-losing kinds are just before new growth begins in

When large trees have to be moved a considerable distance it is usual to attach them securely to wooden platforms and transport them by truck or special tree movers.

spring, and in early autumn about the time the leaves are falling. Evergreen kinds are best transplanted just before new growth begins in spring or in late summer or early fall.

Whatever the kind of tree and its size at planting time, it is of the utmost importance to set it in a hole much larger than the spread of the roots, to have the hole prepared by digging over its bottom and incorporating generous amounts of compost, rotted manure or other humus-forming material, and to fill good, rich soil around and between the roots. Good planting in good soil goes far toward ensuring the well-being of the tree.

The tree should be set at the same depth as it has previously been, or at the most an inch or two deeper. Deep planting is very harmful.

After the tree has been set in place and the hole filled to about three-quarters of its depth with good soil, and this has been rammed firmly, the remainder of the hole should be filled with water once or twice. This should be allowed to soak in before the soil fill is completed.

The surface is finished by making a slight depression over the area the tree roots occupy and encircling the area with a slight ridge or mound of soil. This makes it possible to water the newly planted tree more thoroughly during the first season after it is planted.

Trees may be planted bare-rooted (without soil attached to the roots) or with their roots contained in a mass of soil which is called the "ball" and which is usually tightly wrapped in burlap. Trees handled in the latter manner are said to be balled and burlapped. (See Ball.)

When planting bare-rooted trees, it is very important to spread the roots out in the way they grew naturally and to work good soil between them and pack it firmly. It is harmful to crowd the roots and bunch them together.

When planting balled and burlapped trees, great care must be taken not to break the ball; as much of the burlap as can be removed without damaging the ball is cut away after the tree is in position in the hole and before any soil is filled in. Evergreen trees are always planted with a ball, never bare-rooted.

After planting, bare-rooted trees, and sometimes balled and burlapped specimens, are secured against disturbance by wind by guying them with three stout wires attached to pegs driven into the ground well beyond the spread of the hole. Where the wires pass around the trunk or branches of the tree they are threaded through short pieces of rubber hose to prevent damage to the bark.

It is a good plan to wind a spiral of burlap, or of special paper made for the purpose, around the trunks of newly planted trees that have thin, smooth bark. This is left in position for about a year. It prevents the bark from splitting under the influence of the sun, which it is apt to do before the tree regains its vigor after the shock of moving, and also tends to prevent the entry of borers.

A mulch (surface covering) of two or three inches of coarse compost, littery manure, half-decomposed leaves, peat moss or some similar material placed over the soil occupied by the roots after the tree is planted is beneficial. During the first summer following planting, great care should be taken to soak the roots with water thoroughly at weekly or ten-day intervals during periods of drought. Enough water should be given at each application to soak in to a depth of at least a foot.

Pruning trees at planting time needs considered attention. Because the roots have been reduced in the process of transplanting, it is usually desirable to reduce the size of the top somewhat. This pruning should consist of the thinning out of weak and ill-placed branches and the shortening of some others. The leader (central shoot) should not be shortened. All pruning cuts exceeding 1 in. in diameter should be painted with special tree-wound paint or with ordinary white lead paint into which a liberal amount of powdered sulphur (a fungicide) has been stirred. Before the wounds are painted they should be sealed with a coat of shellac dissolved in alcohol.

Maintenance of Shade Trees

Pests and Diseases. Like all garden plants, shade trees need intelligent attention in order to thrive. Every effort should be made to keep them free of diseases and pests. This means that the trees should be carefully inspected from time to time and that at the first evidence of trouble prompt control or preventive measures should be taken. It is well for the gardener to familiarize himself with the pests and diseases that are most likely to be bothersome to specific trees and to watch for these. (See Pests and Diseases.) Much useful information is available in bulletins on the pests and diseases of shade trees that have been published by State Agricultural Experiment Stations.

Pruning may need periodic attention. Ill-placed, broken and disease-damaged branches should be removed promptly. Sharp tools only should be used and clean cuts should be made. Branches should be shortened to a good side branch or be cut off flush with the trunk. Stubs that rot and encourage decay to spread into healthy parts of the tree should never be left. After each cut is made, it should be painted with shellac dissolved in alcohol in a ring extending for half an inch or so within the bark (this will protect the cambium layer) and then the whole cut surface should be given a coat of tree-wound paint.

Fertilizing is an important routine in keeping shade trees healthy, particularly those growing in poor soils and those that have reached maturity and are growing less vigorously than they were earlier in their lives. Special complete fertilizers or tree foods are available, and these form a simple and effective way of supplying trees with needed nutrients.

An alternative method is to spread a layer of partly rotted animal manure and a dressing of superphosphate over the area occupied by the roots. Such a mulch is of great benefit. Even if fertilizer is relied upon to provide needed nutrients, a mulch of compost, leaf mold or peat moss is highly beneficial because it keeps the roots cool and more evenly moist than would otherwise be the case. When trees are located in lawn or sod such mulches are obviously impracticable; then fertilizers alone must be relied upon.

The fertilizer may be spread over the soil surface, but it is a better plan to bore holes with a crowbar or special power tool in a pattern ex-

Fill the holes to about 4 in. of their tops with a special tree-food fertilizer.

Next, pack the fertilizer firmly in the holes.

To fertilize a shade tree growing in grass, first remove plugs of sod at intervals of about 2 ft.

Finally, replace the plugs of sod and push them firmly into place.

Then, with a crowbar, make holes about 2 ft. deep.

tending over the outer three-quarters of the area in which the roots spread. This area normally extends slightly beyond the spread of the branches and two or three times as far in the case of narrow, more or less columnar trees.

The holes should be about 2 ft. deep and may be spaced 2 ft. apart. They should be about 2 in. in diameter. The holes are filled to within 4 in. of their tops with special tree food. Soil and, if needed, plugs of grass sod are used to complete the filling of the holes.

Manufacturers' directions should be followed

[12–2]
Senecio Doria

[12–2a]
*Spanish Broom
(Spartium junceum)*

[12–2b]
Setcreasea purpurea

[12–2c]
*Shade Trees, newly planted,
trunks protected with wrapping*

The Weeping Beech, Fagus sylvatica pendula, has drooping branches.

The Sugar Maple, Acer Saccharum, colors magnificently in the fall.

The Phellodendrons, hardy, broad-spreading trees of moderate height, are excellent for shade.

Gymnocladus dioica, the Kentucky Coffee tree, has an interesting habit of growth and provides light shade.

The Norway Maple, Acer platanoides, is a favorite shade tree and is suitable for use as a street tree.

The Honey Locust and its varieties are fine shade trees with lacy foliage. They resist disease and pests.

Recommended Shade Trees*

Ash, Green (Fraxinus pennsylvanica variety lanceolata). A fairly narrow tree of quite rapid growth. Hardy to northern Canada. Prefers deep, rich soil but stands dryness remarkably well. A good tree for the Plains and Prairie regions of the Middle West and useful elsewhere in the North.

Ash, Velvet (Fraxinus velutina). A round-headed tree of rather open growth that attains a height of 45-50 ft. It is fast-growing, drought-resistant and stands alkali soils quite well. It is adapted only for mild climates and is recommended for the drier parts of the Southwest. It thrives best in a reasonably fertile soil.

Beech, European (Fagus sylvatica and its varieties). Eventually very large, with a dense, broad head and smooth, light gray bark. Roots near the surface and does not thrive in compacted (packed down) soil. Under old specimens it is not usually possible to grow grass or other plants. There are several fine varieties of this noble tree including cut-leaved or fern-leaved kinds and kinds with purple foliage. The variety called tricolor has variegated leaves and is very handsome. It does not grow so large as the other kinds.

Box Elder (Acer Negundo). For use only where more desirable trees will not grow. Best on moist soil but stands drought well. Plant male trees only; females are hosts of the Box Elder Bug.

Camphor Tree (Cinnamomum Camphora). Evergreen. Well-established trees resist temperatures as low as 15 degrees. Dropping of abundant fruit may be something of a nuisance.

California Pepper Tree (Schinus Molle). A broad-topped evergreen of very attractive appearance. It bears clusters of very beautiful rose-pink berries that follow small, yellowish-white flowers. This tree is drought-resistant and fairly tolerant of alkali soils. It gives light shade. Best suited for California. A related kind, S. terebinthifolia (the Brazilian Pepper Tree), has bright red fruits and is suitable for planting in Florida. Both attain a height of about 20 ft.

Cape Chestnut (Calodendrum capense). An evergreen tree, round-headed, that attains a height of up to 70 ft. It bears attractive, rose-lavender flowers and has handsome, dark green foliage. It is suitable only for very mild climates such as those of southern Florida and southern California.

Cork Tree (Phellodendron amurense). Gives light shade. A low-branched tree with a broad, spreading top. Resistant to pests and diseases and has handsome foliage and attractive bark. Is tolerant of city smoke. Hardy as far north as Newfoundland, southern

	For the Northeast	For the Southeast	For the Plains	For the Rockies	For California	For the North Pacific Area
Ash, Green	X		X	X		X
Ash, Velvet				X	X	
Beech, European	X	X				
Box Elder			X	X		
Camphor Tree		X			X	
California Pepper Tree					X	
Cape Chestnut					X	
Cork Tree	X					

* Based on Selections made in the United States Department of Agriculture Yearbook.

Ontario and British Columbia. A related kind, P. sachalinense, is similar and equally as satisfactory. These trees attain maximum heights of about 50 ft.

Ginkgo (Ginkgo biloba). A tree of somewhat erratic branching habit that casts light shade and is notoriously free of disease and insect pests. A good tree for city planting. Male and female flowers are borne on separate trees. The fruits, which are borne by female trees only, of course, have a very objectionable odor; for this reason male trees only should be planted when it is possible to obtain specimens identified as to sex. At maturity Ginkgos attain a height of 100 ft. or more.

Golden-Rain Tree (Koelreuteria paniculata). Wide-spreading, round-topped, 20-30 ft. tall. Graceful foliage. Large clusters of yellow flowers in summer, followed by attractive fruits in fall. Fairly rapid grower. Stands heat and drought and tolerates alkali soil better than any other tree.

Hackberry (Celtis occidentalis). A wide-spreading tree, 50-70 ft. tall, that gives moderate shade. It has somewhat the appearance of an elm but is less graceful. It is not tolerant of smoke and soot. It is hardy into northern Canada. A less hardy kind, but one that is to be preferred where it can be grown (as far north as southern New England), is C. laevigata. This Hackberry is resistant to the witches'-broom disease that disfigures C. occidentalis.

Honey Locust (Gleditsia triacanthos and varieties). This fine tree gives light shade, and grass grows well beneath it. It is a fairly fast grower and stands city conditions well. The seed pods are something of a nuisance when they fall, but a modern, thornless form of this tree, known as the Moraine Locust, does not produce pods. This is recommended as a substitute tree for the American Elm.

Kentucky Coffee Tree (Gymnocladus dioica). Gives light shade. Prefers moist soil but adapts itself to drier locations. Subject to cotton root rot disease. Do not plant on infected soils.

Linden, Silver (Tilia tomentosa). Eventually large, with dense, broad head. Small, fragrant, creamy flowers in summer. Tolerates heat and drought. Good near the seacoast. Not good in smoky areas. Said to be poisonous to bees when in bloom.

London Plane (Platanus acerifolia). Eventually large and spreading. Stands pruning well. Good in cities. Alkali-tolerant. Subject to some diseases and pests but less so than the native American Plane (Sycamore).

Madrona (Arbutus Menziesii). Evergreen. Grows moderately rapidly. Does not stand cold or wind well. Needs sheltered location.

Maple, Norway (Acer platanoides). Gives heavy shade from a rounded head. Tolerates a wide variety of soils. Good city tree. Has surface roots and so it is difficult to grow grass beneath it. The Schwedler variety has leaves that are deep bronze in spring. The variety Crimson King has deep purplish-red foliage.

	For the Northeast	For the Southeast	For the Plains	For the Rockies	For California	For the North Pacific Area
Ginkgo	X					X
Golden-Rain Tree	X	X			X	
Hackberry	X		X	X		X
Honey Locust	X		X	X		
Kentucky Coffee Tree	X		X			
Linden, Silver	X					
London Plane	X		X		X	
Madrona						X
Maple, Norway	X		X	X	X	X

SHADE TREES

Not hardy in all parts of Rocky Mountain region.

Maple, Sugar (Acer saccharum). Large at maturity. Not suited for polluted atmospheres. Best in moist, rich soil. Gives wonderful fall color. Subject to wilt disease and, in hot, dry weather, to scorching of its foliage.

Oak, Bur (Quercus macrocarpa). Large, slow-growing. Has massive head. Gives moderate shade. Drought-resistant and hardy. Do not plant on soil infected with cotton root rot fungus.

Oak, Coast Live (Quercus agrifolia). Evergreen. At maturity, broad-spreading. Grows slowly at first, faster later. Do not plant in lawns or other constantly irrigated areas.

Oak, Live (Quercus virginiana). Evergreen. Rather slow-growing. Huge at maturity. Broad-topped. Needs plenty of room. Is damaged by severe frosts. Resists insects and diseases.

Oak, Northern Red (Quercus borealis). Eventually large. Has a short trunk and spreading branches. Good fall color. Thrives in gravelly and sandy soils, not in wet ones. Subject to Oak wilt disease where this is prevalent.

Oak, Pin (Quercus palustris). Straight-trunked, with many slender branches and of fine appearance. Good autumn color. Tolerant of a wide variety of soils (except alkaline ones) and of city smoke.

Oak, Scarlet (Quercus coccinea). A fine tree. Prefers dry sandy soil. Endures city conditions well. Foliage colors handsomely in fall.

Oak, Water (Quercus nigra). Eventually large, symmetrical. Grows rapidly in early life. Leaves stay on late in the fall. Tolerant of wide variety of conditions.

Oak, White (Quercus alba). Sturdy, with broad, rounded, open top. Eventually large. Leaves turn brown in fall and hang on late. Subject to wilt disease where this occurs.

Oak, Willow (Quercus Phellos). Handsome, graceful, large tree. Leaves willow-like, light green. Grows quickest in moderately moist soils but stands dry soils also.

Pagoda Tree, Chinese Pagoda Tree, Chinese Scholar Tree (Sophora japonica). Has broad, rounded, spreading top. Casts light shade. Has attractive yellow-white flowers in summer. Young trees more susceptible to winter cold than older, well-established specimens.

Russian Olive (Elaeagnus angustifolia). A small tree. Survives on sandy and alkaline soils but prefers rich, moist soil. Drought-resistant.

Southern Magnolia (Magnolia grandiflora). Large, handsome, symmetrical, evergreen. Beautiful cream-white fragrant flowers. Rather slow-growing. Stands a variety of conditions but not poor soil drainage.

Sweet Gum (Liquidambar Styraciflua). Has a narrow or fairly broad, open top. Trunk straight. Its foliage colors brilliantly, crimson and wine-purple, in fall. For moist, nonalkaline, well-drained soils. A little difficult to transplant. Plant in spring.

Tulip Tree (Liriodendron Tulipifera). Tall,

	For the Northeast	For the Southeast	For the Plains	For the Rockies	For California	For the North Pacific Area
Maple, Sugar	X					
Oak, Bur			X	X		
Oak, Coast Live					X	
Oak, Live		X				
Oak, Northern Red	X					
Oak, Pin	X	X			X	X
Oak, Scarlet	X	X				X
Oak, Water		X				
Oak, White	X	X				X
Oak, Willow	X	X				
Pagoda Tree	X					X
Russian Olive			X	X		
Southern Magnolia		X				
Sweet Gum	X	X			X	X

straight-trunked, with an open top. Its foliage colors bright yellow in fall. Large, greenish-yellow flowers in spring. For fairly moist, loamy soils. Not easy to transplant. Move young specimens only, in spring. Leaves drop over a long period.

Tupelo or Sour Gum (Nyssa sylvatica). Casts moderate shade. Has an irregularly shaped top. Needs rich, moist soil. Brilliant scarlet foliage in fall. Difficult to transplant. Set out small trees only, in spring.

Yellow Wood (Cladrastis lutea). Medium-sized, broad-topped. Foliage colors bright yellow in fall. Fragrant white flowers in June. Prefers rich, moist soil but is drought-resistant. A fine shade tree. Plant in spring. Transplanted specimens re-establish themselves rather slowly.

	For the Northeast	For the Southeast	For the Plains	For the Rockies	For California	For the North Pacific Area
	X	X				
	X					
	X	X				

A magnificent mature specimen of the Pin Oak, Quercus palustris.

The Willow Oak, Quercus Phellos, becomes large at maturity. This specimen grows in Virginia.

Largest of all evergreen flowering trees, the Southern Magnolia or Bullbay is a favorite shade tree in the South.

The Tulip tree, Liriodendron Tulipifera, is distinguished by its straight trunk, its peculiarly shaped leaves and its greenish-yellow tuliplike flowers.

No tree colors more magnificently than the Sweet Gum, Liquidambar Styraciflua. The foliage of this tree becomes brilliant scarlet in fall.

SHADY GARDENS. Many gardeners are baffled by problems caused by shade. However, there are numerous plants which prosper in areas where shade occurs, and from these a selection can be made to suit most situations.

Shade exists in many degrees but to evaluate the variations according to any set rule is almost impossible. Some analysis is, however, advisable to determine the types and degrees of shade in the garden at different times of day and during the changing seasons. Such stocktaking should, if possible, be done before selecting the kinds of plants to be grown.

Perpetual shade may be caused by closely planted or dense evergreens, by high walls or buildings located to the south. A lighter and more cheerful shade may exist where light is reflected from a white wall or where distant

Evergreen Rhododendrons and a ground cover of Pachysandra terminalis provide welcome greenery throughout the year in this shady garden.

Partial shade is beneficial to many plants.

The Plantain Lilies or Hostas grow equally well in sun or shade.

Virginia Bluebells, Mertensia virginica, are excellent spring-flowering plants for shady gardens. They do not retain their foliage long after flowering.

The Spanish Bluebell, Scilla hispanica, is a spring-blooming bulb especially suitable for planting in shady locations. Blue-flowered, white-flowered and pink-flowered varieties are available.

The English Primrose, Primula vulgaris, thrives in shady places where the soil is rich and fairly moist.

that branch high. Kinds such as Honey Locust and Birch give a pleasant, dappled sunlight and shadow effect. When planting against a building facing north, it is well to remember that although the area may receive early and late afternoon sun, this is much less powerful than sun at midday.

It is true that most plants prefer a sunny situation, yet some, including Rhododendron maximum, (Rosebay), Leucothoë, Viburnum acerifolium (Dockmackie), and most Ferns actually prefer a shaded location. Shade-preferring objects only block the sun. Heavy shade may sometimes be reduced by the judicious pruning of offending trees, but amputation of branches requires skill and restraint. Tall shrubs may be pruned to admit more light and at the same time add to the well-being of the trees.

Shade May Be Seasonal. A bright spring garden, gay with flowering bulbs, may be very shaded later when leaf-losing (deciduous) trees are in full leaf. Some trees cast a heavy shadow in summer. Here belong Ash and Beech trees, as well as the Norway Maple, under which practically nothing will grow once the trees are old and big. Trees such as Pin Oak, Black Locust and Sycamore create less shade, and so do trees ground covers include Ajuga, Periwinkle and Pachysandra. Many herbaceous perennials flourish in deep woodlands but languish in sunshine, and a large number of these are adaptable for cultivating in shady beds and borders as well as in wild gardens and less formal areas. When appropriate plants that will fit into cultivated and landscaped grounds are considered, many well-behaved natives should be included.

Soil Variations. In shaded areas in the wild there exists every kind of soil condition. There are plants which flourish in shaded bogs, in shaded soils of extreme acidity, in dry, shaded areas, on fiber-matted woodland floors and in good, loamy soil. In home gardens, conditions are usually more uniform. Yet many cultivated plants set in shade die, not from lack of sun, but from unsuitable soil conditions.

Unless otherwise stated, the plants recommended here all require good, friable (crumbly) garden soil prepared to a depth of 1-2 ft. by spading and by adding generous quantities of compost or other organic matter and some fertilizer. Where the soil is naturally acid, it is prudent to consider planting acid-soil plants only, rather than to recondition the soil, although this may be done by liming. Acid soil exists naturally where Hemlocks, many Pines and other coniferous (cone-bearing) evergreens grow. An acid condition is also usually found under most kinds of Oak trees. If in doubt as to whether a soil is acid or alkaline, the gardener should have a sample soil test made by a State Agricultural Experiment Station or by a qualified person.

If the soil is not acid enough, increased acidity can be built up by incorporating with it leaves and leaf mold or acid peat moss. Peat moss and leaf mold help to condition the soil; sharp (coarse) sand may be used to lighten it if it is of a clayey nature. To conserve moisture and keep the roots cool (shade-loving plants need a moist, cool soil) a mulch should be laid over the soil in shaded parts of the garden. This also prevents packing of the soil by water dripping from trees and shrubs.

Epimediums are splendid ground-cover plants for shade.

The Sweet Rocket, Hesperis matronalis, blooms freely in lightly shaded places.

Chrysogonum virginianum, a native American plant, grows well in partial shade.

The Solomon's-Seals or Polygonatums are handsome herbaceous perennials that thrive in shaded locations.

It is generally best to avoid setting plants too close to surface-rooting trees, such as Maples. Few plants can successfully compete with such trees for the moisture and nutrients they must have.

On the credit side of gardening in the shade is the fact that the plants usually require less watering, because the sun does not dry out the soil rapidly. Flowers in shaded or partly shaded areas tend to hold their color and freshness longer than do flowers grown in the sun, even though their blooms may be less numerous.

Flowers most attractive in the shade are those with warm colors such as yellow-pink (salmon or apricot), orange and yellow. White is also effective. The colder colors seem to recede; however, blues and purples can be used with good effect in the shaded landscape.

Flowering Shrubs for Full Shade. Rosebay, Rhododendron maximum, when planted in shade, tends to become lanky. It may be used effectively by planting it with the following deciduous Azaleas (botanically also called Rhododendrons): R. arborescens, Pinxter-Flower (R. nudiflorum), R. roseum, R. Vaseyi, and White Swamp Honeysuckle (R. viscosum). Drooping Leucothoë (L. Catesbaei), which, like the Rosebay, is evergreen, may also be planted with the above. These shrubs produce white or pink flowers in succession from April through July. Along with these the Hemlocks and Canadian Yew (Taxus canadensis), the only needle-leaved evergreens which will grow in all degrees of shade, may be planted with good effect.

Evergreen Shrubs for Light to Medium Shade. The Rosebay, Rhododendron maximum, and the Leucothoë mentioned above are useful where shade is light to medium, and for planting in the same soil conditions. Other kinds, suitable for mild climates, include Aucuba and Laurel, Laurus nobilis. The following broad-leaved evergreens, which are not content in deeper shade, may be used: Pieris japonica, with white flowers; Mountain Laurel, Kalmia latifolia, with pink or whitish flowers, which bloom in May or June.

Rhododendron (Azalea) obtusum amoenum

Rhododendrons are excellent in light shade.

For the same kind of location there are a number of handsome evergreen shrubs that have insignificant flowers and are grown for their foliage. Yews fit admirably into this picture. Where no great height is wanted, the shrubby Yews with their short, crowded leaves are recommended. These include the dwarf English Yew, Taxus baccata adpressa, and the dwarf Japanese Yew, Taxus cuspidata nana. Several broad-leaved evergreens are excellent for locations where shade is not too heavy—among them, Japanese Holly, Ilex crenata, both the tall and the dwarf kinds, and the looser-branching Inkberry, Ilex glabra. Euonymus Fortunei and its varieties are useful, especially when allowed to climb.

Deciduous (Leaf-losing) Shrubs for Full Shade. In addition to the shrubs mentioned above under Flowering Shrubs for Full Shade, the following, which do not have showy blooms, succeed well in comparatively deep shade: Privet, Ligustrum; Acanthopanax Sieboldianus; Snowberry, Symphoricarpos albus; Japanese Barberry,

Many Azaleas are excellent for growing in partial shade. The three shown here are (Above) Azalea nudiflora, (Below) A. lutea, and (Right) A. Kaempferi.

has red-purple blossoms, and Rhododendron (Azalea) obtusum Hinodegiri has bright rose-red flowers in April and May. The large-flowered Rhododendron (Azalea) mucronatum also does well where shade is not too dense, but its foliage is less glossy than that of the other two Azaleas here mentioned. Camellias, in climates where they can be grown outdoors, are most handsome shrubs or small trees for growing in partial shade.

Berberis Thunbergii; Shrub Yellow Root, Xanthorhiza simplicissima.

Leaf-losing Shrubs for Light Shade. Among spring-flowering shrubs and small trees that thrive in good garden soil and stand some shade are Cornelian Cherry, Cornus Mas; Spicebush, Lindera benzoin; Kerria, and Weigela. All have yellow blooms except Weigela, which has pink flowers. Many shrubby Dogwoods are eligible for use in light shade, as also are most Viburnums, though not Viburnum Carlesii or Viburnum Burkwoodii, because they require more sun. Enkianthus, which requires an acid soil, is excellent and has handsomely colored autumn foliage. Several species of Bush Honeysuckle are recommended, including, especially, Lonicera canadensis, L. Morrowii and L. tatarica.

Kinds that bloom in summer are Sweet Pepper Bush, Clethra alnifolia; Hypericum frondosum; Hypericum densiflorum; and Flowering Raspberry, Rubus odoratus. The latter, on account of its coarse foliage, is best placed where it will be seen at a distance, perhaps along the fringe of woodland, from where its rose-purple blossoms show effectively.

Vines for Shade. Among the most satisfactory vines for shade are the following: English Ivy, Hedera Helix; Virginia Creeper, Parthenocissus quinquefolia; Boston Ivy, Parthenocissus tricuspidata; Euonymus Fortunei; Bittersweet, Celastrus; Silver-Lace Vine, Polygonum Aubertii; Akebia quinata; Dutchman's-pipe, Aristolochia durior; and Climbing Hydrangea, Hydrangea petiolaris.

Ground Covers for Shade. The following are a recommended list of ground covers suitable for planting in shaded locations: Lily of the Valley, Convallaria majalis; European Wild Ginger, Asarum europaeum; Epimedium; Dwarf Lily Turf, Ophiopogon japonicus; Big Blue Lily Turf, Liriope Muscari; Common Periwinkle, Vinca minor; Japanese Spurge, Pachysandra terminalis; and English Ivy, Hedera Helix.

Perennials, Including Bulbs, for Shade. There are a vast number of woodland plants that are well adapted for growing in woodland gardens, wild gardens and rock gardens, and a more limited but still generous number that are adaptable for cultivating in perennial borders that are shaded. When preparing a perennial bed or border in a shaded area, select a location where the shade is not really heavy. Perhaps a spot can be found that gets sunshine filtering through the leaves of trees or even a few hours of direct sunlight; or possibly the shadow is from distant trees or buildings or from trees which branch high so that good light from the sides is received. An airy, fairly light condition is desirable for best results. It is simply impossible to grow many plants suitable for a perennial border where shade is really dense or air circulation is not reasonably good.

One of the first requirements in establishing a border or bed of perennials in a partially shaded place is to make sure that the preparation of the soil is very thoroughly carried out before any planting is attempted. This involves spading it to a depth of 8-12 in. and mixing in liberal amounts of organic matter and fertilizer. For plants in shade it is well to have the soil even more fertile than for plants growing in more sunny locations.

The plants that may be grown include:

For Spring Bloom: Bleeding Heart, Dicentra spectabilis; Dicentra eximia; Christmas Rose, Helleborus niger; False Solomon's-Seal, Polygonatum; Trillium; Bloodroot, Sanguinaria canadensis; Lily of the Valley, Convallaria majalis; Crested Iris, Iris cristata; Blue Phlox, Phlox

The Boston Ivy, Parthenocissus tricuspidata, thrives in shady locations.

Foxgloves are favorite plants for partially shaded locations.

divaricata (needs spring sun); Epimedium; Virginia Bluebells, Mertensia virginica; Violets, Violas; Daffodils, Narcissi; Winter Aconite, Eranthis; Camassia; Snowdrops, Galanthus; Snowflakes, Leucojum aestivum; Grape Hyacinth, Muscari; Glory-of-the-Snow, Chionodoxa; Spanish Bluebell, Scilla hispanica; English Bluebell, Scilla nonscripta; Polyanthus Primrose, Primula polyantha; English Primrose, Primula vulgaris.

For Summer Bloom: Astilbe (needs moisture); Foxglove, Digitalis purpurea; Aquilegia canadensis; Plantain Lily, Hosta; Day Lily, Hemerocallis; Campanula latifolia; Campanula lactiflora; Rocket, Hesperus; Tiger Lily, Lilium Tigrinum; False Dragonhead, Physostegia virginiana; Coral-Bells, Heuchera sanguinea; Balloonflower, Platycodon grandiflorum; Japanese Primrose, Primula japonica (needs a moist or wet soil); Black Snakeroot, Cimicifuga racemosa; Meadow Rue, Thalictrum.

For Autumn Bloom: Day Lily, Hemerocallis; Plantain Lily, Hosta; Cimicifuga simplex; Mistflower, Eupatorium coelestinum; Monkshood, Aconitum.

Ferns for Foliage Effects: Maidenhair Spleenwort, Asplenium Trichomanes; Cinnamon Fern, Osmunda cinnamomea; Interrupted Fern, Osmunda Claytoniana; Christmas Fern, Polystichum acrostichoides; Maidenhair Fern, Adiantum pedatum; Hay-scented Fern, Dennstaedtia punctilobula.

Annuals and Summer Bedding Plants. Not very many annuals and summer bedding plants succeed in shade, and none will endure really dense shade. Among those that thrive in light or partial shade are the following: Balsam, Impatiens; Wax Begonia, Begonia semperflorens; Fancy-leaved Caladiums; Fuchsia, Nicotiana, Lobelia, and Torenia.

SHALLOT. The botanical name of this bulb is Allium ascalonicum; it is a native of Palestine, and belongs to the Lily family, Liliaceae; it is closely related to the Onion, Allium Cepa. The Shallot is a useful winter vegetable which is very easily grown; it is one of the simplest vegetables to manage. The bulbs are chiefly used for pickling.

How to Plant. The Shallot thrives best on deeply cultivated, moderately rich soil. After the ground has been prepared, the bulbs are simply pressed into the soil until they are about half-covered; they should be set 6 in. apart in rows 10-12 in. from each other. Planting should be done as early in spring as possible. During the summer months the only attention needed is to hoe frequently between the rows to destroy weeds and keep the surface soil "fine," thus preventing loss of moisture by evaporation.

Lifting the Crop. When the leaves have turned brown and have almost died down, the Shallots

Many Ferns thrive in shade. This is the Hay-scented Fern, Dennstaedtia punctiloba.

are lifted, set out to dry for a few days, cleaned of dead leaves and soil, and stored until required for use. They keep well in any cool shed or room and are not stored in sand, soil or other material.

Each Shallot bulb produces a cluster of six or more bulbs. When the Shallots are lifted, the bulbs are separated before being stored. A sufficient number should be saved for replanting the following year.

The ordinary Shallot is suitable for general purposes. Those who wish to grow large Shallots should choose the Giant or Russian variety.

SHAMROCK. A name applied to several plants—Medicago lupulina, Wood Sorrel (Oxalis), etc., but the White Clover, Trifolium repens, is generally accepted as the "true" Shamrock.

SHAMROCK PEA. See Parochetus communis.

SHARP SAND. When gardeners speak of sharp sand they refer to sand that consists of fairly large grains and is free of fine clay or silt material. Sharp sand permits the free passage of water and good aeration between the grains. Sharp sand is much used as a propagating medium. See Sand.

SHASTA DAISY. See Chrysanthemum maximum.

SHEARS. Garden shears are indispensable. There are various types, each of which is constructed for a definite purpose.

Hedge and garden shears are used for trimming hedges, as well as narrow grass strips and steep banks, where it is impossible to use a mowing machine. They are made on the same principle as scissors, with blades 9 in. or more long,

Pruning shears are an essential garden tool. They come in many different sizes and types.

and handles 9 in. in length. Some types have a notch at the base of one of the blades to enable thick branches to be cut off. Small shears with 7-in. blades, specially made for ladies, can also be obtained.

Electric hedge shears are available that make it possible to trim a much greater amount of hedge surface in a given time than is possible with hand shears.

Sheep Shears are hand shears especially made for trimming grass edges, around trees, steps and the like. They are available in various types.

Pruning Shears. A strong pair of hand pruning shears forms an indispensable part of the gardener's equipment. They are used for pruning fruit trees and ornamental shrubs. They should be kept sharp and well oiled. There are various types; some, with two cutting blades; others, like the modern Rolcut, in which one blade cuts against a soft metal surface to avoid bruising the stems that are cut.

SHEEPBERRY. Viburnum Lentago, which see.

SHEEP LAUREL. Kalmia angustifolia, which see.

SHEEPS-BIT SCABIOUS. See Jasione.

SHELLFLOWER. A name applied to Alpinia speciosa, Chelone glabra, and Molucella laevis.

SHELTER PLANTINGS. The desirability of shelter plantings may be considered from several angles. Their greatest value is that they reduce injury to plants caused by prevailing winds. They lessen the damage done by sandstorms and diminish the force of harmful salt-laden winds from the ocean. They are also used to moderate

Sheep shears will trim grass around a tree where the lawn mower cannot safely be used.

the drying effect of windstorms on flat lands in the Middle West and other regions. By suitable plantings designed to break their full force, even high winds that blow around corners of houses in suburbs and elsewhere can be reduced before they reach tender plants.

Except for the most exposed areas, there is a wide selection of plant material that may be used as shelter plantings. When trees are used of a size that will produce immediate effect, skilled and careful planting is important and guy wires are needed to support each tree until it is established and well rooted.

Possible Harmful Effects. While the shelter of trees and shrubs often makes possible increased productivity of the soil, and the cultivation, in some locations, of plants that could not otherwise be grown there, at the same time shelter plantings, originally designed, perhaps, for background as well as windbreak, can be harmful or can become harmful. They can be so dense as to obstruct the free circulation of air, resulting in greater incidence of disease among garden plants. For instance, mildew on Lilacs and other plants and black spot on Roses are likely to be more prevalent where air circulation is not adequate. Late spring frosts are often destructive in oversheltered areas, especially if the land is low. Shelter plantings can do damage if they are so close to the garden that they shade sun-loving plants or if they draw moisture and food from the soil in which the roots of garden plants ramify.

Situations Where Shelter Plantings Are Helpful. Shelter plantings or windbreaks can often be used with advantage to protect orchards. When they are so used, however, they should be only just dense enough to reduce the force of prevailing winds so that branches heavily laden with fruit are not broken and so that windfall fruits are reduced to a minimum.

If a windbreak is needed at the corner of a home or other area close to a house, conifers of a rugged nature are usually chosen although a dense planting of a hardy shrub such as Lilac is sometimes used to give the protection necessary. The planting should be made as wide as possible with a view to breaking the velocity of the wind by partly blocking it and spreading it rather than by attempting to stop it completely. If the planting has considerable depth it usually creates a better appearance than does a hedge.

Lilacs form an effective deciduous windbreak in landscaped areas.

When a house is located on high ground and has a beautiful view of a lake, river or valley that it is desirable not to block, but where prevailing winds are a problem and outdoor living cannot be fully enjoyed, a hedge of Privet or other plants suitable for shearing may be used as a windbreak. This may be comparatively tall along most of its length but have its height appropriately lowered in front of the main view.

Near the seashore, shelter is often much needed. The selection of plants that are suitable for such locations is limited, especially if the soil is almost pure sand, as it is very apt to be. Under such conditions it is important that young, vigorous small plants are used rather than attempting to set out those of comparatively large size. Small plants stand the best chance of taking hold and becoming established. If thickly planted, these will get a firmer hold in the soil if for the first year after they are set out they are protected by a fence or other bulwark.

Plants to Use. Evergreens are often preferred for shelter-belt planting and, where they will live, are ideal, but the number of kinds that will grow in exposed places, especially near the sea, is few. For regions of the East Coast north of southern New Jersey the best evergreen trees are Austrian Pine, Pinus nigra; Japanese Black Pine, Pinus Thunbergii (especially useful by the sea); Pitch Pine, Pinus rigida; American Arborvitae, Thuja occidentalis; and the Red Cedar,

The Austrian Pine, Pinus nigra, is a fine evergreen for providing shelter.

Juniperus virginiana. For a low screen, the following have possibilities: Inkberry, Ilex glabra; Swiss Mountain Pine, Pinus Mugo; and Japanese Holly, Ilex crenata.

For the same region, deciduous (leaf-losing) shrubs that grow to 6 ft. or higher under ideal conditions and that are surprisingly resistant to wind and salt water spray include the Privets, Ligustrum amurense and L. ovalifolium; Beach Plum, Prunus maritima; Buffalo Berry, Shepherdia argentea; Groundsel Bush, Baccharis halmifolia (especially good for seashore planting); Chokeberry, Aronia; Elder, Sambucus; Tatarian Honeysuckle, Lonicera tatarica, Lonicera Morrowii; Lilac, Syringa; Red-Osier Dogwood, Cornus sanguinea; Russian Olive, Elaeagnus angustifolia, Rosa rugosa; Shadblow, Amelanchier; Staggerbush, Lyonia Mariana; Sumac, Rhus; Tamarix parviflora; Withe Rod, Viburnum cassinoides; and Arrow Wood, Viburnum dentatum.

Where a hedge is required, the densest growers among the above are the Privets. The other shrubs mentioned are better suited for use in close-set groups to break the force of the wind. Where there is plenty of space a naturalistic and dense planting can be esthetic as well as useful. It can be enriched with low-growing plants on the outside. A selection of these include Bayberry, Myrica; Bearberry, Arctostaphyllos Uva-ursi; Bittersweet, Celastrus; Sweet Pepper Bush, Clethra alnifolia; Sweet Fern, Comptonia peregrina; Cotoneaster horizontalis; Heather, Calluna; Hydrangea macrophylla; prostrate forms of Juniper; Rosa blanda; Rosa carolina; Spireas, Spiraea; and Yucca.

Southward from Cape May suitable plants to use in shelter plantings are Rose of Sharon, Hibiscus syriacus; various kinds of Hydrangea,

Where a low evergreen windbreak shelter planting is needed, the Mugo Pine, Pinus Mugo Mughus, is excellent.

The Red Cedar, Juniperus virginiana, forms a very good evergreen windbreak.

Red Cedar, Juniperus virginiana; Neviusia alabamensis; Rosa hemisphaerica; various kinds of Spiraea; Snowberry, Symphorocarpos albus; Syringa chinensis and Persian Lilac, S. persica. In Florida various kinds of Casuarina are good windbreaks and the shrub Tephrosia candida is also useful.

In wind-swept plains of the Middle West the choice of trees is limited but includes Alder, Alnus; Ash, Fraxinus; Box Elder, Acer Negundo; Buckeye, Aesculus; Cherry, Prunus; Elm, Ulmus; Hickory, Carya; Honey Locust, Gleditsia; Red Maple, Acer rubrum; White Maple, Acer saccharinum; Poplar, Populus; Sour Gum, Nyssa sylvatica; Sweet Gum, Liquidambar styraciflua; and Willow, Salix.

Shrubs suitable for use in the same region include: Acanthopanax pentaphyllum, Amorpha canescens, Colutea arborescens, Cotoneaster hupehensis, C. foveolata, C. racemiflora, Deutzia Lemoinei, Elaeagnus umbellata, Exochorda racemosa, Kerria japonica, Rhodotypos tetrapetala, Stephanandra incisa, Syringa amurensis and native Viburnums.

For areas in the Pacific Northwest exposed to strong winds the following kinds are useful, as well as kinds recommended above for northeastern areas: Abelia grandiflora, Ligustrum Henryi, L. obtusifolium Regelianum, Berberis triacanthophora, B. oblonga, B. aggregata, B. Wilsoniae, Buxus microphylla koreana, Rhododrendron ciliatum, R. hippophaeoides, R. rubiginosum and R. yunnanense.

In California drifting sand and strong winds are checked by the use of the native Tree Mallow, Lavatera assurgentiflora; as a windbreak, the Monterey Cypress, Cupressus macrocarpa is frequently used. Various kinds of Eucalyptus are also successfully used as shelter plantings. Vineyards and some other orchards are sometimes protected by a row of Almond, Fig, Olive or Pittosporum planted along the side from which the prevailing winds blow.

SHE-OAK. Casuarina, which see.

SHEPHERDIA—*Buffalo Berry* (Shepherd'ia). Leaf-losing shrubs of North America. In all of the known kinds the leaves are more or less silvery, and in one of these the branches are rather spiny. Male and female flowers are on separate bushes. In neither case are they very attractive, but when plants of both sexes are grown together a crop of edible, red or orange, acid fruits may be expected. The plants are allied to Elaeagnus and belong to the family Elaeagnaceae. The name honors John Shepherd, a Curator of the Botanic Garden, Liverpool, England.

Propagation is by seeds sown outdoors or in frame or greenhouse in spring. These shrubs thrive in loamy soil and may be planted in gardens near the sea. No regular pruning is required. The known kinds are: S. argentea, a spiny-branched shrub up to 12 ft. high, bearing silvery leaves; S. canadensis, 6-8 ft. high, with spineless branches; and S. göttingensis, a hybrid between the two.

The shrubs are extremely hardy and may be grown far north in the United States and in Canada. They withstand poor soils and dry, windswept locations as well as extreme cold. S. argentea is valued for planting to form hedges where other hedge shrubs will not survive.

SHEPHERD'S-SCABIOUS. See Jasione.

SHIELD FERN. Dryopteris, which see. See also Polystichum Braunii.

SHINLEAF. Pyrola, which see.

SHINLEAF, ONE-FLOWERED. Moneses uniflora, which see.

SHIRLEY POPPY. A race of annual Poppies, selected from the common Papaver Rhoeas or Corn Poppy, by the Reverend W. Wilkes, Secretary of the Royal Horticultural Society. The strain has since been further improved by seedsmen. See Papaver.

SHOO-FLY PLANT. Nicandra physaloides, which see.

SHOOT. This term is commonly used by gardeners to indicate the fresh young growth of a tree, shrub or other plant.

SHOOT, LEADING. A name given to the shoot at the end of a branch. It is generally used in reference to the shoots at the end of tree branches.

SHOOT, SIDE OR LATERAL. See Side Shoot or Lateral.

SHOOTING STAR. See Dodecatheon.

SHORTIA (Short'ia). A small genus of very beautiful woodland plants belonging to the Diapensia family, Diapensiaceae, and named in honor of Dr. Charles W. Short, a Kentucky botanist. Shortias are not always easy to grow,

Shortia galacifolia is a charming woodland plant. A native of North Carolina, it has bell-shaped white flowers tinged with pink, which are produced on 4-5 in. stalks in spring. It is a gem for a cool spot in open woodland or in the rock garden.

but they are so exquisitely beautiful that no trouble is too great to expend on them.

These are clump-forming plants with wiry stems and fine roots. They must be grown in moist but well-drained acid soil that contains an abundance of organic matter such as leaf mold or peat moss. It is hopeless to attempt their cultivation in alkaline soil. They enjoy half-open woodland conditions and are suitable for associating with Azaleas, Rhododendrons and similar acid-soil shrubs and for planting in a cool spot in the rock garden where they are protected from the hottest rays of the sun.

Raising Plants from Seeds. Shortias may be propagated by very careful division in spring when the plants are large enough and strong enough, or seeds may be sown, in spring, in a pan containing leaf mold or peat moss and fine loam with plenty of sand added; the pan is kept in a shaded cold frame until the seedlings are large enough to pot individually in small pots containing soil similar to that in which the seeds were sown. The young plants grow slowly in the early stages, and when potting them the greatest care must be taken that the roots are not exposed to the air long enough for them to dry out.

Oconee Bells, Shortia galacifolia, is a native of the mountains of North Carolina. It has rounded leaves of leathery, glossy texture, on wiry, 4-5-in. stems, and bears large bell-shaped flowers of exquisite waxy texture on stems a little taller than the leaves; the flowers are five-lobed and of delicate pink color. The plant blooms in early

Shortia uniflora variety grandiflora has exceptionally large flowers.

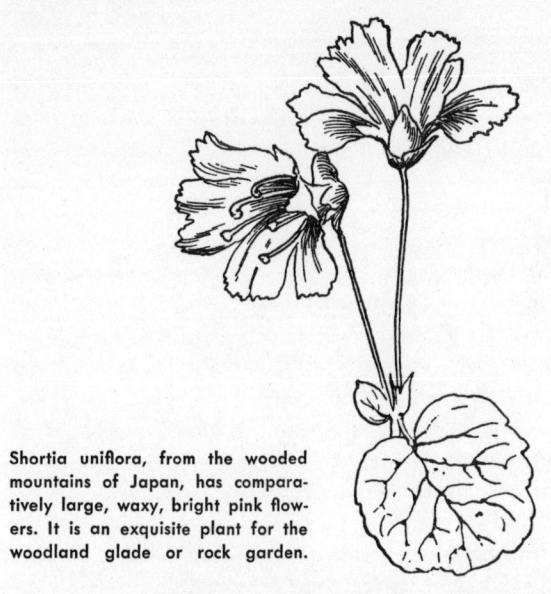

Shortia uniflora, from the wooded mountains of Japan, has comparatively large, waxy, bright pink flowers. It is an exquisite plant for the woodland glade or rock garden.

summer. In order to obtain seeds it is worth while to fertilize the flowers with the aid of a camel's-hair brush. In autumn and winter the glossy green leaves often turn a fine red color, particularly when the plants are exposed to a fair amount of sunshine, though too much sun is not good for this woodlander, unless the soil is absolutely suited to its requirements, especially in regard to moisture.

An interesting history surrounds this plant. It was first collected in 1781 in the mountains of North Carolina by a French collector and then was not found again for nearly a hundred years. The search for it and the tale of its rediscovery read like a modern detective story.

Nippon Bells, Shortia uniflora, is from the wooded mountains of Japan, and its requirements as to soil are the same as those of S. galacifolia. If anything, however, it requires more shade. It has much the same leathery glossy leaves, which, however, are not so prone to color in winter. The leaf and flower stalks, too, are somewhat shorter. The waxy, five-lobed, bell-shaped flowers are considerably larger and range in color from almost white through pale pink to rose-pink. It is one of the most exquisite of all plants for the rock garden or for a choice place in the wood garden or in the shade of Rhododendrons.

An even finer plant is Shortia uniflora grandiflora, with larger flower bells. The color varies through pale and dark pink, and plants with white flowers occasionally occur.

Shortia uniflora may be raised from seeds in the same way as S. galacifolia; this is a more satisfactory method than division of the roots, for the plant is comparatively slow in forming clumps strong enough to bear division. It seems a pity to risk the dangers of division, which at best can give a few plants, whereas by carefully hand fertilizing the flowers, considerable quantities of seeds may be secured. Although raising seedlings requires some skill and care and is somewhat slow, a far greater number of healthy plants is obtained in less time from seeds than by waiting for plants large enough to divide.

Shortia is closely related to the almost equally beautiful Schizocodon and it is possible to cross-fertilize the two.

Raising Shortia from seeds has much to recommend it, especially as the stocks of these plants at present in cultivation are almost entirely collected from the wild. They are slow of increase in nature, and must therefore be in danger of gradual extermination. If large stocks could be raised from seed it would do much to discourage the trade in collecting the plants. Home-raised seedling plants are, moreover, far more satisfactory than collected plants, which are so difficult to establish, and there is always a high rate of mortality among them.

The plant which is by some botanists called Shortia soldanelloides is by others named Schizocodon soldanelloides. In this encyclopedia it is treated under Schizocodon, which see.

SHRIMP PLANT. Beloperone guttata, which see.

SHRUB. A perennial plant, the woody branches of which normally live for many years, although it does not develop a dominant central trunk. The line of demarcation between trees and shrubs is not, in all cases, sharply defined. See Planning The Garden, Planting The Garden.

SHRUB ALTHAEA. Hibiscus syriacus, which see.

SHRUB YELLOWROOT. Xanthorhiza simplicissima, which see.

SIBBALDIA (Sibbald'ia). A small group of low, perennial herbaceous plants belonging in the Rose family, Rosaceae, and nearly related to Potentilla. They occur as natives in the cooler parts of the Northern Hemisphere, including Canada and the United States as well as Europe and Asia. The name honors Robert Sibbald, who was a professor of medicine at Edinburgh, Scotland, in the seventeenth and eighteenth centuries.

Sibbaldia procumbens is grown in rock gardens and wild gardens. It is a spreading or tufted plant about 4 in. tall and bears rather inconspicuous, small yellow flowers. For its successful cultivation this plant needs a partly shaded location and a woodsy, moderately moist soil. It is easily increased by seeds and by division in spring or early fall.

SIBIRAEA LAEVIGATA (Sibirae'a). A hardy deciduous shrub, 5 ft. high, closely related to Spiraea and requiring the same culture. A native of Siberia, it has small greenish flowers.

SIBERIAN CRAB. Malus baccata, which see.

SIBERIAN IRIS. Iris sibirica, which see.

SIBERIAN SQUILL. Scilla sibirica, which see.

SIBERIAN WALLFLOWER. Cheiranthus Allionii, which see.

SIBTHORPIA — *Cornish Moneywort* (Sibthorp'ia). Hardy and tender, trailing, herbaceous plants, which belong to the Figwort family, Scropulariaceae. The principal kind, S. europaea, is found growing wild in the Channel Isles, the south of England and Ireland, and other parts of Europe. It has slender, creeping stems, rooting at the joints, small, kidney-shaped, green leaves, 1 in. in diameter, and tiny yellow or pinkish flowers in summer.

In nature this plant grows in moist, shady places, and is therefore suitable for bog gardens or damp positions in the rock garden. The variegated kind, S. europaea variegata, is more tender than the typical kind, and is therefore suitable only for fairly mild climates and for growing in pots for decorating the greenhouse, and as a house plant. The name Sibthorpia commemorates John Sibthorpe, a professor of botany at Oxford.

A Carpeting Plant for Damp Places. The hardier, green-leaved kind may be planted in moist, shady or semishaded places, to carpet the soil around taller-growing plants: ordinary garden soil is suitable. When planted in a bog garden, it needs very little attention beyond trimming back the shoots to prevent their encroaching beyond their allotted positions. The trailing shoots root at the joints as they run along the soil, so that they quickly spread; the plants are easily propagated by detaching pieces of shoot with roots attached and dibbling them in fresh soil.

An Attractive Pot Plant. The variety with colored leaves may be planted out of doors for the summer, but it needs protection in winter. As a pot plant it is very attractive; its long trailing shoots, covered with golden variegated leaves, hanging downwards over the sides of the pots are very ornamental.

The best way to obtain an effect quickly is to fill a well-drained 5-in. pot with soil, and dibble in three small plants near the edge at equal distances apart. The tips of the shoots are pinched out occasionally to make the plants spread and cover the sides of the pot. Very pretty effects can be produced by planting the variegated-leaved kind in hanging baskets. The baskets are lined with moss, then filled with compost, and small pieces of rooted shoots are dibbled in 2 in. apart all over the surface of the soil.

The soil must be kept moist during the summer, but during the winter it must be kept moderately dry.

The chief kinds are S. europaea, green-leaved, trailing; S. europaea variegata, leaves green and yellow; and S. peregrina (Disandra prostrata), from Madeira, with small yellow flowers, which needs greenhouse protection.

SICANA ODORIFERA — *Curuba, Cassabanana* (Sican'a). A tendril-bearing, tender vine belonging in the Gourd family, Cucurbitaceae. It is a native of South America and is grown outdoors in the warmest parts of the South for its ornamental and edible fruits. The name is a Peruvian one.

Sicana odorifera has stems 40 ft. and more long. It is a perennial but only persists from year to year where winters are almost or quite frost-free and where hot summers are experienced. Elsewhere it may be grown as an annual by raising a fresh stock of plants each year from seed in the same manner that Gourds and Melons are raised. In the North the plants may not flower and fruit.

The flowers of this vine are yellowish, the

males and females separate but borne on the same plant. The cylindrical fruits are 15-24 in. long and when ripe are orange-crimson. They are very fragrant.

SIDALCEA (Sidal'cea). Herbaceous perennial plants which belong to the Mallow family, Malvaceae, and are natives chiefly of western North America. The name is derived from Sida and Alcea, related plants.

In recent years, owing to the introduction of numerous new varieties, the Sidalcea has become one of the most attractive of hardy flowering plants. The various kinds reach a height of 3 to 4 ft., and are in full beauty in July and August. The blooms, an inch or so across, like a small single-flowered Hollyhock, are of various shades of rose and red, and there are white varieties.

In general, Sidalceas are better suited for growing in gardens on the West Coast than elsewhere in North America.

Hints on Cultivation. Sidalcea, which may be planted in autumn or spring, thrives in ordinary, well-tilled garden soil; if this is clayey, it will benefit by the addition of compost, farmyard or stable manure or leaf mold and sand; if light, manure should be added as a top-dressing in April or May. A sunny position is necessary. The plants should, if possible, be left undisturbed for several years to allow them to develop into large clumps which will yield a profusion of bloom.

The stems are of upright and fairly stiff growth and need little support; it is, however, wise to place two or three bamboo canes around large plants, and encircle them with string, to keep them erect in rough weather.

Propagation. Although it is best to leave the plants undisturbed as long as they remain flourishing, Sidalcea can be increased by division in autumn after the stems have died down. The plants are lifted and separated into pieces for immediate replanting in the positions where they are to bloom the following and succeeding years. The pieces on the outsides of the clumps should be chosen for replanting; those near the inside are older and weaker and should be discarded.

The herbaceous perennial Sidalcea malvaeflora Listeri produces spikes of fringed bright pink flowers in July-August.

The species are easy to raise from seed. These may be sown out of doors in a nursery border in early May, or in a flat of sifted sandy soil, in a greenhouse in March; if potted separately in 3-in. pots and grown in a cold frame for a month or six weeks, the seedlings will be large enough to be planted out of doors, either where they are to remain, or in a reserve border.

The Best Kinds and Varieties. The two chief

The herbaceous perennial Sidalcea has pale pink flowers.

species or wild types of Sidalcea are S. candida, with white flowers, and S. malvaeflora (Checkerbloom), of lilac-mauve shade. The former is a beautiful plant which is still popular, but most of the other Sidalceas now in cultivation are varieties which have been raised by crossbreeding and selection.

The best of the older ones is Sidalcea malvaeflora variety Listeri, which has flowers of rose coloring. Of the newer European varieties, not all of which are yet available in North America, the following are attractive: Crimson King, soft rose-crimson; Interlaken, pink, 2½ ft.; Monarch, bright rose; Elsie Hugh, 3 ft., pale pink; Sussex Beauty, pale pink; Scarlet Beauty, amaranth-red; and Rose Queen, rich rose.

SIDERASIS FUSCATA. This is the name given by some botanists to the plant described in this Encyclopedia under its better known name of Tradescantia fuscata. It is also called Pyrrheima fuscata.

SIDERITIS (Siderit'is). Mostly tender herbs, shrubs and subshrubs that are native to the Mediterranean region, adjacent Asia and the Canary Islands. They belong in the Mint family, Labiatae. The name is an ancient Greek one used by Dioscorides and refers to the fact that the plant was believed to cure wounds caused by iron or *sideros*.

The kinds cultivated are shrubs and subshrubs that need a well-drained soil in full sun. They are propagated by seeds and by cuttings. They are chiefly adaptable for growing outdoors in climates such as that of southern California. S. candicans also makes an attractive window or greenhouse plant for a location where it is exposed to plenty of sunshine and where the temperature is fairly cool.

The kinds most likely to be cultivated are S. canariensis, a tall shrub with wrinkled velvety leaves; S. candicans, 3 ft., with leaves covered with white-woolly hairs; S. incana, 1 ft., also covered with white-woolly hairs; S. scordioides, 1 ft., hardier than the others mentioned here; S. taurica, 18 in., densely covered with white-woolly hairs and comparatively hardy.

SIDESADDLE FLOWER. Sarracenia, which see.

SIDE SHOOT OR LATERAL. A term used by gardeners to indicate the secondary or small shoots which develop on the trunks and main branches of trees and other plants.

SIEVE. Various sizes of sieves are indispensable in the garden. They are used chiefly for preparing seed-sowing and potting composts. The following sizes of mesh are useful for various purposes: ⅛ in., ¼ in., ½ in., ¾ in., and 1 in. The largest is used for sifting the compost when plants are potted in pots 6 in. in diameter, or larger. A sieve of ¾-in. mesh is used for preparing the compost for potting plants in 4-in. and 5-in. pots. For potting in 3-in. pots the compost is sifted through a sieve with ½-in. mesh, and for preparing soil for seed sowing a sieve with ¼-in. or ½-in. mesh is used. Leaf mold should be rubbed through a ½-in. or ¾-in. sieve, to avoid wastage.

To cover fine seeds with soil after sowing, a ¼-in. or ⅛-in. sieve or one made of window screening is satisfactory. This consists of a small wooden (cigar) box about 3 in. deep, the bottom of which is replaced by the screening.

When sifting coal ashes for covering potted bulbs, a sieve with ¼-in. or ½-in. mesh should be used.

SIEVEKINGIA (Sieveking'ia). Only a few kinds of this Orchid are known. All are evergreen epiphytes (kinds that grow on other plants) with small ovoid, clustered pseudobulbs, each bearing one evergreen leaf, and few-flowered, pendent spikes. The flowers, which do not last long, are about 2 in. across, the petals are narrower and smaller than the sepals. The plants are wild in Brazil, Costa Rica and the neighboring countries. These Orchids usually flower in summer and autumn. The name commemorates Dr. Sieveking, a burgomaster of Hamburg, Germany.

As the flower spikes are pendent, the plants are grown in Orchid baskets. The potting compost may consist of cut osmunda fiber, Tree Fern fiber or of Fir bark or Redwood bark. Root disturbance should be avoided as much as possible, but if the compost has to be entirely renewed it should be done in spring when new roots appear. The baskets should be suspended near the glass in a greenhouse with a tropical temperature in summer, and a winter temperature of not less than 60 degrees at night. In winter, water should be given infrequently, but the leaves must not be allowed to shrivel through drought.

The Chief Kinds. S. suavis is greenish-yellow spotted with black; S. Reichenbachiana has yellow flowers with red spots; S. Jenmanii is reddish-yellow, and S. peruviana, yellow.

SIGMATOSTALIX RADICANS (Sigmat'ostalix). A pretty, small-flowered evergreen epiphytal Orchid found wild in Brazil. It has small pseudobulbs set at short intervals on a rhizome. Each of the pseudobulbs has two narrow leaves. The sepals and petals are greenish-yellow, and the lip is white with yellow crest. The plant is very free-flowering and the blooms last a considerable time; they usually open in summer. The name Sigmatostalix is derived from *sigma,* the letter S, and *stalix,* a stake.

This Orchid is of easy cultivation, requiring a subtropical temperature and atmosphere in summer, and a winter temperature of 60 degrees; occasional falls below this, however, do no harm. The plant is sometimes grown with Odontoglossums, but does better in rather warmer conditions. Flower pans are preferable to pots for this Orchid, and the potting compost may be cut osmunda fiber or Tree Fern fiber or of Redwood bark or Fir bark.

Repotting is done in spring or early summer; it should be carried out only when the old compost is much decayed. Shading is necessary during bright weather. This Orchid must be watered throughout the year, and liberally in the summer.

SIKKIM COWSLIP. See Primula sikkimensis.

SILENE—*Catchfly, Campion* (Sile'ne). An extensive group of hardy annual, biennial, and perennial herbaceous plants, which are found wild in most temperate climates, principally in Europe. A few kinds are also found in North America, China, Japan and central Asia.

Silene belongs to the Pink family, Caryophyllaceae; the name is derived from *sialon,* saliva, and refers to the sticky fluid on the leaves. In this sticky fluid flies are often entrapped, hence the common name of Catchfly. The origin of the name Campion is not determined, but it is supposed to be derived from *campus,* a field, because many of these plants are found growing wild in fields.

As the cultivated kinds do not exceed usually 12 in. in height, they are principally used in the rock garden. S. pendula and its varieties are,

Silene Armeria is a showy hardy annual Catchfly, with glaucous leaves and heads of rose-colored flowers. It can be sown in spring or autumn where the plants are to grow.

however, good for use as spring bedding plants.

For Rock Gardens and Wild Gardens. S. alpestris, the Alpine Catchfly, is a pretty white-flowered perennial of very easy culture. It grows about 6 in. tall and blooms freely in spring and summer. It is a native of the mountains of Europe and prefers a location in full sun. S. alpestris variety grandiflora has larger blooms than the type plant. S. alpestris flore-pleno has double flowers.

S. acaulis is a dwarf plant of tufted habit, about 2 in. in height, with tiny, green, linear leaves and bearing small, rose-colored flowers in

The Moss Campion or Cushion Pink, Silene acaulis, a dwarf rock-garden plant of cushion-like growth bearing rose-colored blooms in summer.

early summer. It is commonly known as the Cushion Pink, or Moss Campion. There is also a white-flowered variety, alba, and one with pink flowers, exscapa.

S. acaulis and its varieties are natives of the high mountains of North America and Europe; they are not difficult to grow in a moraine or scree but in cultivation they rarely flower well away from their mountain homes.

S. caroliniana (S. pensylvanica), the Wild Pink, grows natively in eastern North America. It is an extremely pretty spring-flowering plant which grows to a maximum height of 9-10 in. Its flowers, which are clear, deep pink or more rarely white, are borne in profusion. It is a plant for partial shade. S. Wherryi is very closely allied to S. caroliniana, differing chiefly in having the calyx densely covered with whitish hairs.

S. Elizabethiae (Melandrium Elizabethiae) has large, rose-colored flowers in May. It has narrow, lanceolate (lance-shaped) leaves, 2-3 in. long, is of compact habit and grows 4-6 in. in height.

S. maritima, the Sea Campion, is a caespitose (tufted) kind, with gray-green lanceolate leaves and white or reddish flowers in July and August.

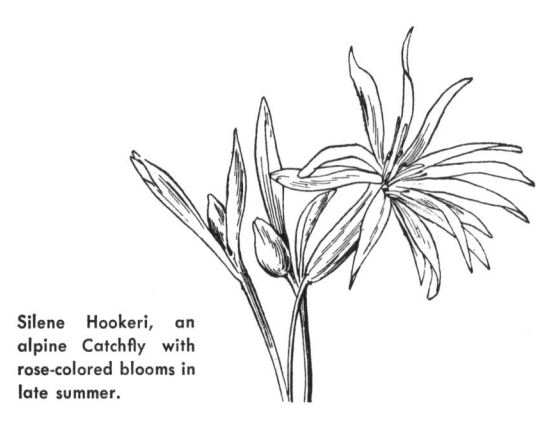

Silene Hookeri, an alpine Catchfly with rose-colored blooms in late summer.

The Wild Pink, Silene caroliniana, is a beautiful spring-flowering species that is native to eastern North America.

Silene Zawadskii is an easy-to-grow perennial. It bears a profusion of white flowers in summer.

The annual Silene pendula is a summer-flowering kind that has pink or white flowers.

The double-flowered variety of this is much superior, the flowers being larger and lasting longer. The variety with reddish or pink flowers is named rosea.

S. rupestris is a charming little plant, about 6 in. in height, with narrow blue-gray leaves and white to pink flowers in June and July.

S. Schafta is an autumn-flowering plant with rosy-purple flowers; it grows 6 in. in height and has rosettes of small oblanceolate (the reverse of lanceolate) leaves. It is one of the best of the dwarf kinds and is easily raised from seed, which it sets freely.

S. virginica, the Fire Pink, is a grand plant for light shade and woodsy soil. It is native from New York to Georgia and Arkansas, grows 1-2 ft. tall and bears large crimson-scarlet blooms in spring and summer.

There are a number of other perennial Silenes that are sometimes cultivated in gardens. S. Hookeri, a 5-in.-tall rock native of the Pacific Northwest, has beautiful fringed pink flowers. This kind is suitable for rock gardens, but considerable skill is needed to grow it successfully. S. quadridentata, a white-flowered plant from the mountains of Europe, grows 4 in. tall. S. Zawadskii, which grows 6-8 in. tall, has white flowers. It is a native of Europe.

S. laciniata, the Indian Pink, grows to a height of 5 ft. and is a native of Mexico and southern California. Its flowers are bright red. S. laciniata variety Purpusii is a dwarf kind with cardinal red flowers. Neither of these kinds is hardy where severe winters prevail.

Details of Cultivation. A sunny location is required by all the perennial Silenes listed above except S. caroliniana, S. virginica and S. Wherryi, which thrive best where they receive light shade. The shade lovers prefer a moderately moist but well-drained soil that contains liberal amounts of organic matter (humus). The lower-growing kinds are suitable for rock gardens. S. laciniata is adaptable for planting in wild gardens and borders. The rock-garden kinds need light, well-drained soil. S. acaulis and S. Elizabethiae are liable to decay at the collar in winter unless grit or small stones are mixed with the soil. They also do well in the moraine or scree.

Planting is done in fall or early spring. Those raised in pots may, however, be planted at almost any time of the year. They should be lifted and replanted only when it is necessary to divide them, or they show signs of deterioration. Healthy vigorous growth can be maintained by top-dressing them annually in March with gritty soil.

Propagation is by division in spring or by seeds and cuttings. Seeds are sown in well-drained pans of sandy soil in spring. The seeds are sown thinly on the surface and lightly covered with fine soil. The pans are then placed in a cold frame, which is kept closed and shaded. As soon as the seedlings are large enough to handle they are transplanted into other seed pans, and later on are potted singly in 3-in. pots, from which they are planted in the rock garden.

Cuttings are taken in summer. Basal shoots are selected and, after being trimmed, are inserted in a close shaded frame until rooted, when they are potted off and treated as the seedlings.

Lovely Hardy Biennials. Silene pendula is a free-flowering biennial Catchfly, about 6 in. in height, which has small velvety leaves and bears terminal clusters of rose pink flowers in spring. There are various forms of this; S. pendula compacta is one of the best for spring bedding. S. pendula Bonnettii has purple stems. S. pendula alba is pure white.

These plants are raised annually by sowing seeds out of doors in August. The seedbed is prepared by digging the soil and raking the surface to a fine tilth. Drills 6 in. apart and ¼ in. deep are then made, the seeds sown thinly and covered.

When the seedlings are an inch in height they are transplanted in a cold frame or nursery bed, 6 in. apart, and set in their final positions in early spring.

Other showy biennial Silenes are the closely related S. Armeria and S. compacta, with loose panicles of rose-pink flowers on erect stems up to 15 in. tall. From seeds sown outdoors in early autumn they will bloom from June onwards. S. Armeria is naturalized in eastern North America and is known as the Sweet William Catchfly.

SILK OAK. Grevillea robusta, which see.
SILK TREE. Albizzia Julibrissin, which see.
SILK VINE. See Periploca graeca.
SILKWEED. See Asclepias.

SILPHIUM—*Compass Plant, Cup Plant, Rosinweed* (Silph'ium). Coarse-growing, hardy, herbaceous perennials which are only suitable for large perennial borders and wild gardens. There are about ten kinds, all natives of North America, but only two are in general cultivation, and even these are not popular garden plants. The name Silphium is derived from *silphion*, the Greek name of an African plant, but the application is obscure.

The Compass Plant. S. laciniatum is given the name of Compass Plant because its leaves, which are arranged in pairs, are supposed to point due north and south. It is a stately plant with stout stems, 6-8 ft. in height, with lance-shaped, deeply divided leaves, 12 in. long, and terminal spreading clusters of bright yellow flowers. S. perfoliatum, Cup Plant, is of about the same height, but the leaves are undivided and sessile (without stalks).

For the Wild Garden. Silphiums flourish in ordinary garden soil, or even in clay. Very striking effects are obtained by planting them in bold groups in the wild garden, or a plant or two set at intervals at the back of the herbaceous border is effective. Planting may be done in spring or fall, when the ground is in a workable condition. They may be left undisturbed for several years, or until they show signs of deterioration, when the clumps should be lifted, divided into smaller portions and replanted in fresh soil. When dividing the clumps, the outside portions only should be selected for planting. This method of division is the principal means of propagation.

The chief kinds are S. laciniatum, 6 ft., and S. perfoliatum, 6 ft. Other kinds are A. trifoliatum, 7 ft.; S. integrifolium, 6 ft.; and S. terebinthinaceum, the Prairie Dock, 8 ft. All have yellow flowers in summer.

SILVER-BELL TREE. See Halesia.

SILVERBERRY. Elaeagnus commutata, which see.

SILVER FERN. Pityrogramma, which see.

SILVER FIR. Abies alba, which see.

SILVER HEATH. See Cassinia.

SILVER-LACE VINE. Polygonum Aubertii, which see.

SILVER MAPLE. See Acer saccharinum.

SILVER SAW PALM. See Paurotis.

SILVER TREE. Leucadendron argenteum, which see.

SILVERVINE. Actinidia polygama, which see.

SILVER WATTLE. See Acacia decurrens variety dealbata.

SILYBUM — *Milk Thistle, Blessed or Holy Thistle* (Sil'ybum; Silyb'um). Hardy, herbaceous perennials, cultivated for their ornamental foliage. These thistle-like plants are rather coarse-growing and are most suitable for planting in less formal parts of the garden.

S. Marianum, the chief kind in cultivation, is a native of the Mediterranean region. It has naturalized itself in California and occurs there spontaneously, principally on waste ground. It sends up robust prickly stems, 5 ft. in height, and has large, prickly-edged leaves which clasp the stems. These leaves are very ornamental, being light green and shiny, and having milk-white veins and blotches. The flowers appear in summer and are terminal, thistle-like, rosy purple in color and not very attractive.

The Holy Thistle. The common names Milk Thistle, Blessed or Holy Thistle have been given from the superstition that the milky veins were caused by milk falling on them when the Infant Jesus was being fed. The species name Marianum also reflects this superstition. The origin of the Latin name Silybum is not determined. It

Silphium perfoliatum bears small sunflower-like blooms in summer.

Sinningia barbata has dark colored foliage and creamy colored flowers.

is said to be the name given by Dioscorides to thistle-like plants. Silybum belongs to the Daisy family, Compositae.

The roots were at one time boiled and eaten, like Artichokes, the young leaves used as a salad, and the flower heads as a substitute for Globe Artichokes.

A Fine Foliage Plant. Good effects are obtained in the wild garden, on rough ground, or in front of dark-leaved shrubs, by planting this Thistle in irregular groups. No special preparation of the ground is necessary, and ordinary soil is suitable. Planting may be done at any time in fall or spring, when the ground is in a workable condition.

Seed sown outdoors in spring, where the plants are to mature, produce flowering plants the first season.

SIMPLE LEAF. A simple leaf, as distinct from a compound leaf, is one in which the leaf consists not of two or more leaflets but of a single blade. See Leaf.

SINGLE. This term is correctly used in the description of flowers which have a single row of petals; it is, however, used in reference to various flowers which have few petals, even though they are arranged in more than one row.

SINGLING. A gardening term sometimes used to denote the thinning of seedlings.

SINK GARDENING. This name is given to a type of gardening that has become popular in Great Britain in recent years but is not much practiced in Canada or the United States. It consists of cultivating alpines and other dwarf rock plants in old stone sinks, troughs and similar receptacles. Sometimes sinklike containers are made of concrete especially for the purpose, but devotees of sink gardening do not regard these with favor. If old containers are not available they prefer to cut new ones out of stone; sandstone is especially suitable for the purpose. The "sink" must have one or more holes in its bottom for drainage.

Sink gardens are made by placing a layer of stones, broken brick or similar material in the bottom of the container, then filling it with a soil consisting of 1 part each of loam, leaf mold or peat moss, coarse sand and finely crushed stone. This mixture may be varied by adding more peat, some crushed limestone, or other ingredients that are considered favorable to the growth of particular plants.

When the container is filled, attractive rocks are embedded in the soil surface or placed upon it in such a manner that the illusion of a miniature rock garden or mountain scene is obtained. The plants are then set in place and the garden is watered and placed where it is to stand outdoors, either directly on the ground or on a paved surface or pedestal.

Almost any rock-garden plants of suitable size and not too rampant growth may be used. Among the many possibilities are tiny dwarf evergreens, Androsaces, Armerias, Campanulas, Dianthus, Drabas, Erinus, Gentians, Primulas, Saxifragas, Sedums, Sempervivums, Silenes, Thymus and Wahlenbergias.

SINNINGIA—*Gloxinia* (Sinning'ia). This is the genus to which the showy florist's Gloxinias belong, the species chiefly responsible for their production being Sinningia speciosa, which, like other members of the genus, is a native of Brazil. Sinningia belongs to the family Gesneriaceae, and is named after W. Sinning, a head gardener at the University of Bonn. The species or wild types are becoming popular and they respond to treatment similar to that recommended for Gloxinia, which see. The cultivation of the hybrid Sinningias commonly known as

Sinningia speciosa.

Sinningia eumorpha.

Gloxinias is treated in this Encyclopedia under Gloxinia, which see.

Kinds. S. eumorpha, 6-8 in., flowers nodding, white marked inside with yellow and lavender; S. pusilla, 2 in., lilac with darker veinings; S. regina, 9 in., leaves with ivory-white veins, flowers nodding, violet-purple; S. speciosa, 9-10 in., flowers violet, red or white; S. barbata, 12-15 in., flowers creamy white.

SINUATE. A botanical term used in describing leaves which have waved edges.

SIPHONOSMANTHUS DELAVAYI (Siphonosman'thus). This attractive, flowering, evergreen shrub is often known by the name of Osmanthus Delavayi. Its name is derived from *siphon*, a tube, and Osmanthus, a genus of closely related plants, and refers to the fact that the flowers possess cylindrical tubes. It belongs in the Olive family, the Oleaceae.

Siphonosmanthus Delavayi is a native of China that was introduced to Western gardens in 1890. It withstands some frost but is adaptable for cultivating outdoors in the milder parts of the United States only; it is not hardy in the North. This plant forms a rounded, spreading shrub 6-10 ft. tall that is well clothed with small, dark green leaves and in spring bears a profusion of pure white, fragrant flowers.

A loamy soil and an open, but not windswept, location suits this evergreen. It may be propagated by cuttings in late summer and fall and by grafting on Ligustrum, although this last method is less satisfactory.

SISAL HEMP. A fiber which is obtained from the leaves of Agave sisalana.

SISYRINCHIUM — *Blue-eyed Grass* (Sisyrinch'ium). Dainty hardy and tender perennial flowering plants which belong to the Iris family, Iridaceae. They vary in height from 12 in. to 3 ft., have narrow, grasslike leaves and produce slender flower spikes, surmounted by a cluster of small, rotate (wheel-shaped) blue, yellow or white flowers in summer. Most kinds are natives

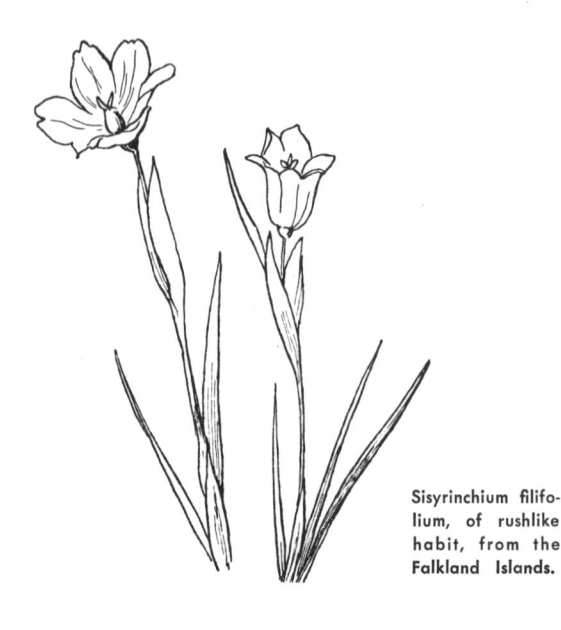

Sisyrinchium filifolium, of rushlike habit, from the Falkland Islands.

of the Americas, mostly from the temperate parts, but a few are from the tropics.

The name Sisyrinchium is one used by the Greek, Theophrastus. The name Blue-eyed Grass refers to the grasslike leaves and small blue flowers.

Delightful Rock and Border Plants. The hardy kinds are ideal plants for the border and rock garden. They require a cool, moist location, and a compost of loam and peat in equal parts. Planting may be done in fall or spring; they should not be disturbed unnecessarily, for they do best when well established. A top-dressing of fresh compost annually in spring is all that is necessary. During the summer months the soil must be kept moist.

These plants are easily increased by dividing them in spring.

Tender Kinds. The tender kinds are grown out of doors in mild climates or in a greenhouse where the minimum night temperature is 45-50 degrees. Repotting is done in September. At that time the plants are taken out of their pots, divided if large enough, and repotted in a compost of loam and peat in equal parts, to which a small amount of sand is added.

After potting, the plants are placed in a cool greenhouse and watered moderately until growth becomes active in spring; then the soil is watered more freely until the flowers have faded. After blooming, the plants are placed in a cold frame, where they remain until potting time in September.

The Chief Hardy Kinds. S. californicum, 12 in., bright yellow; S. Douglasii (grandiflorum), 12 in., purple, and its white variety album; S. angustifolium, 9 in., pale blue.

Tender Kinds. S. chilense, 12 in., purple; S. iridifolium, 8 in., ivory; S. micranthum, 8 in., yellow; S. Bermudianum, 18 in., blue; S. striatum, 3 ft., light yellow; S. filifolium, 8 in., white.

SITKA SPRUCE. Picea sitchensis, which see.

SIUM—*Skirret, Water Parsnip* (Si'um). Hardy, herbaceous perennials, of little horticultural value. Like the majority of the Parsnip family, Umbelliferae, to which they belong, they have thick fleshy roots, divided leaves, and large umbels of small whitish flowers in summer. S. suave, Water Parsnip, grows natively in North America but is not considered to have any garden value.

S. Sisarum (Skirret), a native of eastern Asia, was at one time cultivated for its edible roots, but it is rarely grown nowadays.

Seeds Are Sown in Spring. The method of raising this plant is to sow the seeds annually in early spring, in deeply cultivated soil in a sunny position. Ground manured for a previous crop produces the best results.

The seeds are sown thinly in drills ½ in. deep, and the seedlings thinned out to 12 in. apart. As the flower heads appear, they are removed in order to throw all the energy of the plants into the production of large roots. In dry weather the plants should be watered. In fall, after early frosts, the roots are taken up and stored for cooking.

To obtain seeds for sowing in the following year, the roots should be planted in spring and allowed to flower, the seeds being harvested in the autumn. See also Skirret.

SKIMMIA (Skim'mia). Low-growing evergreen shrubs of considerable decorative merit, bearing fragrant, white flowers in late spring; in some kinds these are followed by attractive, bright red fruits, which remain on the plants for several months. In some kinds male and female flowers

Skimmia Foremanii is a hybrid that produces its red fruits very freely.

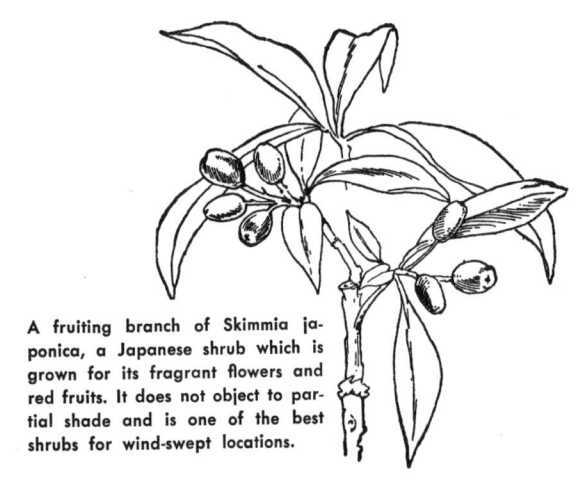

A fruiting branch of Skimmia japonica, a Japanese shrub which is grown for its fragrant flowers and red fruits. It does not object to partial shade and is one of the best shrubs for wind-swept locations.

are produced on different plants; therefore it is necessary to have bushes of both sexes growing together in order to ensure berries. These shrubs are natives of China, Japan and the Himalayas, and have long been grown in our gardens.

Skimmia belongs to the Rue family, Rutaceae, and the name is derived from the Japanese word *skimmi,* meaning a beautiful fruit.

Propagation by Seeds and Cuttings. Skimmias are easily increased by seeds sown in sandy soil in a greenhouse in spring, and cuttings of short shoots, 3-4 in. long, can be rooted in summer if dibbled in sandy soil in a warm and close frame. By propagating in the latter way it is possible to know whether a satisfactory proportion of male and female plants is being maintained, and to keep the sexes apart in order that they may be planted in the right proportion, five to six females to one male.

A very good fruiting Skimmia named S. Foremanii is worth growing in pots for winter decoration. In this case the plants are grown in a greenhouse and the flowers are hand-pollinated in order to obtain a profusion of fruits.

The Skimmias will thrive in open places and in partial shade. They require moist, but not waterlogged, loamy soil, and grow into shapely bushes without pruning.

Skimmias are not considered generally to be reliably hardy north of Washington, D. C., but both S. japonica and S. Reevesiana have thrived for a great many years outdoors in sheltered places in the vicinity of New York City.

Shrubs with Fragrant Flowers. S. Reevesiana (Fortunei) is a spreading bush, 3-5 ft. high, with thick leathery leaves, $2\frac{1}{2}$-4 in. long and 1 in. wide. The white fragrant flowers open in April and are followed by red fruits. This species is hermaphrodite—that is, the flowers bear both male and female organs, thus differing from S. japonica.

S. japonica is a dense bush, $2\frac{1}{2}$-4 ft. high, with aromatic leaves 3-4 in. long and $1\frac{1}{4}$ in. wide. Its fragrant white flowers appear in April, and are followed by very attractive red fruits. It is a native of Japan. Two especially fragrant-flowered male forms are fragrans and fragrantissima. S. Foremanii, previously mentioned, is a very fine hybrid between S. japonica and S. Reevesiana (Fortunei). S. Foremanii Rogersii is a variety.

S. Laureola is a Himalayan bush, 2-3 ft. high, with laurel-like leaves, 3-6 in. long and $1\frac{1}{2}$-2 in. wide, clustered about the ends of the shoots. They emit a rather disagreeable odor when crushed. The flowers are white and the fruits red.

SKIRRET. This vegetable (Sium Sisarum) is a native of eastern Asia and is generally believed to have been introduced into British gardens in the reign of Henry VIII or Edward VI. There is no definite information on this point. It is quite possible that the plant was among the numerous vegetables grown in Roman days and lost again until reintroduced in Tudor times. The Emperor Tiberius valued Skirrets so highly that he accepted them for tribute.

In all sixteenth-, seventeenth- and eighteenth-century gardening manuals Skirrets figure among the commonly grown vegetables. Gerard says of them: " 'Tis reported they were heretofore something bitter; see what culture and education effects." Parkinson, in his *Paradisus,* gives them the first place among root vegetables and describes the taste as "very pleasant, far beyond any Parsnip as all agree that taste them."

This is true, for Skirrets taste like very superior Carrots, but they are white. John Evelyn described them as "exceedingly nourishing, wholesome and delicate."

Joseph Cooper, who was cook to Charles I, gives a recipe for Skirret pie. This was made with boiled Skirrets dipped in yolks of eggs, cooked chestnuts, sliced hard-boiled eggs, put into a pie, with butter, and flavored with lemon, cinnamon and nutmeg. Skirrets were also served fried in batter, flavored with ginger, cinnamon or nutmeg. Worledge, writing in 1682, described Skirrets as "the sweetest, whitest and most pleasant of roots." For cultivation, see Sium.

SKULLCAP. Scutellaria, which see.

SKUNK CABBAGE, YELLOW. Lysichitum americanum, which see.

SKY FLOWER. Duranta repens, which see.

SLIME FUNGI, or Myxomycetes, are a remarkable group of organisms related to the lower fungi, but possessing some animal characteristics. They form spores, as do fungi, but also have a free-living stage in their life history when they move about slowly like animals.

Most of these organisms live on rotten wood, decaying leaves or other plant refuse and are perfectly harmless. A number of species cause plant diseases, the best example being club root of Brassicas.

SLIP. A term used in describing a shoot which is pulled off a plant for the purpose of providing a cutting, and which is planted without further preparation. The term is also commonly used for any cutting, whether it is pulled or cut off the parent plant and even though it may be prepared for planting by cutting across the base of its stem.

SLIPPERFLOWER. Calceolaria, which see. See also Pedilanthus tithymaloides.

SLIPPER ORCHID. See Cypripedium.

SLIPPERWORT. Calceolaria, which see. See also Pedilanthus tithymaloides.

SLOE. Known to many as the Blackthorn, the Sloe (Prunus spinosa) is a hardy tree or shrub of the Rose family, Rosaceae, which grows wild in hedgerows throughout many parts of Europe. The tree is dense in growth, with numerous stiff, hard-wooded branches and short twigs which usually end in very sharp spines, to form a thick, impenetrable hedge. The small white flowers open early, before the leaves appear.

The fruit, which is about the size of a small Plum, is black or very dark purple with a pale bloom on the skin; it is very sour to the taste and is used mainly for making Sloe gin and a few preserves.

SLUG. See Pests and Diseases.

SMILACINA—*False Solomon's-Seal* (Smilaci′na; Smila′cina). Hardy herbaceous flowering perennials of North America, the Himalayas, and eastern Asia, including Japan. About twenty-five kinds are known, but only two or three are commonly grown.

The name Smilacina is a diminutive of Smilax; the plant's leaves are somewhat similar to those of the Smilax. It belongs to the Lily family, Liliaceae.

The most popular kind is S. racemosa, which has slender arching stems, averaging 2-3 ft. in height. These are covered with oblong or oval sessile (stalkless) leaves, 3-6 in. in length, and terminated by feathery spikes of small white flowers. The shoots of the Smilacina are somewhat similar to those of the Solomon's-Seal, hence the common name.

For Moist, Partly Shaded Places. These plants are not suitable for exposed locations. They are ideal for planting in light woodlands and other partly shaded places. They require a moist soil. Very heavy soils, and those of a sandy or gravelly nature, need the addition of large proportions of humus to make them suitable for these plants.

Planting may be done in October or spring. The plants require very little attention after planting, and are best left undisturbed for many years. They benefit from a top-dressing of well-decayed compost applied each fall or early spring.

Propagation. The usual method of propagation is to lift the plants in spring and divide the clumps into pieces, these being immediately planted in their permanent positions. Seeds may be sown in a pan or flat of light soil in summer or fall. After the soil has been thoroughly moistened, a pane of glass is laid over the seed receptacle, which is placed in a cold frame or cool greenhouse. As soon as the seedlings appear, the glass is removed and they are exposed to the light. When 2 in. high, they are lifted and set 2 in. apart in a deep flat filled with light soil or in a bed of similar soil in a cold frame, and grown until large enough to plant out in the garden.

Useful for the Greenhouse. S. racemosa makes a very attractive pot plant when forced into bloom in early spring. The roots are dug up in October or November and set in pots just large enough to hold them. A light porous compost is used for potting, and the potted plants are

[12–5]
Jerusalem Cherry
(Solanum Pseudo-Capsicum)

[12–5a]
Yellow-fruited Jerusalem Cherry
(Solanum Pseudo-Capsicum variety)

[12–5b]
Compass Plant
(Silphium laciniatum)

[12–5c]
Brazil Cress
(Spilanthes oleracea)

SMITHIANTHA. A name used by some botanists for the plants described in this Encyclopedia under the name Naegelia.

SMOKE TREE. See Cotinus.

SMUT. See Pests and Diseases.

SNAIL. See Pests and Diseases.

SNAILFLOWER. Phaseolus Caracalla, which see.

SNAKE PALM. See Hydrosme.

SNAKE PLANT. Sansevieria, which see.

SNAKEROOT, BLACK. Cimicifuga racemosa, which see.

SNAKEROOT, BUTTON. Eryngium aquaticum and Liatris, which see.

SNAKEROOT, VIRGINIA. Aristolochia Serpentaria, which see.

SNAKEROOT, WHITE. Eupatorium rugosum, which see.

SNAKE'S-BEARD. See Ophiopogon.

SNAKE'S-HEAD FRITILLARY. See Fritillaria meleagris.

SNAKE'S-HEAD IRIS. See Hermodactylus.

SNAPDRAGON. Antirrhinum, which see.

SNEEZEWEED. Helenium, which see.

SNEEZEWORT. See Helenium.

SNOW. When snow falls, it washes down with it impurities in the air, including soot, ammonia compounds, etc. It thus has a certain fertilizing value, indirectly, and may be said to enrich the ground in a small degree. When it lies on the ground it acts as a nonconducting blanket; plants beneath it are safe from severe frost and the heat of the soil is conserved. In this respect it is helpful, and a fall of snow may be heralded with pleasure in districts where plants of doubtful hardiness are kept out all winter.

Much of the snow that falls, however, is of a moist, clinging nature. It collects on the branches of trees, shrubs and plants in thick billows. These gradually weigh down the branches, and unless precautions are taken the branches may break off. In large shrubberies and in orchards a fall of snow often does much damage.

It is advisable to look over the trees and especially evergreens at intervals and to dislodge the snow from heavily weighted branches. Specimen trees and shrubs, and especially conifers, call for particular attention.

Snow on the top of a garden frame may be a blessing in so far as it keeps out cold, but when it begins to melt there is the danger of a cold and destructive drip getting through to the plants underneath. When the thaw comes it may be advisable to remove the melting snow from the frame and to substitute a mat.

SNOWBALL. See Viburnum Opulus roseum, also Viburnum tomentosum sterile.

SNOWBERRY. Symphoricarpos, which see.

SNOWBERRY, CREEPING. Chiogenes hispidula, which see.

SNOWDROP. Galanthus, which see.

SNOWDROP ANEMONE. Anemone sylvestris, which see.

SNOWDROP TREE. Halesia, which see.

SNOWFLAKE. See Leucojum.

SNOWFLAKE, WATER. Nymphoides indicum, which see.

SNOW-IN-SUMMER. See Cerastium tomentosum.

SNOW-ON-THE-MOUNTAIN. See Euphorbia marginata.

SNOW WREATH, ALABAMA. See Neviusia.

SOAPBERRY. Sapindus, which see.

SOAP PLANT. Chlorogalum pomeridianum, which see.

SOAPWORT. Saponaria, which see.

SOBRALIA (Sobral'ia). Orchids which are very different in appearance from most other kinds. They are found in Brazil, Mexico and Guatemala, and most of them flower in May and June. All are terrestrial and have reedlike stems, well furnished with evergreen leaves, the bases of which clasp the stems. The flowers are large and showy and are produced from the tops of the stems in succession. Thus, although the life of the individual flower is only three or four days the flowering period is extended. The name commemorates Don Francisco Martin Sobral, a Spanish botanist.

Hints on Management. The roots of Sobralia are large and fleshy and should be grown in large pots in a mixture composed of fibrous loam, cut osmunda fiber and crocks, sphagnum moss being added. Drainage should be free. The plants need not be repotted annually, but when necessary; this should be done in early March. From spring to September the plants must have an abundance of water; the compost is kept moist in winter but less water is needed then than in summer. If necessary, these Orchids may be increased by division when repotting is done.

In summer the plants require a moist warm atmosphere and slight shading. In winter a minimum temperature of 55 degrees by night is suitable.

The Chief Kinds. S. macrantha has bright crimson-purple flowers on stems 3-7 ft. high; there is a white variety, S. macrantha Kienastiana, and one named nana with slightly smaller flowers on stems 3 ft. in height. S. xantholeuca has yellow flowers on 3-ft. stems. In S. leucoxantha, the flowers are palest yellow, while in S. Charlesworthii they are bright rose and deep purple. S. Sanderae has pale sulphur-colored flowers with a crimson-purple lobe to the lip.

SODIUM CHLORATE. This chemical is a nonselective weed killer that is toxic to plants. It is most useful in clearing weed-infested neglected ground and in keeping paths and driveways weed-free. It is nonpoisonous to warm-blooded creatures, but it is inflammable.

The chemical kills on contact with plant tissues and may be absorbed and translocated within the plant to other parts. It may also be absorbed by the roots. In effect, its use partially sterilizes the soil by destroying all plant life in it. This effect persists until the salt is washed out of the soil, which takes 4-6 months, according to the strength of the application and the ease with which the soil drains. Light soils will be clear of the chemical effects more quickly than heavy ones.

Application can be made in dry powder or fine crystalline form, letting the rain dissolve and wash it into the soil. It is safer, however, to apply the salt in solution with water. The rate of application depends upon the weeds to be controlled. For deeply rooting weeds, such as Goutweed, Bindweed, Docks, etc., and heavily infested areas, a solution of 8 oz. per gallon water is not too heavy, and will treat 10 square yards. For clearing paths, etc., a solution of $\frac{1}{4}$ lb. in 10 gallons of water for 150 square yards is satisfactory.

For maximum effect, sodium chlorate should be applied when the weeds are in leaf and growing actively. The top growth should be allowed to wither before being removed.

The chemical has two disadvantages. First, it tends to spread into the soil somewhat beyond where it is applied. Care is needed not to apply it within 6-12 inches of lawns or borders. Second, it is inflammable when dry. It must be stored in sealed containers under cool conditions. The solution should not be allowed to soak and dry on clothing or to wet the fur of animals or the feathers of poultry. Rubber boots and overalls, which can be washed, should be worn while spraying.

Potassium chlorate is sometimes used as an alternative weed killer of similar properties to sodium chlorate, but it is more expensive.

SOIL: ITS IMPROVEMENT AND MAINTENANCE

A knowledge of the soil—its origin, characteristics and capabilities—is a fundamental requirement of all who would obtain the finest results from their gardening efforts. Armed with this information, the gardener is in a position to work and fertilize his garden so that the most satisfactory results are produced. Without such knowledge he works in the dark.

The meaning of the term soil is generally well understood. It is applied to the loose upper layer of the land surface of the Earth, which is composed for the most part of disintegrated rock intermingled with a greater or lesser proportion of decayed organic matter—the remains of dead plants and animals. The rocks have decomposed as a result of countless ages of weathering, through such influences as exposure to rain, wind, and alternate freezing and thawing. The depth of the soil varies from zero (in places where the rock itself forms the surface) to many feet in those regions where soil has been carried and piled up by the action of water or wind. Speaking broadly, the deeper soils and more fertile places on the Earth are the valleys and level lands, while the mountain tops and hillsides have often but a superficial covering of soil, and this frequently poor in fertility. To this statement there will be found, however, important exceptions, for Nature is decidedly capricious in her distribution of fertile soils.

If water lies for long periods on the soil surface as it does here, it is a sure sign that the subsurface drainage is poor. This condition needs remedying for most garden plants.

As gardeners it is usually only within certain limits that we can choose the site of our garden with special reference to soil conditions; many other factors (such as convenience to the house) enter into the selection of the site for a garden. It is axiomatic however, that practically any soil can be improved by appropriate treatment, and it is the business of the gardener to know how this can best be accomplished.

The soil serves three chief purposes in the economy of the plant. It forms an anchorage for the roots so that the plants are held firmly in position. It supplies the water used by the plant and it affords certain mineral elements essential to the plant's growth and well-being.

Soils vary greatly in their origin, depth, physical texture, chemical composition, and fertility and in other ways. The components of all soils include small rock particles, water, air, humus, dissolved material, and living organisms, and each of these we must consider in turn.

Rock Particles. The bulk of most soils consists of small, more or less angular particles of rock. Up to 90 per cent of the weight of most good soils is formed of such material, and it is this component which furnishes the anchorage for the roots. Nutrient materials are slowly dissolved from the surfaces of these rock particles and are absorbed by the plant.

Rock particles vary greatly, ranging from ultra-microscopic size to that of coarse gravel and stones. They also differ in shape and in chemical composition, depending upon the type of rock from which they have resulted. Because of their irregularity of shape, small spaces or pores occur between the particles, and these spaces are occupied by air or water.

Humus. Humus is the name of all decayed

By spading or plowing, the soil is loosened and new portions are brought to the surface to receive the beneficial effects of weather. It also becomes easy to mix manure and other organic matter with the soil.

The application of fertilizers to soil is a standard garden practice.

organic matter, whether of plant or animal origin. It is a necessary component of all fertile soils and in the practice of gardening we increase the amount present in the soil by various methods, such as mixing with it manure, compost and peat moss and digging in green manure or cover crops.

After incorporation with the soil, organic matter gradually decays and is finally broken down into simple substances such as carbon-dioxide, water and ammonia. This destruction of organic matter is brought about by a series of complex chemical changes, in the process of which it becomes characteristically dark in color and loses its original structure. It is when this stage is reached that this substance is known as humus, and it gives to the topsoil a color usually noticeably darker than that of the subsoil.

Humus not only liberates nitrogen compounds and other nutrient materials which ultimately become available to plants, but it also forms the food supply for the soil bacteria which are indispensable in plant nutrition.

Because of its fragmentary character, humus tends to separate the soil particles and increase materially the air content of the soil. Due to its spongelike properties, humus absorbs water readily, so that its presence also adds to the water-holding capacity of the soil. Generally speaking, any treatment of the soil which increases its humus content tends to increase fertility, and a decrease in humus content results in an impoverishment of the soil.

Soil Water. Water is of vital importance to the living plant, and all the water used by the plant is obtained from the soil. Rain is the chief source of the soil water, and indeed in most cases affords the only supply. A considerable portion of the total rainfall may never enter the soil, but may be lost by surface drainage. This "run-off" is particularly severe on sloping ground, when the rainfall is heavy or if the surface is hard. Excessive "run-off" may result in serious harm, due to the washing away of a part of the surface soil, and erosion of this type must be guarded against.

Of the water which actually enters the soil a portion is held as a film surrounding each individual particle. The remainder drains downward between the soil particles until it reaches a level below which all the soil spaces are completely filled with standing water. This level is known as the water table.

The position of the water table in the soil differs from place to place and may vary greatly in any given location. It is often below the reach of the roots and thus unavailable directly to plants. The level of the water table can be ascertained by digging a hole and covering it over so that no surface water enters. The level of the standing water in this hole indicates the height of the water table. The water table forms a reservoir from which water constantly rises by capillary attraction.

Dissolved Substances. Soil water is not pure, but contains in solution a great variety of substances, many of which are absorbed by the root hairs of plants. Since all material so absorbed must be in solution it is obvious that these substances form the only portions of the soil, apart from the water itself, which are directly available for the nutrition of the plant. The solvent power of soil water is increased by the presence in it of carbon-dioxide liberated by the respiration of plant roots and of lower organisms. The soil water attacks and dissolves not only the surfaces of the rock particles, but also takes into solution any soluble material which may be formed in the humus or as a result of bacterial activity.

Of the many substances which are commonly

absorbed by the roots at least seven are essential for normal plant growth. These are sulphur, phosphorus, calcium, magnesium, potassium, iron and nitrogen. A soil which is deficient in any one of these is unable to support vegetation successfully. Most soils, however, contain sufficient supplies of all but three of these elements—nitrogen, phosphorus and potassium—and in garden practice our fertilizing routine is usually directed towards increasing the proportion of these elements in the soil.

Air. The presence of a plentiful supply of air in the soil is necessary because oxygen is essential for the respiration of the roots. If the spaces between the soil particles become filled with water, most of the air is driven out; when this condition of saturation is long maintained, ordinary land plants suffer. Water and bog plants are especially adapted for living in water or wet soils and are able to obtain sufficient oxygen for their needs from the water.

In most cultivated soils 20-30 per cent of the soil volume consists of air spaces. The air in the soil usually differs somewhat in composition from the atmosphere, the proportion of carbon-dioxide being higher. Working the soil by tools and implements tends to increase greatly the air content, since the structure of the whole mass is loosened and the particles are more widely separated. A soil in such a condition is said to be in good tilth and is in an ideal state for the growth of most plants.

A soil in good tilth contains water only as a film surrounding the individual particles; air occupies the larger spaces. Such a condition is clearly most favorable for plant growth, since then, and then only, is there available to the roots a plentiful supply of soil water together with a sufficient supply of oxygen.

Soil Organisms. The uninformed frequently regard soil as a dead, inert and messy substance. They may refer to it as "dirt," and think of it only in terms of the labor required to move it. Actually, a fertile soil is decidedly pleasant to handle and, far from being dead, is literally teeming with countless millions of minute living organisms, some favorable and others detrimental to plant growth. These organisms, in the course of their growth and multiplication, modify the chemical and mechanical condition of the soil.

Most important of the soil organisms are the bacteria. These are tiny one-celled plants which lack chlorophyll. Many of them obtain their food material by decomposing complex organic substances into such simple end products as carbon-dioxide, water and ammonia. These are the bacteria of decay. Still other bacteria seize upon the ammonia and transform it by a process known as nitrification into nitrate salts, the only form in which most plants can use nitrogen. The bacteria which do this work are of two types, those which convert ammonia into nitrites and those which in turn convert nitrites into nitrates.

Through the activity of another group of these minute organisms certain of the plants belonging to the Pea family are able to make use of the free nitrogen of the air. These bacteria form nodules on the roots of Beans, Peas, Clovers, etc., and convert the free atmospheric nitrogen into nitrogenous compounds which are available to the plant on whose roots the bacteria grow. Thus these leguminous plants are able to acquire an abundant supply of this important element.

Yet other seed plants live with their roots in intimate association with species of fungi forming unions known as mycorrhiza. These fungi surround the roots with a weblike jacket of mycelium threads which largely take the place of root hairs in aiding the plant to absorb water. Certain plants are quite unable to grow except in the presence of the particular species of fungus to which they have been accustomed.

Soil Tillage. From the above it is obvious that soils must be considered from their chemical, physical and biological aspects and our gardening practice must be directed towards such matters as the deepening of shallow soils, the maintenance of a desirable physical or mechanical condition, the encouragement of the development of favorable soil organisms and the addition of plant foods which are not present in sufficient quantities. All too often the beginner considers only this point, yet unless the other conditions are favorable the addition of fertilizers is largely wasted effort.

Classification. Ordinary garden soils may be classified into four main groups, based on the size of the particles of which they are predominantly formed and the amount of organic matter they contain. Each of these groups has definite characteristics and presents distinct problems for the gardener.

Clay soils are heavy, sticky and difficult to cultivate. Being retentive of moisture, they do not dry out rapidly; they are consequently cold and unsuitable for early crops. To bring a clayey soil into a state of fertility and to render it easy to work, the soil needs liberal applications of humus in the form of compost, peat or manure. Sand also is desirable to make it porous, and lime helps to keep it in a workable condition. It is also important that clay soils be properly drained to get rid of excess water.

Because the structure of clay soils is severely damaged if they are manipulated when they are wet, every effort should be made to avoid walking on them, plowing them, pushing wheelbarrows or carts over them, trucking over them, or in other ways disturbing or compacting them at such times. It is important to work on clay soils only when they are so dry that they do not stick unpleasantly to shoes and tools. Such timing of operations will do much to prevent them from becoming excessively sticky and impervious to air when they are wet, and from baking into hard clods when they are dry.

Clay soil is improved by burning, and burnt clay is an excellent dressing for Rose beds and shrub borders. To burn clay, a fire of wood logs is first made, and, when well lit, is covered with a mixture of the clay and garden rubbish. As the fire breaks through, more clay and rubbish are added; provided openings are left at the base to ensure a free draft, the fire can be kept lit indefinitely and a large quantity of clay burned.

Sandy soils, being porous, lose their moisture rapidly and are consequently warmer and more suitable for early crops. They can be improved by digging in plenty of humus, which not only renders them more fertile but helps to conserve moisture.

Because sandy soils lose solubles rapidly by leaching (the action of liquid that percolates through), more frequent fertilization is needed than with loams and clay soils. In dry weather more frequent applications of water are also necessary.

Peat, Bog and Muck Soils. These are formed of dead and decaying roots, rhizomes, leaves and stems of bog plants, consequently this type of soil is acid and can only be brought into a state of fertility by draining and liming and, if practicable, by the addition of loam or good soil.

Loam is a blend of sand, clay, and humus. If sand preponderates, it is a sandy loam, and when clay is in excess it is clayey loam. Loam of a medium texture is the gardener's ideal soil. It is the chief constituent of most potting composts.

A good loam is friable (crumbly) and easy to work with gardening tools such as spade, spading fork, rake and hoe. It permits water to drain through it fairly rapidly yet is retentive enough to hold sufficient moisture to supply the plants over a reasonable period. Fertilizers do not leach as rapidly as from sandy soils.

Color of the Soil. The color of the soil varies according to the amount of humus and iron it contains. Red soils derive their color from the oxide of iron which is present, and the bluish color in soils is due to iron sulphide. Humus makes the soil dark when wet, grayish when dry.

Drainage. No matter what the soil type is, good drainage is essential for the successful cultivation of most garden crops. Drainage is usually thought of as being the removal of surplus water, but actually drainage serves to make available to plants an increased proportion of the actual rainfall. Plants on poorly drained soils often suffer more severely during periods of drought than plants on adequately drained land. This is explained by the fact that on well-drained ground root development extends to a considerable depth and even during dry periods the plants are able to make use of supplies of water held deep in the ground. On poorly drained ground where a high water table exists during the spring and early summer the plant roots are confined to a shallow depth, and when, in periods of drought, the water table sinks rapidly, the plants having shallow root systems are unable to avail themselves of the water at any considerable depth.

In most situations encountered by the gardener appropriate tillage operations are sufficient to ensure proper soil drainage, but in particular cases these measures may not be enough and an installed drainage system becomes necessary. Such systems are always costly in labor and should not be undertaken without due consideration being given to all circumstances. However, if the permanent water table lies within 2-2½ ft. of the surface, need for artificial drainage is indicated. See article on Drainage.

Digging, Plowing and Rototilling. Deep cultivation effected by the proper use of the spade, digging fork, plow or rototiller is perhaps the most important of garden tillage operations. The fullest possibilities of any piece of garden devoted to the growing of flowers or vegetables cannot be realized unless it is properly worked, and this implies turning it over thoroughly at intervals. This operation permits the incorporation with the soil of manures and other humus-forming material and ensures the various weathering agencies the opportunity to bring their ameliorating influences to bear upon portions of the soil which would otherwise remain buried and unchanged over long periods. By such means, in course of time, the depth of good soil is increased and plants grown on such ground find more nutrients available and are able to send their roots deeper into the earth so that in time of drought they are far less likely to suffer. See Digging, the Basis of Good Garden Cultivation.

Fertilizing. The addition to the soil of fertilizers and manures is an important factor in the maintenance of soil fertility. The kinds and amounts used should depend to a considerable extent upon the character of the soil and the plants that are being grown. See Fertilizers.

Lime is desirable for various reasons. It granulates the particles of clayey soil and renders it more friable or crumbly. It neutralizes acid in the soil, prevents or cures sourness, and liberates some plant foods, particularly potash, present in the soil, so that they become available to the plants.

A simple method of testing for lime is to obtain a representative sample from the garden and place it in a jar with sufficient hot water to make it of a creamy consistency. Then pour into it about two fluid ounces of hydrochloric acid. If it effervesces freely, sufficient lime is present, but if feebly or not at all, it is deficient in lime and a dressing should be given, unless plants that are known to require acid soils, such as Azaleas, Blueberries, Heathers and Rhododendrons, are being grown. A surer method of testing for lime is by the use of a soil testing kit. See Soil Testing.

Potting Soils

In gardens it is common practice to prepare special soil mixtures or composts for plants that are to be grown in pots or other containers. Experience proves that such mixtures are usually productive of better results than ordinary loam or topsoil no matter how well adapted it is for growing plants outdoors.

There are two reasons why most plants grown in containers do not prosper as well in topsoil

Loam for use in potting soils may be prepared by stacking alternate layers of grass sods and compost or manure in a heap outdoors in a sheltered location.

(loam) as in topsoil mixed with various other ingredients. First, when plants are potted the soil is normally packed fairly firmly and frequent subsequent watering tends to make it even more compact, so that unless the soil is naturally very porous the free passage of water and air through it is seriously retarded. Second, because the amount of soil available to the roots of a potted plant is limited, frequent watering causes the nutrients it contains to leach out more rapidly than in outdoor gardens.

To counteract the tendency of soil used for potting to become excessively compacted and leached of nutrients, materials that help to make it more porous and fertilizers that supply nutrients are added to it.

In recent years attempts have been made to develop a number of standard soil mixtures for seed sowing, potting, etc. (see entry in this Encyclopedia, John Innes Seed and Potting Composts) and also to develop soil substitutes in which to grow plants in containers. Among the latter much success has been had with finely sifted or milled sphagnum moss (see Sphagnum Moss) and with the U.C.-Type Soil Mixes discussed at the end of this article.

The basis of all potting soils is good loam. Fertile topsoil taken directly from a field or garden may be used, but a better source is a loam heap made by stacking grass sods cut from a rich meadow or field. The sods should be 4-5 in. thick and piled grass side down to form a heap 3-5 ft. high and of any convenient length and width. When the heap is made it is beneficial to add a 3-in. layer of manure between every two 8-10 in. layers of sods. The loam heap should be in a shaded location. At the end of about 6 months it will be ready for use. The loam is at its best when the grass roots have partly rotted but not completely decayed. A generous amount of fiber in the soil gives it a springy character and prevents it from packing.

When preparing soil for potting, the loam used should be in a moist but not wet condition. It should not be so muddy that it sticks to the hands. It should be chopped to suitable-sized pieces or sifted through a sieve so that it is not in too coarse a condition, but great care must be exercised not to remove all or most of the fibrous parts or to have it excessively fine. Except for use in very small pots (for which the loam may be sifted through a $\frac{1}{2}$-in. mesh) soil for potting should never be sifted through a mesh smaller than $\frac{3}{4}$ in., and usually a 1-in. mesh or larger is more appropriate.

Decayed organic matter in the form of leaf mold, commercial humus, sedge peat, peat moss or other appropriate material is added to the loam for most potting composts. If necessary, these materials are sifted through a $\frac{1}{2}$-in. or $\frac{3}{4}$-in. sieve. The amount of organic matter added varies according to the character of the loam and the type of plant being potted, but quite usually is approximately $\frac{1}{3}$ by bulk of the amount of loam used. The organic matter helps porosity, slows down leaching and, as it decays, supplies some nutrients.

Porosity is usually further assured by adding such materials as coarse sand, finely broken brick, or sifted coal cinders (but not fine ashes). Such materials usually constitute $\frac{1}{3}$ part or less (by bulk) of the finished potting mixture.

Fertilizers added to the mixture may include dried cow manure (up to $\frac{1}{10}$ or $\frac{1}{8}$ part by bulk of the finished mixture), bone meal (up to about one pint to each bushel of mixture), unleached wood ashes (up to two quarts to each bushel of mixture) and a commercial fertilizer, in smaller amounts, depending upon the character and analysis of the fertilizer and the type of plants for which the soil is being prepared.

Other additions sometimes include crushed limestone or lime and chopped charcoal. The exact materials selected and the proportions in which they are used vary according to the needs of the particular plants to be potted. For very young plants it is common to use less fertilizers than for mature ones of the same kinds.

Because loams, sands, leaf molds and other ingredients used in potting and seed-sowing soils vary in texture and other characteristics it is not possible to state with exactness the proportions in which they should be mixed. The following soil mixtures (potting and seed-sowing composts) are approximations rather than absolutes.

For Seed Sowing. All ingredients should be fine enough to pass through a $\frac{1}{2}$-in. mesh. Rub the loam and leaf mold through so that as much of their fibrous parts as possible are retained.

A soil mixture for the seeds of the great ma-

Loam, peat moss, and sand are the chief ingredients of potting-soil mixtures. Leaf mold or humus may be substituted for the peat moss. For most plants some bone meal or other fertilizer may be added. It helps to add broken charcoal to soil mixtures that contain much organic matter.

jority of plants consists of loam, one part; leaf mold, peat moss, or humus, one part; coarse sand, one part.

A mixture suitable for sowing seeds of Cacti and other succulents: loam, one part; leaf mold, peat moss, or humus, one part; coarse sand, four parts; crocks, broken brick or gritty cinders (passed through a ¼-in. sieve and with all fine dust removed), four parts.

A soil mixture suitable for plants that require a woodsy, humus soil such as Begonias, Gloxinias and African Violets: loam, one part; leaf mold, peat moss, or humus, two parts; sand, one part; crocks, cinders, or broken brick (passed through a ¼-in. sieve and with all fine dust removed), ¼ part; charcoal (passed through a ¼-in. sieve), ¼ part.

For Transplanting Seedlings. Soil for the first transplanting of seedlings should be similar to that recommended for seeds of the same plants, except that it may be coarser and may have a little fertilizer added. If it passes through a ⅜-in. mesh it is fine enough. Add half a pint of bone meal and a pint of dried sheep manure (or two quarts of dried cow manure) to each bushel.

For Potted Cuttings. Cuttings rooted in sand, vermiculite and other well-aerated media need a loose, porous soil at their first potting. Use the same type of mixture that the plant is known to favor at later pottings but leave out all fertilizers and double or treble the proportion of sand used. Pass all ingredients through a ½-in. sieve.

For Potting Established Plants. The mixture should not be finer than necessary to permit packing it about the roots. Within reason, the coarser the soil the better. When potting in large pots or tubs, coarser material may be used than for smaller receptacles.

A general-purpose mixture suitable for most strong-rooted plants such as Geraniums, Chrysanthemums, Fuchsias, Palms, Snake Plants and English Ivy consists of loam, four parts; leaf mold, peat moss, or humus, two parts; dried cow manure, one part (or one-third as much dried sheep manure); coarse sand, two parts (this may be replaced in part by chopped crock, brick or gritty cinders); bone meal, a pint to each bushel; wood ashes, two quarts to each bushel; complete garden fertilizer, half a pint to each bushel.

A woodsy mixture for plants that need a soil having a high organic content, such as Begonias, African Violets, Gloxinias and Ferns, may consist of loam, two parts; leaf mold, peat moss, or humus, two and a half parts; coarse sand, half a part; broken crock, brick or gritty cinders, one part; charcoal, half a part; dried cow manure, one part; bone meal, a pint to each bushel.

A soil mixture for succulent plants such as Cacti may be made from loam, two parts; leaf mold, peat moss, or humus, two parts; coarse sand, two parts; broken crocks, bricks, or gritty cinders, two parts; bone meal, a pint to each bushel; lime, a pint to each bushel; wood ashes, two quarts to each bushel. For strong-growing kinds such as Century Plants and Aloes add one-tenth part by bulk of dried cow manure.

For acid-soil plants such as Heathers, Azaleas, Camellias and Gardenias the soil may consist of loam, two parts; leaf mold or humus, one part; peat moss, two parts; coarse sand, two parts; dried cow manure, one part.

For forcing bulbs and plants such as Daffodils, Hyacinths, Tulips, Spiraeas and Fuchsias a good mixture is loam, four parts; leaf mold, peat moss, or humus, two parts; coarse sand, three parts; and bone meal, a pint to be added to each bushel.

U.C.-Type Soil Mixes. These are standardized potting soil substitutes developed at the University of California and now widely used for container-grown plants, especially in the West. Basically they consist of mixtures of fine sand and peat moss. It is emphasized that the sizes of the grains comprising the fine sand are important; maximum and minimum dimensions should be 0.5 mm and 0.05 mm, respectively. Grains of these sizes should comprise preferably 85 per cent and certainly not less than 70 per cent of the sand used. Of the remainder, not more than 15 per cent should be silt and clay (finer particles than the smallest of the fine sand grains) and not more than 15 per cent should be larger particles than the largest of the fine sand grains. The peat moss used should be finely ground.

The proportions of fine sand and peat moss vary in different mixes. U. C. Soil Mix A is based on 100 per cent fine sand. In U. S. Soil Mix B 75 per cent fine sand and 25 per cent peat moss is used. U. C. Soil Mix C employs 50 per cent fine sand and 50 per cent peat moss. U. S. Soil Mix D consists of 25 per cent fine sand and 75 per cent peat moss. U. C. Soil Mix E is based on 100 per cent moss.

Because the fine sand and peat moss are devoid of or are deficient in plant nutrients it is necessary to add fertilizers in carefully measured amounts. Dolomite lime and calcium carbonate are added to correct excessive acidity. Several different fertilizer formulas for each of the six basic U. C. Type Soil Mixes are recommended and are listed in publications of the University of California College of Agriculture, obtainable from Agricultural Publications, 22 Gianni Hall, University of California, Berkeley 4, California. One of these publications, Manual 23, "The U. C. System of Producing Healthy Container-Grown Plants" is priced at one dollar and should be in the hands of everyone who intends to use these soil mixes.

The fertilizers used (in varying amounts in different mixes and for different uses of the same mix) are potassium nitrite, potassium sulphate, single superphosphate, hoof and horn or blood meal and, in addition, dolomite lime, calcium carbonate lime, and gypsum.

SOIL BLOCKS AS SUBSTITUTES FOR POTS
Excellent for Seedlings and Cuttings If Made Properly

Raising plants in soil blocks is a practice developed in Europe but not much used in the United States and Canada. The blocks consist of suitably constituted soil compost molded under pressure and cohering by compression.

For Seedlings and Cuttings. The blocks are most suitable for the raising of plants from seeds or cuttings that are to be transplanted into greenhouse benches or out of doors. They are less suitable for plants eventually intended to be

(Above) Making soil blocks with a simple and easy-to-handle soil-block maker. (Right) A greenhouse full of seedling Tomatoes that were transplanted in soil blocks, which retain their form until planting time.

grown in pots and for continuous growing throughout a season.

Sturdy seedling Tomatoes grown in soil blocks and ready for planting.

In the soil block the root system develops more naturally and evenly through the rooting medium in contrast to the pot plant which develops roots which tend to wrap around the inside of the pot itself. It is not only easier to transplant the soil-block plant but it can be done without any check to growth.

Block-making Tools. Block-making machines range from the mechanically operated capable of producing up to 1,000 blocks an hour, to the small tools which make one block at a time. The more evenly and uniformly the machine compresses the block, the better. Although blocks may be made in various sizes, the most common are 3-in. diameter, and $2\frac{1}{4}$-in. diameter.

Suitable Compost. The primary essential of a successful soil block is a well-mixed and balanced soil compost. Any proven formula used for ordinary potting may be adopted.

The loam should be a medium loam with not too much or too little clay content. A turf loam is ideal. A light sandy loam does not cohere well. A silty loam makes a too dense block, and a heavy clay loam makes a bricklike block. The loam should preferably be sterilized, as any necessary weeding may pull the block apart. A good sedge or moss peat in moist condition, and a coarse lime-free sand without gravel particles, are best for blocks.

Soil composts should be well mixed with fertilizing ingredients and uniformly moist, so that a handful will bind together when squeezed and yet fall readily apart when slightly shaken. Correct moistness is the key to a successful soil block, and it is worth experimenting a little to gain familiarity with the effect of moisture conditions on the consistency of the block. The aim must be to make a block that will stand up to use with a minimum of compression. To get uniformity the same quantity of soil compost must be used for each block.

Management. Once made, soil blocks should be used as soon as possible, and never allowed to dry out. The planting hole in the block should be filled with the same soil compost as used for the block.

In transplanting seedlings, etc., into blocks it is wise to leave a small depression to catch water around each plant. When set out on benches the blocks should be spaced slightly apart to prevent inter-rooting. They should be on firm, flat surfaces and not on slatted benches, unless covered by stout paper. It helps to conserve moisture to stand the blocks on a ¼-in. layer of peat. The blocks should not stand on earth or ash beds which the roots may enter and suffer damage when removed.

Watering. In watering soil blocks the aim is to prevent the surface from becoming too dry. Watering must be done with a spray to avoid breaking down the block structure. Too little watering will result in the blocks becoming hard, with growth checked. Too much will cause excessive root development to the outsides of the blocks, and such roots will be vulnerable to drying out. In practice, therefore, moderate watering is best for plants in soil blocks.

Apart from the superior results given by the soil block when compared with the clay pot, the initial cost of the machine is offset by the saving of time and effort and of breakages in the use of clay pots.

SOILLESS CULTIVATION. This subject is dealt with fully under Hydroponics, which see.

SOIL, POTTING. See Potting Soils under Soil: Its Improvement and Maintenance.

SOIL SOAKER. A porous hose that permits water to soak out all along its length and moisten the soil on which it is laid. Soil soakers are used for watering trees, shrubs and other garden plants.

SOIL STERILIZATION. The logical way of getting rid of fungus diseases and pests in the soil is to kill these organisms by chemicals or by heat. The practical problem is, however, a serious one. The difficulty with chemicals is to make certain that the whole of the soil is permeated by the substance used. For this reason sterilization by chemicals is less efficient than sterilization by heat, as a rule.

Sterilization by Chemicals. Among materials available are formalin, carbon disulphide (corrosive sublimate), D-D mixture and V.C. 13. See Insecticides and Miticides and also Fungicides, under Pests and Diseases.

Chemicals used for soil sterilization are either diluted with water and poured on to the soil until it is soaked to a considerable depth (in some cases, as with formalin, it is necessary to cover the treated areas for a few days with tarpaulins or other suitable covers to prevent the escape of gases) or are injected into the soil with a special tool, as is usually done with chloropicrin. When manufacturers supply directions, these should be closely followed; in other cases care should be taken to ascertain the amounts needed for given areas before applying them.

Sterilization by heat is very much more efficient than by chemicals. The soil is raised to a temperature of 210-212 degrees F. (just at or below the boiling point of water) and is kept there for 15-40 minutes. The heavier the soil, the longer the time necessary for satisfactory results, but 30 minutes will be ample with most soils. Heat may be applied by steaming, baking or by electrical methods.

In steaming small quantities of soil it is necessary to remove the soil and place it in a box or bed to which a steam supply is connected. A box 4 ft. 6 in. long, 3 ft. wide and 2 ft. 3 in. deep holds about a ton of soil. Iron sheets are bolted to the inner sides of the box and there is a false bottom consisting of a perforated iron plate. Steam is introduced below the false bottom. Instead of the perforated plate a grid made up of 1-in. piping can be used if preferred.

Steam is passed until the temperature of all parts of the soil is raised to 210-212 degrees, and continued for 20-30 minutes afterwards. It is very important to use reliable thermometers to make certain of this. The top of the box should be covered with burlap or tarpaulin to keep the steam in.

Still smaller quantities of soil can be sterilized in a metal container; steam is introduced through a pipe placed in the bottom and separated from the soil by a false bottom of perforated metal. This is quite satisfactory for about 300 lbs. of soil.

The condition of the soil at the time of treating is important. It must be uniformly moist but not too wet. If it is too dry the steam blows through too quickly. If it is too wet it bubbles through in channels and the soil is very muddy when it comes out of the sterilizer. Generally speaking, a soil sufficiently dry for potting is ready for steaming.

Steaming has the advantage that the temperature of the soil cannot rise above 212 degrees F., and there is no danger of destroying the organic matter in the soil.

Baking the Soil. In the method of baking, the soil is placed in a metal box and heated for 12 hours over a slow fire. For safety it is better to have a reliable thermometer inserted and, after it has reached between 205 degrees and 210 degrees F., the heating need be continued only another hour or two. The soil must be fairly dry for satisfactory baking, but not too dry, or there is a danger of overbaking. Plants will not grow in an overbaked soil until untreated soil is mixed with it. This is because the organisms that determine soil fertility have been killed as well as the disease organisms and it is thus necessary to introduce to the soil favorable organisms.

Home soil-testing kits are satisfactory for making simple soil tests. Here, a small portion of soil is about to be placed in a test tube.

Electric soil sterilizing apparatus is available in several types, including small outfits suitable for amateur gardeners. These are simple to use and are quite satisfactory.

Efficient sterilization, whether by heat or by chemicals, not only eliminates pests and diseases from the soil, but also, by its action on the substances making up the soil, and on other soil organisms, actually increases the fertility of the soil. A sterilized soil will usually, therefore, need less nitrogenous manure than is customarily applied. It has been found, however, that the application of phosphatic fertilizer, such as superphosphate, is often distinctly beneficial.

Great care must be taken not to contaminate the soil after it has been sterilized; reinfected soil is just as dangerous as the original diseased soil. The water supply is also important, if it is contaminated it may reintroduce the disease organisms, and the soil become rapidly infected again.

The time of the year to sterilize soil is in the late autumn and winter. After sterilization by chemicals such as formalin and D-D mixture, two or three weeks should elapse before planting is begun.

SOIL TESTING. The chemical analysis of soils is a prolonged and difficult scientific process, which can be carried out only in a chemical laboratory. Ordinarily a complete analysis is not necessary. Simple tests that indicate the degree of acidity or alkalinity, the proportions of humus and nitrogen, phosphorus and potash present are usually sufficient. Such tests are made by

A liquid from the kit is added to the soil in the test tube (concealed here by the hand).

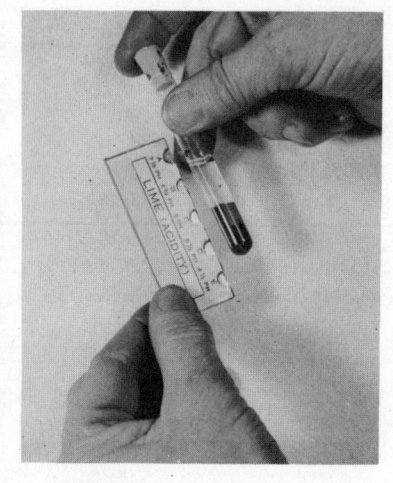

The color of the liquid, after it has been in contact with the soil, is compared with a standard scale to determine the amount of a given element in the soil.

County Agricultural Agents and State Agricultural Experiment Stations, or can be made with soil-testing kits available from dealers in garden supplies.

Meaning of *p*H. Most gardeners seeing the symbol *p*H for the first time, want to know just what it means and why it is considered so important. The *p*H of anything indicates its active acidity or alkalinity expressed in units. It is generally used in horticultural science to indicate a condition of the soil. This is important to know because many plants thrive only when the *p*H value of the soil closely approximates the optimum for their particular kind.

Soil acidity may be of two kinds, active and potential. It is a state in which the concentration of hydrogen ions (H+) exceeds that of hydroxyl ions (OH−). When you have an exact balance of H+ and OH− ions, you have neutrality. When the OH− ions are greater than the H+ ions you have alkalinity.

Active soil acidity represents the excess of H ions over the OH ions present in the soil solution. It is expressed in *p*H units on the *p*H scale. On this scale 7 represents neutrality; higher readings indicate alkalinity, lower ones acidity. It is rare to find a soil with greater acidity than that represented by 3.5, or with great alkalinity than 8.0. But it should be noted that the relationship between the figures is geometric. Acidity at *p*H 5 is ten times as great as at 6, and at *p*H 4, one hundred times.

It is usual to term soils extremely, slightly, moderately or strongly acid or alkaline in correlations with their *p*H reading.

The Acid-Alkaline Balance. Soils are rarely static in their acid-alkaline balance. Most, under cultivation, tend to become more acid. This is because they have a potential acidity in the H ions held in the colloidal matter of the soil. These ions do not move freely like those in the soil solution, but they are in equilibrium with them. It can be said that the potential or reserve acidity of the soil is reflected in the active acidity of the soil solution and, indeed, conditions it.

To neutralize acidity the gardener adds lime, a base or alkaline mineral. This quickly neutralizes the active acidity. When this happens, H ions are released from the potential acidity of the soil, from the colloids, and in time make the soil solution acid again. In soils with a high potential acidity, such as clay or peat, this happens relatively quickly. In chalky or limy soils, acidification increases slowly. Sometimes it is desirable to increase soil acidity. This may be done by adding acid peat moss, powdered sulphur or aluminum sulphate. One to 2 pounds of sulphur to each 100 sq. ft. are needed to lower the soil each ½ *p*H.

The importance of ascertaining the *p*H of a soil with reasonable accuracy is twofold. It tells you what plants you can expect to grow successfully; and it also indicates how much lime you need to apply if the soil is too acid.

Simple Outfits Available. Precise determinations of *p*H are made electrically with the use of a potentiometer. In the garden and for novice use, sufficiently accurate readings can be best obtained by using a simple, inexpensive soil-testing outfit based on colored dyestuff indicators, by which different colors or shades correspond to different *p*H values. Such outfits are of great value to the keen gardener, permitting repeated tests to be made of different soil levels, different plots, year by year.

Efficient Liming. The first step in efficient liming is to find out the measure of soil acidity we have to reduce. This is done by ascertaining the *p*H value of the soil. The next is to take into account the optimum *p*H for the plants we intend to grow.

If the soil has a *p*H value of 4 to 5, the only plants it is likely to grow well are Azaleas, Rhododendrons, Laurels, Holly, Cranberries and other members of the Ericaceae and Vacciniaceae and a few other kinds. A *p*H 5 to 5.5 suits lawn grasses, Melons, Cucumbers, Squash and certain alpine plants, and is all right for Potatoes and Tomatoes otherwise well fertilized. Most vegetables and many herbaceous plants do best when the soil's *p*H is between 6 and 7.

Raising the *p*H Value. To raise the *p*H from a low value to a high one, we add lime. The actual amount needed depends on the readiness with which the lime disperses in the soil and the kind of lime used. The lighter and coarser the texture of the soil the more quickly lime works, so that less lime is needed for a sandy soil than a clay to reduce a stated acidity. The accompanying chart shows the importance of this point.

Amount of Hydrated Lime Needed to Reduce Soil Acidity to pH 6.5

Soil acidity	Pounds per Rod (30¼ sq. yd.)			
	Light sandy soils	Medium sandy soils	Loam and silt soils	Heavy clays
From pH 4.5	14	18	21	30
" pH 5.0	13	17	19	28
" pH 5.5	11	14	18	24
" pH 6.0	8	11	15	20

The rapidity with which lime acts is also determined by the form in which it is applied. Slaked or hydrated lime is usually a fine powder and, when evenly distributed, it reacts quickly and within a few days. Hydrated lime is the form to use when time presses. The same is true about quick or burnt lime, for as this is wetted it is converted into hydrated lime.

If, however, you use ground limestone, you must use more of it and preferably some weeks ahead of when you want it to be effective. This is because it acts more slowly, and, to be really effective, must be finely ground. It takes 30-50% more ground limestone than hydrated lime to have the same effect. But ground limestone remains longer in the soil and thus is effective for a longer period.

Types of Lime to Use. Because it is effective for 3-4 years, ground limestone is often the best form of lime to use and is certainly best on sandy soils. Hydrated lime may be used on all types of soil.

Whatever material is used, it is best applied to the soil surface and raked or harrowed in. The feeding roots of plants crowd the upper level of the soil, and it is here that the correction of acidity is most needed.

Testing for Physical Condition. Sometimes it is desirable to make a physical test of the soil to determine what proportions of humus, clay, silt, sand and other soil fractions it contains. Such a test can be made at home in the following manner, the result giving a rough analysis of the soil contents. Weigh about 1 lb. of soil and spread it out thinly on a tray; keep in a dry room for a week, or in a warm oven for a day. Weigh again. The difference represents "soil water"; it may be calculated to a percentage. Roast the dry soil thus obtained until it ceases to give off smoke and weigh again when cool. The difference now represents the organic matter or humus, which is dissipated in the roasting process. It should be calculated again to a percentage.

The matter which remains may be looked upon as mineral soil, containing fertilizing salts, clay, sand, grit, stones, etc. Place it in a jar, add distilled water, and shake up. Carefully pass off the muddy water into another jar. Repeat this three or four times until the water poured off is almost clear. Dry what is left and place the jar of muddy water in the oven; in a few days it, too, will dry up. The former jar contains sand, grit and stones only; the latter contains clay. From the weight of each you can then calculate the percentage of clay and sand.

SOLANDRA—*Chalice Vine* (Solan'dra). Tropical climbing shrubs which grow wild in tropical America and belong to the Solanum or Potato family, Solanaceae. They have woody stems, large, somewhat oval leaves, and immense flowers similar in shape and size to those of the Datura. The flowers are funnel-shaped, five-lobed, and average 12 in. in length. They are white or yellowish and some kinds are fragrant. They are solitary (produced singly in the axils of the leaves) and open in late spring. The name Solandra commemorates Daniel C. Solander, a Swedish naturalist.

Flowering Plants for a Warm Greenhouse. The plants require a minimum winter temperature of 55 degrees, and a soil compost of equal parts of loam, leaf mold, peat and well-decayed manure, to which sufficient sand is added to make it porous. The plants are grown in large,

Solandra nitida has purple-striped flowers which are creamy yellow when they first open, but soon become deeper yellow.

well-drained pots or tubs, and the shoots are trained to wires or a trellis fixed to the greenhouse wall, roof or pillars.

Details of Cultivation. Well-rooted plants in 5-in. pots are planted in the tubs in February or March. After planting, the compost is kept slightly on the dry side until the plants are well established, but for the remainder of the summer it is kept moist.

As the plants are at rest during winter very little moisture is needed then; it is therefore sufficient to water the soil only when it becomes quite dry. By keeping them short of water after growth is complete the wood becomes well ripened and will bear flowers more profusely. Shading is only necessary during the hottest time of the day in summer.

From March to September the atmosphere is kept moderately moist by damping the floor and benches, and the foliage is syringed twice a day. During the resting period very little damping or shading is required.

Little pruning is necessary; the strongest shoots should be shortened slightly and the weaker ones thinned out after flowering.

Propagation Is by Cuttings. Shoots 3 in. long are taken off in March or April and, after being trimmed, are inserted in sand, sand and peat moss or vermiculite in a propagating case with a bottom heat of 65-70 degrees. The case is kept close and shaded. More light and air are admitted when roots have formed, and the cuttings are eventually removed from the propagating case and potted separately in 3-in. pots. As soon as they are well rooted they are repotted in 5-in. pots, and finally planted into the large tubs or pots.

The chief kind is S. grandiflora, 30 ft., flowers cream with purple streaks. Other kinds are S. longiflora, 6 ft., white with purple streaks, and S. nitida, 20 ft., cream turning to deep yellow as they age and with purple stripes.

SOLANUM — *Potato, Eggplant, Christmas Cherry* (Sola'num). A very extensive group of over one thousand species or kinds of tender and hardy, herbaceous, shrubby or climbing plants. They are found wild in many countries, but principally in Chile, Costa Rica, tropical Africa and Europe. Several kinds are found wild in North America.

Young Eggplants — a species of Solanum, like the Tomato and Potato.

The Solanums are easily distinguished by their flowers, which are rotate (wheel-shaped), five-petaled, white or blue or purple, with five stamens set close together. They are in pendent clusters in the axils of the leaves. The Potato flowers are typical of this genus.

Solanum belongs to the Solanaceae, the Nightshade family. The derivation of the name is rather uncertain; it is supposed to be from *solamen,* quieting, in reference to the soothing and narcotic principles of some of the species.

Eggplant. S. Melongena variety esculentum,

The Jerusalem Cherry, Solanum Pseudo-Capsicum, is a favorite pot plant for winter decoration.

Staking

[12–6]
Tying Chrysanthemum stems to a single, central stake

[12–6a]
Freesias with four stakes around outside of each pot

[12–6b]
Peas supported by chicken wire

[12–6c]
Method of staking or guying newly planted tree

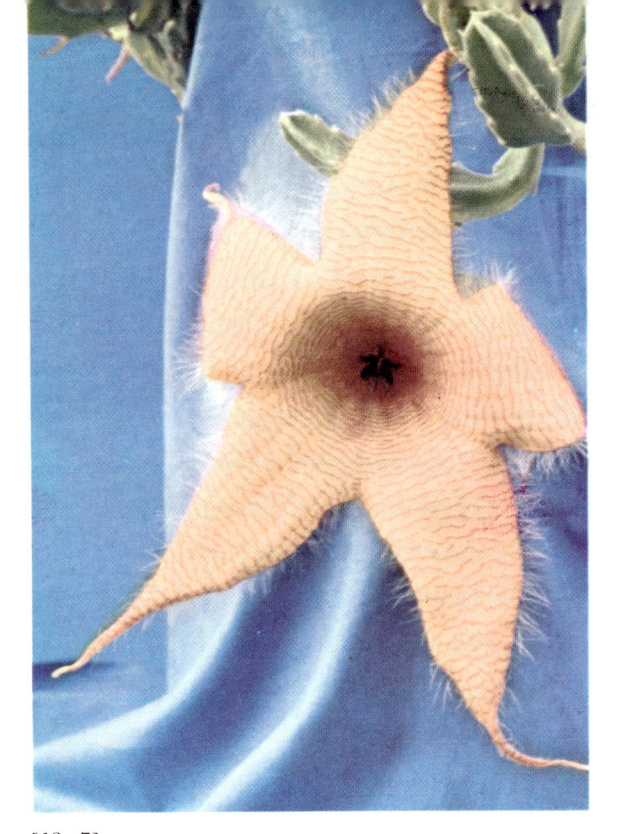

[12–7]
Carrion Flower
(Stapelia nobilis)

[12–7a]
Carrion Flower
(Stapelia grandiflora)

[12–7b]
Spathiphyllum **Wallisii**

[12–7c]
Sobralia Galleottiana

Solanum jasminoides, the Potato Vine, a tender climber for the greenhouse or for outdoors in warm climates.

commonly known as Eggplant, is grown for its ornamental and edible fruits. So are two other varieties of this species, S. Melongena variety depressum, the Dwarf Eggplant and S. Melongena variety serpentinum, the Snake Eggplant. These annuals, which are natives of tropical Africa and Asia, grow 2-3 ft. in height and have ovate, entire (undivided) leaves. The violet-blue flowers are produced in long-stalked clusters, and these are followed by egg-shaped or elongated, white, purple, or yellow fruits, up to 12 in. in length. The fruits are edible and are highly esteemed. For details of cultivation, see Eggplant.

The Potato is S. tuberosum and is available in many varieties. For its cultivation, see Potato. Although commonly known as Irish Potato, the wild forms are natives of South America.

Solanum crispum is a tender small tree or shrub which has ovate, slightly hairy leaves, 2-4 in. long. The flowers, which are produced during late summer, are light purple and borne in large, spreading clusters. This plant is adaptable for outdoor cultivation in mild climates only.

Ordinary garden soil is suitable and a well-drained site is necessary. Planting should be done in spring. Pruning consists of thinning out the weak shoots and slightly shortening the vigorous branches in spring when growth is commencing. This shrub may be kept in the form of a dwarf shrub by hard pruning in spring.

Solanum Wendlandii is one of the most handsome of climbing kinds. Here it is seen trained to the rafters of a large greenhouse.

Solanum jasminoides, the Potato Vine, is a tender climber that is popular for planting outdoors in mild climates such as those of Florida and California. It grows up to 20 ft. in height, has small, oval, green leaves, and bears large trusses of star-shaped white flowers in late summer and autumn. It is a useful plant for a cool greenhouse, but, being vigorous, it requires drastic pruning each spring. There is a large-flowered form, grandiflorum, and one with variegated leaves named variegatum.

A Splendid Climbing Plant. S. Wendlandii is a handsome climbing plant for a greenhouse in which the temperature does not fall below 45 degrees in winter. It forms a thick woody stem, and has large glossy leaves, some of which are ovate, while others are pinnate, or divided into five or more sections. The flowers are pale blue, 2½ in. in diameter, in large pendulous clusters.

The plants are grown in large tubs, or planted out in a prepared bed of soil in the greenhouse. Good drainage is necessary, and a compost of equal parts of peat, loam and leaf mold is required, together with a scattering of sand. The plants, well rooted in 5-in. pots, are planted in March, and the shoots, as they develop, are trained to wires or a trellis. They should be shaded from the hottest rays of the sun. During the summer the soil is kept moist and occasional applications of liquid fertilizer are given as the flowers develop. Very little water is required in winter, sufficient only being given to prevent the stems from shriveling.

Pruning consists of slightly shortening the strong shoots and cutting back the weak ones to two or three buds in spring. Young plants are obtained by inserting shoots, 2 in. in length, in a bed of sand, sand and peat moss or vermiculite in a warm propagating case in spring. A little bottom heat is necessary and they must be kept close until rooted. Then they are potted in 3-in. pots, and later in 5-in. pots, from which they are planted in large pots, or tubs or in a bed of soil.

Plants which will bloom in 7-in. pots are grown from cuttings in spring; each is restricted to a single stem until flowers are produced. In the very warmest sections of the United States this magnificent vine may be grown outdoors.

The Jerusalem Cherry or Christmas Cherry, S. Pseudo-Capsicum, is very valuable as a pot plant for winter decoration of the house or greenhouse. It is a semiwoody plant with dark green shoots and small oblong leaves. In summer it bears small white flowers in abundance, which are followed by roundish scarlet or yellow berries, ½-1 in. in diameter. The berries commence to ripen in the autumn and remain on the plant for several months. This decorative kind is useful at Christmas, when its colorful berries are particularly welcome for decorative purposes.

Plants Are Raised from Seeds or Cuttings. Seeds are sown in a well-drained pot or seed pan filled with finely sifted sandy soil, in February or March. The soil is moistened, and the pots are set in a greenhouse with a minimum temperature of 50 degrees. When the seedlings have two leaves they are set 1½ in. apart in a seed pan or box filled with light rich soil. They are watered, shaded from strong sunlight until established, and then exposed to full light.

When large enough, they are potted singly in 3-in. pots; a week or two later the ends of the main shoots are cut off. As soon as side shoots appear, repotting is done in 5-in. pots, and after the lapse of a week, the tips of the side shoots are pinched out. No more repotting or stopping is required. Afterwards they are allowed to develop naturally.

Hints on Management. In their early stages the plants are grown in a warm greenhouse, and the atmosphere is kept moderately moist by damping the floor and benches. The foliage is also syringed mornings and evenings. As the plants develop in size they are gradually hardened off and placed out of doors in a sunny position in June. They may be plunged in ashes to the rims of the pots, to keep the roots cool and moist.

By this time the plants are well rooted in the final pots. Watering must be done regularly and the foliage syringed daily. When the flowers have set young fruits, dilute liquid fertilizer is given twice a week.

Instead of the plants' being plunged in their pots they may be transplanted from the pots to beds of soil and there left until frost threatens, when they are dug up and repotted. After this potting they should be well watered and be kept shaded from strong sunshine, in a close atmosphere for at least one week or possibly two.

Before frost the plants are removed to a sunny cool room or greenhouse with a minimum temperature of 45 degrees. Many of the berries are colored by this time, and the remainder will become well colored by winter. For the plants to stay in good health they must be cool, have free ventilation (not cold drafts), be kept away from gas fumes, and the compost must be always moist. Very dry or excessively wet conditions of the soil cause the leaves to fall, and are fatal.

Treatment after Fruiting. It is advisable to raise new plants each year, the old ones being discarded after they cease to be decorative. If old plants are to be kept to furnish cuttings or to be grown on for another year the following procedure is advisable.

Early in the New Year, when the berries have fallen, less water is given, in order to let the plants have a short rest. In February the side shoots are pruned to two or three buds. By syringing them twice a day, new side shoots are assisted to form. The plants may then be shaken free of the old soil, and repotted to make large plants, or cuttings may be taken.

When cuttings are required, the side shoots are allowed to develop to 2 in. in length; they are then taken off and inserted in sand or vermiculite. After the soil has been moistened, the pots of cuttings are set in a propagating case in a warm greenhouse and are kept close until rooted. They are then potted separately in 3-in. pots and treated as advised for seedlings.

The secret of success with this plant is to grow it in airy conditions when in bloom, so that fruits will form freely.

The False Jerusalem Cherry, S. Capsicastrum, a native of Brazil, closely resembles the true Jerusalem Cherry, S. Pseudo-Capsicum, and requires the same culture. It grows about 2 ft. tall. Its foliage is more grayish than that of S. Pseudo-Capsicum and its twigs are covered with fine hairs. Its fruits do not hang on the plants so long as those of the true Jerusalem Cherry. S. Capsicastrum variegatum has variegated leaves.

S. aculeatissimum is a spiny-leaved native of the tropics that has rounded orange-colored fruits that measure about 2 in. in diameter. The flowers are white and the plant grows about 2 ft. tall. It is easily raised from seeds sown in a warm greenhouse in late winter or spring and the plants may be grown in pots and fruited in greenhouses or, in warm climates, may be planted outdoors and grown as perennials.

S. integrifolium, the Scarlet or Tomato Eggplant, is a native of Africa. It is a spiny plant that grows about 3 ft. tall and has large, decorative leaves, white flowers and globular fruits that are red or yellow in color. This is a highly ornamental kind. It may be grown in the same manner as S. aculeatissimum.

S. Rantonnetii, which is a native of Paraguay and Argentina, is one of the most handsome of the shrubby Solanums. It bears its beautiful dark lavender-colored or violet flowers in clusters over a long period in summer. In frost-free and nearly frost-free climates it may be planted outdoors as a permanent shrub; in more severe climates it may be grown as a pot plant and may be set outdoors during the summer.

S. Rantonnetii is very easily propagated by cuttings inserted in a propagating case in a greenhouse in spring or summer and it is easily trained into standard (treelike) form, in which shape it is particularly useful for placing in flower gardens, on terraces and at other vantage points.

S. Seaforthianum is a shrubby vine that attains a height of 10 ft. or more and bears lavender-colored, purple or white flowers in summer. The flowers are succeeded by clusters of scarlet fruits each about the size of a pea. This attractive species, which is a native of South America, may be cultivated outdoors only in the very warmest parts of the United States; elsewhere it is an elegant plant for the warm greenhouse.

S. Dulcamara, the Bittersweet or Woody Nightshade of Europe and of tradition (not in any way closely related to Celastrus, which is commonly known as Bittersweet in America), is a slender vine or somewhat shrubby climber, that may attain an ultimate height of about 8 ft. It is a native of Europe and Asia and occurs wild as a naturalized plant in America.

This kind is scarcely worth cultivating, although its lavender-blue flowers and bright scarlet flowers are by no means unattractive. Both its fruits and its foliage, especially when the latter is wilted, are poisonous.

S. nigrum, which in its cultivated forms is

known as Wonderberry, Garden Huckleberry and Sunberry, is a native of many parts of the world, and some of its wild forms are somewhat poisonous; its wilted foliage is dangerously poisonous if eaten. This plant is of weedy appearance and has no decorative value. The garden forms, the fruits of which are used for making pies, are easily grown in any fairly good garden soil in full sun. The seeds are sown outdoors in spring.

For Summer Bedding. Several kinds of Solanum are grown chiefly for their attractive foliage, especially for subtropical bedding effects. They are 2-5 ft. in height, have large, entire or deeply divided leaves, which are either green or variously colored, and in most cases armed with stout spines. The following are some of the most popular: S. marginatum, 30 in., large sinuate leaves covered with a dense growth of silvery hairs; S. aviculare (lacinatum) 9-10 ft., leaves deep green; S. giganteum, 10-20 ft., leaves hairy underneath; and S. macranthum, 5 ft., leaves deeply lobed, pale green with purplish veins.

These plants, when used for summer bedding, are grown from seeds sown in deep, well-drained pans of sandy soil in February. A minimum temperature of 55 degrees is necessary. The seedlings are first potted singly in 3-in. pots, and later in 5-in. pots; they are gradually hardened off and planted out of doors in the flower beds in June.

S. giganteum is known as African Holly in southern California, where it is grown as a shrubby perennial outdoors.

SOLDANELLA (Soldanel'la). A small group of only six kinds of dwarf alpine plants, belonging to the Primrose family, Primulaceae. The name Soldanella is from *solda,* a piece of money; the plant is so named because of the shape of the leaves.

These plants are widely distributed in the Alps of Europe and are always found at considerable elevations. The Soldanellas are typical high alpines and are plants of the greatest beauty, all having a strong family resemblance to one another in their thick leathery leaves, either round or kidney-shaped, and the pretty flowers, bell-shaped or funnel-shaped and deeply fringed. In the Alps they flower directly after the snow has melted, and may often be seen at the edges of snow patches with fully expanded flowers actually pushing up through the snow.

Soldanellas are generally difficult to grow. They should be given open, well-drained pockets of loam in which has been mixed a liberal proportion of well-rotted leaf mold. They are intolerant of drought, and so must receive attention in the matter of watering during dry weather.

For the Rock Garden and Unheated Greenhouse. Soldanellas may not only be grown in the rock garden, but they are amenable to cultivation in pots or pans in the unheated alpine house, where they should be given the same type of soil as that suggested for their rock-garden cultivation.

Propagation. The Soldanellas may be increased by careful division of the roots, the best time for which is just after flowering. They may also be propagated by seeds, sown as soon after gathering as possible, in a pan of loam, leaf mold and sand in a cold frame. Although the young plants are somewhat slow in attaining size, this is by far the best and most satisfactory means of propagation, as it provides healthy, vigorous stock in large quantity.

Soldanella alpina, a choice plant for the rock garden.

Soldanella alpina is perhaps the kind most often met with in the European Alps, where it often grows in profusion, sheeting the ground with a film of amethyst as the snow recedes. The small rounded leathery leaves are untoothed at the edge, and the small lavender fringed flower bells, marked on the inside with reddish lines, are in a loose spray on 3-in. stems. The bells do not spread out at the mouth as do some of the others, but are more or less straight. S. alpina is not more difficult to cultivate than others, and it is certainly one of the daintiest and prettiest of them all.

S. hungarica is confined to the eastern Alps. It grows 4-5 in. high, and has a few blue-lilac flowers on each stem. It is seldom seen in gardens.

S. minima is the smallest; it grows only 1 in. or so tall, and has tiny narrow flower bells, usually solitary on their stems. The perfectly round leaves, not kidney-shaped, are very distinctive. The flowers are white or palest lilac with violet lines within the bell.

S. montana is one of the largest, most handsome, and easily grown of all Soldanellas. It is usually found at lower, almost subalpine elevations than the others, and chiefly in the eastern Alps. The large, round, dark green, leathery leaves are of somewhat uneven, waved outline. The violet-lilac flowers are in fives or sixes on stems 6-9 in. tall. The deeply fringed flowers are spread open widely at the mouth. This is a grand plant for the rock garden and the alpine house.

S. pindicola is of local occurrence and is little known in gardens though a really fine plant. It is found on the summit of Pindus in Greece. It is said to be even larger and stronger than S. montana, and to be further distinguished from that plant because the lower surface of its leaves is pale gray with small dots.

S. pusilla is not unlike a larger edition of S. minima. The flowers, borne singly or in twos on stems 2 or 3 in. tall, are narrow and tube-shaped, as opposed to the spreading bells of the others, and they vary from pale lavender to white, and occasionally pale rosy-lavender. The flowers are fringed, but not so deeply cut as in the others. It is a beautiful plant and not difficult to manage in the rock garden in favored climates.

A large number of hybrid Soldanellas have been recorded by botanists and they seem to occur fairly frequently wherever two species overlap and grow together. They are, however, of little horticultural importance, as they do not exhibit any special virtues not possessed by their parents. The only one of these hybrids that seems ever to have found a place in gardens is the pretty S. Ganderi, a cross between S. alpina and S. minima. This grows 2 or 3 in. tall, and has palest lilac or almost white flowers in twos and threes on a stem.

SOLIDAGO—*Goldenrod* (Solida'go). A group of hardy herbaceous perennial plants, some of which are grown in Europe as garden plants and provide a display during the late summer and early autumn months. In North America they are rarely accepted as garden plants, even though they are natives chiefly of North America. The name Solidago is derived from *solido,* to join or strengthen, and refers to the plant's supposed virtues. These plants belong to the Daisy family, Compositae.

The Goldenrods or Solidagos, although little appreciated in North America, are distinctly decorative herbaceous plants.

SOLIDASTER LUTEUS (Solidas'ter). This is the plant grown commonly in gardens as Aster hybridus luteus. It is a bigeneric hybrid between Solidago and Aster ptarmicoides, produced at Lyons, France, about 1909, and the name combines those of its parents. It is an interesting, and not unattractive, hardy herbaceous perennial, 2½ ft. tall, with much-branched sprays of small aster-like flowers that open bright yellow, then become creamy yellow. It thrives in any average garden soil and is easily increased by division.

SOLLYA—*Australian Bluebell Creeper* (Soll'-ya). These evergreen tender climbing plants are found wild in Australia and belong to the family Pittosporaceae. They were named in honor of Richard Solly, an English botanist of the early eighteenth century.

The principal kind cultivated is S. heterophylla. It has slender, woody, twining stems, clothed with both small narrow lanceolate to oblong and divided leaves. The flowers are bright blue, bell-shaped, ½ in. long and are in pendent clusters in summer.

In the warmer parts of the South this plant may be grown outdoors and is effective when used either as a vine or ground cover.

Charming Climbing Plant for a Greenhouse. This plant, which grows about 6 ft. in height, is suitable for a greenhouse with a minimum temperature of 45 degrees. It may be grown in pots and trained to stakes, or in a prepared bed of soil to cover the wall or pillars of the greenhouse or conservatory. The best compost consists of equal parts of loam and peat with sand added freely.

When the plants are grown in pots, repotting is done in March. The plants are removed from their pots, all loose soil is carefully taken off with a pointed stick, and they are repotted in slightly larger pots. The potting compost must be made firm.

The bed of soil is prepared by digging a hole 30 in. deep. A layer of broken bricks or small stones is placed in the bottom for drainage and the hole is filled with the prepared compost. When planting, the roots are well spread out and the compost made firm.

After potting or planting, the soil is not watered until it becomes moderately dry. It is then thoroughly watered and kept moist during the summer. During the winter less water is required, but the soil must not be allowed to remain dry for long periods, as these plants are evergreen. The atmosphere should be kept moderately moist at all times and the foliage syringed during summer and winter on warm days. No shading is required.

Propagation. New plants are obtained by inserting short side shoots, or the tips of young shoots, in a propagating bed in sand and peat moss in spring or summer. When the cuttings are rooted, they are potted separately in 3-in. pots and subsequently into larger pots.

SOLOMON'S-SEAL. See Polygonatum.

SOLOMON'S-SEAL, FALSE. See Smilacina.

SONERILA (Soneri'la). Tropical ornamental foliage plants which are chiefly grown in small pots or earthenware pans in warm, moist greenhouses. They belong to the family Melastomaceae, and are natives of Asia and the East Indies. Sonerila is the original native Malabar name.

Plants with Colored Leaves. These dwarf herbaceous perennials have ovate or lance-shaped leaves, 2-5 in. long, and grow from 4-12 in. in height. The leaves, which are the most ornamental feature of most kinds, are beautifully marked with cream-white, crimson and white, white and green, or silvery white and green. The tubular flowers are about ½ in. in diameter, and are produced in short racemes or spikes in summer. The most popular kind is S. margaritacea, which grows about 6 in. high, has small rosy flowers and ovate-lanceolate leaves which are reddish-purple beneath and silvery gray on the upper surface.

A very moist atmosphere is required for these plants and a minimum winter temperature of 55 degrees. Good drainage is essential and shade from strong sunlight is necessary. The best

Sonerila margaritacea variety Mme. van Longenhot.

compost consists of equal parts of peat moss and chopped sphagnum moss, with the addition of a liberal quantity of sand and a small amount of crushed charcoal.

Propagation. As young plants are the most vigorous, and have the most brilliantly colored foliage, it is usual to maintain the stock by raising a few plants annually. These are obtained by taking cuttings in spring. Tips of the shoots, 2 in. in length, are removed from the old plants, trimmed, and inserted in a sand and peat moss bed in a propagating case in a warm greenhouse.

The cuttings, when rooted, are potted separately in small pots; or several rooted cuttings may be set in a 4-in. pot to produce an effect more quickly. They may also be placed 3 in. apart in deep, well-drained flower pans or hanging baskets.

After potting, they are watered moderately until established, then they are given abundance of moisture during the summer. An exceptionally moist atmosphere is maintained by damping the floor and benches as soon as they approach dryness, and the ventilators are only opened when the temperature rises above 70 degrees.

In mixed collections it is often necessary to grow these plants under large bell jars to keep them sufficiently moist.

The chief kinds are S. laeta (maculata), rosy-purple, 12 in., leaves white and crimson; S. margaritacea, leaves copper-green spattered with pearly silver spots, and its several varieties including argentea, leaves silver with olive-green veins, and Hendersonii, a taller kind with coppery red leaves freely marked with silver spots; and S. speciosa, 12 in., leaves green, flowers mauve.

SOOT. Soft-coal soot has a definite value as a fertilizer on account of the nitrogen it contains; and plants to which it is applied are stimulated to increased growth. An excellent liquid fertilizer is made by steeping soft-coal soot in water. The soot is placed in a bag suspended in the water. Fresh soot must not be used on plants. It should be stored in a dry place for six months before use. See Fertilizers.

SOPHORA (Soph'ora). Hardy and tender deciduous (leaf-losing) and evergreen trees and shrubs. Sophora belongs to the Pea family, Leguminosae, and the name is derived from *sophera*, an Arabic name given to trees of the Pea family.

The Japanese Pagoda Tree, Sophora japonica, forms a broad rounded head and bears showy panicles of creamy-white flowers in summer.

The most popular member of this group is S. japonica, the Japanese Pagoda Tree or Chinese Scholar Tree from China. This deciduous tree grows up to 80 ft. in height, has large, bright green pinnate (feather-like) leaves, averaging 9 in. in length, and composed of about twelve elliptic leaflets. It does not bloom until it attains about 30 years of age, and then bears panicles of cream-white, pea-shaped flowers in late summer. S. japonica pendula is a variety with pendulous branches.

A flowering branch of the evergreen or semi-evergreen Kowhai, a small tree from New Zealand. Its yellow flowers are produced freely in May.

The bluish-white flowers of Sophora viciifolia, a free-blooming hardy shrub.

Another excellent kind is S. tetraptera, the Kowhai, an evergreen tree from New Zealand. S. microphylla is similar but hardier. Neither is hardy in the North; they can only be grown out of doors in mild localities. S. tetraptera reaches a height of 20 ft., forms a bush or small tree with twisted, stunted, short-jointed branches and pinnate leaves, and bears yellow flowers in May. S. microphylla has smaller leaflets and smaller flowers than S. tetraptera.

S. viciifolia, from China, forms a compact shrub about 7 ft. in height; it has graceful pinnate leaves, 2 in. in length, and terminal racemes of bluish-white Pea-shaped flowers in June. This free-flowering shrub is hardy in the North.

S. affinis, a native of Arkansas and Texas, attains a height of 20 ft. and has white or pinkish flowers. This is a deciduous (leaf-losing) kind; it blooms in spring.

S. secundiflora, Mescal Bean, is an evergreen shrub or small tree that is a native of Mexico and Texas. It bears fragrant, violet-blue flowers in spring. It is not hardy in the North.

Planting and Pruning. Deep, sandy loam is the most suitable soil, and planting is done in October–November, or March–April. S. japonica is only suitable for large gardens where it has ample room for development. This tree requires no special attention after it has become established.

When S. tetraptera is grown out of doors in the North, it should be placed in a sheltered location where it is protected from cold winds by other trees or shrubs, or near a wall. No pruning is necessary except to shorten excessively long side branches. Out of doors in the North it does not retain all its foliage during the winter, although it is naturally an evergreen in its native country and in mild climates it behaves as such. In colder parts of the country it may be grown in a large tub for decorating the greenhouse or conservatory. In such a restricted space more pruning is necessary to keep it shapely and within bounds. Pruning should be done after the flowers have faded.

Propagation is by seeds, cuttings and grafting. Seeds are sown in a deep, well-drained pan of sandy soil in March; the soil is well moistened, and the vessel is set in a warm greenhouse. The seedlings are potted separately in 3-in. pots and, when well established in these, are placed in a cold frame to harden off. Later in the season they are repotted into 5-in. or 6-in. pots, and from these are planted out in a nursery bed the following spring.

Cuttings are made in spring from young shoots. They are inserted in sand in a warm greenhouse; when rooted, they are potted and treated as the seedlings.

Trees of the weeping kind, S. japonica pendula, are obtained by grafting shoots of the pendulous variety on stocks 8 or 10 ft. high of the typical S. japonica.

SOPHROCATTLEYA (Sophrocatt'leya). A name given to Orchids raised by crossbreeding between Sophronitis and Cattleya. Their cultivation is much the same as for Cattleya, but each plant must be studied for its particular needs, especially during the resting season.

SOPHROLAELIA (Sophrolae'lia). A name given to Orchids which have been raised by crossbreeding between Sophronitis and Laelia.

SOPHROLAELIOCATTLEYA (Sophrolaeliocatt'leya). A name given to Orchids which have been raised by crossbreeding between Sophronitis, Laelia and Cattleya.

SOPHRONITIS (Sophroni'tis). Sophronitis coccinea (commonly grown as S. grandiflora), is a charming low-growing epiphytal Orchid which is found wild in Brazil at a considerable altitude. The growth is compact, the pseudobulbs being set closely together on branching rhizomes. They are only about 1 in. in height, and each bears one evergreen leaf; the flowers, of bright scarlet

Sophronitis coccinea, an easily grown Orchid which produces scarlet blooms in winter.

or orange-scarlet, 2 in. in diameter, are freely produced in winter.

As in Cattleya, to which Sophronitis is closely allied, the flowers are produced from the junction of the pseudobulb and leaf, but in Sophronitis neither the bulb nor leaf has reached maturity when the flowers appear. The season of flowering may extend from November to March, when several plants are grown. Sophronitis is derived from the Greek *sophron,* modest.

An Orchid for Amateurs. S. coccinea is easily grown and particularly well suited to the amateur. A greenhouse in which a night temperature of 50 degrees in winter is maintained is suitable; the summer minimum temperature should be 60 degrees with a moist atmosphere. The small size of the plants renders flower pans preferable to pots; they should be suspended about 15 in. from the glass, in a position where air can be admitted freely without drafts. Shading must be provided during the summer. Water is given throughout the year.

Hints on Management. The critical period is when the plants have to be repotted. The plants are in growth when they bloom, and by the time the flowers have died the roots are in full vigor. Potting can, however, often be avoided by replenishing the compost from time to time; old and partially dead pseudobulbs should be carefully removed and new orchid peat (osmunda fiber) inserted. If, eventually, the plants must be repotted, they should be taken out, the decayed compost removed, and replaced by cut osmunda fiber. These Orchids can also be grown in Tree Fern fiber and in Redwood bark and in Fir bark. Free drainage is necessary.

The time to repot must be judged from the condition of the plants; late-flowering varieties may be potted in January, early-flowering ones may be repotted in the autumn. Some growers attach the plants to blocks of wood or sections cut from a branch of a tree.

SORBARIA—*False Spirea* (Sorb'aria). Hardy and tender deciduous (leaf-losing) shrubs of graceful habit, growing 10 ft. or more tall, the stems furnished with long pinnate leaves and bearing large panicles of white flowers in July–August. They were previously included in the genus Spiraea, from which they are distinguished by their pinnate leaves. The name alludes to their resemblance to Sorbus. Sorbaria belongs to the Rose family, Rosaceae.

Easy to Grow. Sorbarias thrive in any average soil in open, sunny positions. They can be kept fairly compact by cutting the previous year's flowered growths hard back in early spring; and most of them produce suckers freely, by which they can be increased. They may also be propagated by seeds, cuttings and root cuttings.

Favorite Kinds. S. Aitchisonii, from Afghanistan and Kashmir, 10 ft. tall, has leaves up to 15 in. long, and flower panicles 12-18 in. long. S. arborea, from China, is the tallest, growing up to 20 ft. tall, with leaves of up to 19 leaflets and very large, pyramidal flower panicles. S.

The False Spiraea, Sorbaria sorbifolia, is a Japanese kind that has large plumes of small white flowers in summer.

sorbifolia, from Japan, up to 6 ft. tall, has erect panicles up to 10 in. long. S. tomentosa (Lindleyana), is a graceful shrub up to 18 ft. tall, its arching shoots terminated by large pyramids of small, white flowers. The last-mentioned is hardy in the South only; the others listed here are hardy in the North.

SORBARONIA. A group of bigeneric hybrids between Sorbus and Aronia. They are hardy, leaf-losing shrubs or small trees of no great decorative value. They thrive in any ordinary, well-drained soil in sunny locations and may be propagated by grafting onto understocks of Sorbus. The kinds grown are S. alpina, a hybrid between Sorbus Aria and Aronia arbutifolia, which bears white flowers in May and has red fruits; S. Dipplei, a hybrid between S. Aria and A. melanocarpa, a bushy shrub that bears blackish-purple fruits; S. fallax, a hybrid between S. Aucuparia and A. melanocarpa, similar in appearance to S. hybrida (next described) but with blackish fruits, and S. hybrida, a reputed hybrid between S. Aucuparia and A. arbutifolia. S. hybrida forms a shrub or small tree. The fact that it has black-purple fruits, although both of its supposed parents have red fruits, suggests that its parentage may be misreported. It is an old plant in gardens, having been known since 1785.

The name Sorbaronia is formed of the names of the plants' parent genera, Sorbus and Aronia. Sorbaronia belongs to the Rose family, Rosaceae.

SORBUS—*Mountain Ash, Whitebeam* (Sor'-bus). This group of mostly hardy ornamental trees and shrubs was for long included in the genus Pyrus. They rank among the most ornamental of the smaller trees suitable for garden cultivation, especially in their foliage and fruit, and thrive in any average soil. The name is from the Latin *sorbum,* applied to the fruit of Sorbus domestica.

The Service Tree. Sorbus domestica, the Service Tree, is a native of southern Europe, northern Africa and western Asia; it may reach a height of 50 ft. with a trunk several feet in girth, or, under very exceptional conditions, it may grow 60-70 ft. high. The pinnate leaves are 5-9 in. long, and made up of thirteen to twenty-one leaflets with toothed margins. The white flowers are in large clusters in May, and they are followed by green or brownish red-tinged fruits which are round in the variety pomifera, and pear-shaped in the variety pyrifera. The fruits are sometimes eaten, but they are not very palatable.

The European Mountain Ash or Rowan. S. Aucuparia, the Rowan or Mountain Ash, is a much more decorative tree than the last-named. It is commonly cultivated in North America, where it is always popular by reason of its large clusters of red berries in August. Unfortunately, the berries are eagerly eaten by birds, therefore they are seen at their best for a very short period. On hill and mountainsides in its native haunts it often appears as a stunted bush, but in good soil it may grow 30-60 ft. high, with a wide spread of branches. Its green, pinnate leaves and clusters of white flowers in May are well known.

Some Attractive Varieties. Many forms have been selected and given variety names. Good ones are asplenifolia, with deeply cut leaf margins; fastigiata, with stiff, closely arranged, erect branches; xanthocarpa, with yellow fruit; moravica, with berries larger than the type, and pendula, with weeping branches.

The American Mountain Ash. S. americana, the American Mountain Ash, is a small tree attaining a maximum height of about 30 ft. and is of stiffer habit of growth than the European kind. It has large leaves with dark-green leaflets and large heads of flowers followed by very fine heads of red fruit.

This species occurs as a native from Newfoundland to North Carolina and Michigan.

Other American kinds include S. decora, a small tree that grows 30 ft. tall, found from Labrador to New York and Minnesota; S. dumosa, a shrub 15 ft. tall that is found from Oregon to Colorado and New Mexico; S. occidentalis, a shrub 10 ft. tall, native from British Columbia to Oregon and Idaho; S. scopulina, a shrub 15 ft. tall that occurs from South Dakota to British Columbia and southwards to New Mexico and Arizona; and S. sitchensis, a shrub up to 15 ft. tall that is native from Alaska to Idaho and Oregon.

Pink-fruited Mountain Ash. One of the loveliest of all the Mountain Ashes is Sorbus Vilmorinii, a dainty small tree or large shrub from China, with pretty fernlike foliage and clusters

The fruits of the European Mountain Ash, Sorbus aucuparia are bright red.

Sorbus alnifolia in winter.

of very beautiful rosy-red fruits which become pale pink as they ripen.

The Whitebeam Tree. S. Aria, the Whitebeam Tree, is a native of Europe, where it is often found on limestone rocks or growing in chalky ground. It differs from the Mountain Ash by having simple—that is, not divided—leaves. The tree may be of small dimensions or it may attain a height of 40-45 ft., with a widely spreading head. The leaves are elliptic, 2-4 in. long, and nearly two thirds as wide, green above and prominently veined, and covered with white felt-like hairs beneath. The white flowers are in dense heads in May, and are followed by orange and red oval fruits about ½ inch long which provide a gay display in fall.

Many varieties have been given distinguishing names. Some of the best are Decaisneana (majestica), with large leaves, which are very silvery on the undersurface, and bright-red fruits; chrysophylla, of which the young leaves are yellowish, though they turn green later; and salicifolia, with narrow leaves which are decidedly silvery on both of their surfaces.

White Flowers and Red Fruits. S. intermedia, the Swedish Whitebeam, is a very hardy tree, sometimes 40 ft. high, found wild in northern and central Europe. The leaves are 2-5 in. long, with deeply lobed margins, the flowers white and the fruits red. In addition to being very hardy it withstands impure atmospheric conditions better than many trees, and is suitable for planting in town gardens.

The Wild Service Tree. S. torminalis, the Wild Service Tree, is a European tree found wild on chalk formations in the south of England and also in other parts of Europe, northern Africa and Asia Minor. It grows 30-45 ft. high, bears glossy green, coarsely toothed leaves, white flowers in May, and clusters of small, brownish fruits in autumn.

S. alnifolia, a tree 50-60 ft. high in China, was introduced into cultivation in 1892. It has small, ovate to elliptic, alder-like leaves, white flowers, and small red fruits. It forms a slender tree with fine, rather erect branches here. An allied tree is S. caloneura. S. discolor is remarkable because of its white or yellowish-white fruits. It is a native of northern China and is hardy in southern New England.

S. Folgneri is a very graceful tree with arching branches, elliptic-ovate leaves which are white on the undersurface, white flowers and small red fruits. It was introduced from central China in 1901. The variety pendula, with weeping branches, is of particularly pleasing habit of growth. Both are excellent trees for small gardens.

Other Sorbus species of merit are S. japonica, S. Chamaemespilus, S. hybrida and S. Koehneana, the last-named a very dainty small bush with pinnate leaves, white flowers and white fruits. Allied to it are S. Prattii and S. scalaris.

SORGHUM (Sorgh'um). Grasses from tropical and subtropical regions, which belong to the family Gramineae. Sorghum is from *sorgho,* its original Italian name. These plants have little decorative value, but are of economic importance, being cultivated for various purposes. S. vulgare variety saccharatum is grown for its stems, from which a sweet syrup is extracted. S. vulgare variety technicum, Broomcorn, is cultivated for its bristly inflorescent branches, which are used for making whiskbrooms. S. vulgare is grown for its seeds, which are ground into meal to form an article of food in India and other tropical countries.

The only kind of any decorative value is S. halepense, Johnson Grass, a tropical Grass with stems up to 10 ft. in height; it bears purplish, grasslike flower plumes, and has broad green leaves with a white midrib. This species, a native of the Mediterranean region, is grown for forage in the South; it sometimes becomes a troublesome weed.

The Sorghums thrive best where the summers are long and hot. They succeed in a variety of soils, including those of a decidedly sandy character. They are cultivated in the same manner as field corn, but the rows are spaced more widely apart (6-8 ft.) and, as prop roots are not produced from the lower parts of the stems, hilling up (drawing soil up around the stems when the plants are partly grown) is not necessary.

SORREL. Some kinds of Sorrel (Rumex) are very troublesome garden weeds and difficult to eradicate, unless they are dug out or are eliminated by using a selective weed killer, because the roots descend deeply. One kind, Rumex scutatus (French Sorrel), is occasionally grown in gardens for the sake of its leaves, which are used in salads. When grown as a salad plant, Sorrel is raised from seeds sown out of doors in April; the seedlings are planted finally in autumn to supply leaves for picking the following year. The plants are perennial and will remain productive for several years, but owing to the acid taste of the leaves, they are not very popular. Further details will be found under the heading of Rumex.

Another kind of Rumex that is grown for its edible leaves is the Garden Sorrel, R. Acetosa, the principal cultivated variety of which is Large Belleville. R. Patientia, the Spinach Dock or Herb Patience, is a European native that is naturalized in North America. It produces leaves that in spring may be cooked and eaten as greens.

SORREL, JAMAICA. Hibiscus Sabdariffa, which see.

SORREL TREE. See Oxydendrum.

SORREL, WOOD. Oxalis, which see.

SORUS. As applied to Ferns, a sorus is a cluster of spore-bearing organs (one of the fruit dots). The plural is sori.

SOURBERRY. Rhus integrifolia, which see.

SOUR CHERRY. See Cherry.

SOUR GUM. See Nyssa.

SOUR ORANGE. Citrus Aurantium, which see.

SOURSOP. Annona muricata, which see.

SOURWOOD. Oxydendrum arboreum, which see.

SOUTH CAROLINA, GARDENING IN. See Regional Gardening.

SOUTH DAKOTA, GARDENING IN. See Regional Gardening.

SOUTHERN BEECH. See Nothofagus.

SOUTHERN CANE. See Arundinaria.
SOUTHERN CYPRESS. Taxodium distichum, which see.
SOUTHERNWOOD. Artemisia Abrotanum, which see.
SOWBREAD. A name sometimes given to the hardy Cyclamen. The cultivation of these plants is dealt with under Cyclamen.
SOWBUG. See Pests and Diseases.
SOYBEAN. This native of China and Japan is botanically Glycine Max and has been known also as G. Soja and Soja Max. It belongs in the Pea family, the Leguminosae.

Although of comparatively small horticultural importance, this is one of the great agricultural crops of the world. It is grown for forage, human food and as a green manure crop and a cover crop as well as to provide materials for industrial purposes. Many distinct varieties of Soybeans are in existence. These vary in height from 3-6 ft. and are of bushy growth.

Soybeans thrive best in warm, well-drained soils and are usually sown, after settled warm weather has arrived, in drills spaced 2½-3 ft. apart, the plants being spaced 18-20 in. apart in the rows. During their early stages of growth the ground between the rows should be shallowly cultivated at frequent intervals. In many regions it is desirable to sprinkle the seeds, before they are sown, with a special bacterial culture which is sold by seedsmen especially for this purpose.

SPADE. A good spade is a most valuable gardening tool, and its uses are too well known to need description. There are several types on the market, each of which is suitable for its special purpose. The ordinary garden spade, with a 27-in. handle and 12 by 7¼-in. solid steel blade, is the most useful type. This may have either a T- or a D-shaped handle, and may or may not be fitted with a tread. The top edges of a treaded spade are turned over so that they do not cut into the shoes so much as the ordinary kind.

When buying a spade, it pays to purchase one of a good make, as cheap spades are liable to buckle at the blade and snap off at the handles. The more a good spade is used the sharper and more serviceable it becomes, provided it is kept clean.

A spade must be kept clean, otherwise it soon becomes rusty, is difficult to push into the soil and rapidly becomes caked with mud. Each time after the spade is used, the soil should be scraped off with a piece of wood; then the blade should be wiped with a piece of burlap and finally rubbed with an oily rag.

SPADIX. A fleshy flower spike which is surrounded by or has growing from near its base a spathe (a green and leafy, or a colored, petal-like organ). Spadices (the plural of spadix) are found in plants that belong in the botanical family Araceae, in some Palms and certain other plants. The central columns in such "flowers" (inflorescences) as Calla Lily, Jack-in-the-Pulpit and Anthuriums are spadices.

SPANISH BAYONET. Yucca aloifolia, which see.
SPANISH BLUEBELL. See Scilla hispanica.
SPANISH BROOM. Spartium junceum, and Genista hispanica, which see.
SPANISH CHESTNUT. Castanea sativa, which see.
SPANISH DAGGER. Yucca gloriosa, which see.
SPANISH FIR. Abies Pinsapo, which see.
SPANISH GORSE. See Genista hispanica.
SPANISH IRIS. See Iris.
SPANISH LIME. See Melicocca.
SPANISH MOSS. Tillandsia usneoides, which see.
SPANISH SQUILL. Scilla hispanica, which see.

SPARAXIS—*Wandflower* (Sparax'is). Beautiful bulbous plants from South Africa, allied to Ixia and Dierama. In mild climates they are suitable for growing in the garden, but are best grown in pots for greenhouse decoration. They have crocus-like corms (bulbs), long, sword-shaped leaves, similar to those of Montbretia, and produce flowers in spring or early summer. The plants average 18 in. in height. Sparaxis belongs to the Iris family, Iridaceae, and the name is from *sparasso*, to tear, referring to the lacerated spathes.

Treatment in Greenhouses. The corms (bulbs) are potted in September. Six are placed in a well-drained 5-in. pot, the tops 1 in. below the soil. The best potting compost consists of three parts sandy loam, two parts of leaf mold and one part of dried manure with a scattering of sand.

After potting, the bulbs are set in a cold

Sparaxis grandiflora is a handsome South African plant for growing in pots in cool greenhouses. It blooms in spring.

Sparmannia africana, the African Hemp, is an evergreen shrub from South Africa. In a warm greenhouse it produces showy white flowers, with conspicuous stamens, in spring.

frame, and covered with peat moss to a depth of 4-6 in. When the shoots are 1 in. long, the bulbs are set in a light position in the frame until the shoots have become green; then they are set in a greenhouse with a minimum temperature of 45 degrees.

Water is given moderately until growth becomes vigorous; afterwards the soil is kept moist until the flowers have faded and growth is finished. The ripening process then commences. This is assisted by gradually withholding the water supply and exposing the pots containing the corms to full sunlight. The soil is kept quite dry until repotting time in autumn.

The chief kinds are Sparaxis grandiflora, purple and white, and S. tricolor, orange and black. There are numerous named varieties of both of these species.

SPARKLEBERRY. Vaccinium arboreum, which see.

SPARMANNIA—*African Hemp* (Sparmann′ia). Tender evergreen flowering shrubs from South Africa, which were at one time popular as pot plants, but are much less common nowadays. The most usual kind is S. africana, which forms a large, spreading bush, up to 10 ft. in height. It has large, evergreen, hairy, cordate (heart-shaped) leaves, and in winter and spring produces terminal trusses of white four-petaled flowers, with conspicuous yellow stamens. This shrub's name is sometimes spelled Sparrmania.

Sparmannia belongs to the Linden family, Tiliaceae, and the name commemorates Dr. Anders Sparrman, a botanist who accompanied Captain Cook on his second voyage around the world.

In frost-free regions Sparmannias are good shrubs for outdoor planting and they are interesting greenhouse plants. Of special interest is the fact that the stamens are sensitive and move outwards when touched.

Vigorous, Free-blooming Plants. These plants may be grown to flower in small pots, but they

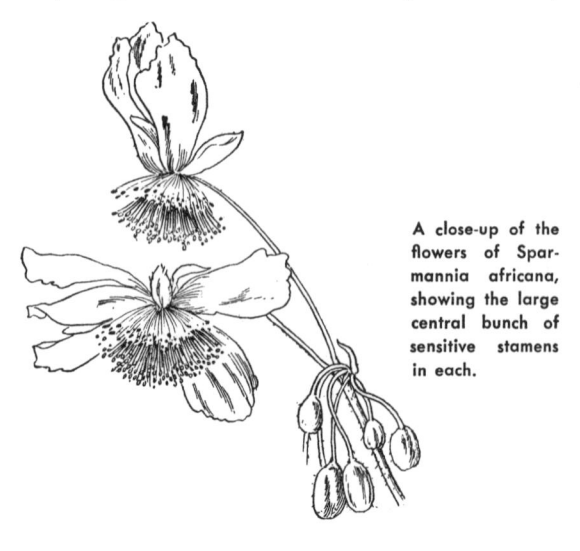

A close-up of the flowers of Sparmannia africana, showing the large central bunch of sensitive stamens in each.

are seen at their best in large tubs. When allowed plenty of room for development, they make handsome bushes and bloom with great freedom. The tubs are well drained, and plants taken out of 7-in. pots are set in them. The soil is made firm with a potting stick, but it is not moistened until it becomes moderately dry. The foliage is syringed twice daily and the plants are shaded from bright sunlight until established, when they are exposed to full sunlight. During the summer months the plants may be set out of doors in a sunny position, and returned to a greenhouse with a minimum temperature of 45 degrees for the winter. From October to April the soil is only moistened when it approaches dryness, but during the summer copious supplies of water are necessary.

Pruning and Propagating. Pruning consists of trimming the plants into shape in March. Young plants are easily obtained by inserting cuttings, which form roots with remarkable freedom. The cuttings are firm shoots, 4 in. in length; they are removed from the plants in April, and inserted in sand or other suitable material in a propagating case. Care must be taken to provide sufficient ventilation, otherwise the leaves (which, being hairy, collect moisture) will quickly decay. When rooted, the cuttings are potted separately in 4-in. pots, and subsequently in larger pots.

If the plants are allowed to grow without the shoots' being pinched, flowers will form in the first season; large bushy plants will develop if the main shoots are cut back to four buds. Plants which are allowed to flower the first season may be hard-pruned in the second year.

The chief kinds are S. africana, 10-20 ft., white, and S. africana flore-pleno, double, white. S. palmata, which has purplish flowers, is also sometimes cultivated.

SPARRMANIA. See Sparmannia.

SPARTIUM JUNCEUM — *Spanish Broom* (Spar'tium). This very decorative shrub loses its leaves in the winter but they are scarcely missed, as the rushlike shoots are green and attractive throughout their leafless time. It is widely distributed in the Mediterranean region and Canary Islands, and in warm countries is scarcely ever without flowers. In the North it blooms well in June, and intermittently until September, when another good display is sometimes made. As the

The Spanish Broom, Spartium junceum, has bright yellow flowers that are produced over a long period in summer.

golden flowers are as large as those of ordinary garden Pea flowers, their showy character is evident. Spartium belongs to the Pea family, Leguminosae, and the name is derived from *sparton,* the old Greek name for the shrub.

Propagation Is by Seeds. Seeds are the usual means of propagation; they are so freely produced, and the plants are so easily raised that no other method of propagation need be tried, except for one or two varieties, which are grafted under glass in spring on stocks of the type plant previously established in pots. Seeds may be sown in a cold frame in spring and the seedlings potted singly in small pots, using loamy soil. As they do not transplant well from the open border, they should be kept in pots until they can be planted in permanent positions. If repotted once or twice, and the tips of the shoots are removed now and then, bushy plants should be ready for setting out by the first autumn.

As Spartium junceum thrives in light sandy soil as well as in that of better quality, there is no need for elaborate ground preparation. If in an exposed place, the plants should be staked until the roots have established themselves.

Pruning consists of shortening the previous year's shoots to within a few buds of the base in early spring, but do not prune back into old wood, for such wood produces few young shoots.

Bushy plants 4-6 ft. high are the most satisfactory; they are obtained only by pruning from the earliest days. This shrub will grow 12 ft. high, but then it is often bare of branches at the bottom. Old, bare-stemmed plants should be destroyed and replaced by seedlings. At the best it is not a very long-lived shrub, but seeds are produced freely every year.

Spartium junceum thrives in gardens near the sea as well as inland, and rarely fails to flower well. There is a variety, flore pleno, with double flowers but it has no advantage over the type and is more difficult to grow. The variety ochroleucum has paler flowers than the typical kind. Spartium junceum is hardy in sheltered places as far north as New York City.

SPATHE. A botanical term which describes a prominent bract encircling or subtending (growing from near the base of) the flowers, as in Calla Lily or Zantedeschia, Jack-in-the-Pulpit, and Anthurium.

SPATHICARPA (Spathicar'pa). Tropical evergreen herbaceous plants belonging to the Arum family, Araceae. These natives of Brazil are little cultivated except in choice botanical collections. The name is derived from *spathe,* a spathe, and *karpos,* fruit, and refers to the curious fact that the flowers and fruits of these plants are adnate (joined to) the spathes.

Spathicarpas have lanceolate or more or less arrow-shaped green leaves which arise from tuberous rhizomes. The stalks bearing the spathes and flowers rise above the leaves. Both spathes and flowers (which are minute) are green.

Culture. These plants need a warm, humid greenhouse for their satisfactory cultivation. One in which Cattleyas or other hothouse Orchids can be successfully grown suits them. Shade from bright sun and a minimum winter temperature of 55-60 degrees is needed. Propagation is effected by means of division or by seeds. The latter should be fresh. Spathicarpas thrive in well-drained sandy soil that contains an abundance of organic matter. The soil should be watered sufficiently frequently to keep it always moist.

Kinds. The kinds most likely to be cultivated are S. hastifolia, with distinctly three-lobed leaves, 8-10 in. tall; and S. sagittifolia, with arrow-shaped leaves, 6-12 in.

SPATHIPHYLLUM (Spathiphyl'lum). Tropical evergreen, herbaceous plants belonging to the Arum family, Araceae, which are grown for their ornamental flowers and foliage. They are found wild in tropical America. The name Spathiphyllum is derived from *spatha,* a spathe, and *phyllon,* a leaf, and refers to their leaflike spathes.

Most of these plants have lanceolate, green leaves which rise straight up from the rootstock,

Spathicarpa sagittifolia is a rare aroid suitable for growing in moist tropical greenhouses.

The white bracts of Spathiphyllum Wallisii are very decorative and contrast well with the dark green foliage.

Spathiphyllum floribundum is a low-growing kind with broad leaves and white bracts.

and vary from 6-20 in. in length. The flower spathes are produced on short stems, average 3 in. in length, and are white or greenish in color.

For a Moist Hothouse. These plants revel in a moist, tropical atmosphere, and require a semi-shaded location. The minimum winter temperature should be 55 degrees, and the greenhouse must be moistened frequently. Repotting is done in February, when the old plants are taken out of their pots, a little of the old soil is removed from the roots with a pointed stick, and they are repotted in slightly larger pots.

The plants are given very little water until the roots have entered the new soil; throughout the summer the soil must be kept moist. In winter it is moistened only when it becomes fairly dry.

As House Plants. Despite the fact that these plants thrive in a humid atmosphere, they last remarkably well as house plants and succeed in comparatively poor light. Well-rooted specimens benefit from fertilizing regularly with dilute liquid fertilizer.

The principal method of propagation is by division of the roots at potting time in spring.

The chief kinds are S. cannaefolium, 20 in., white; S. floribundum, 9 in., white; S. Patinii (candidum), 10 in., white; S. Wallisii, 20 in., white; and the kind called S. Clevelandii which is very similar to S. Wallisii but larger in all its parts. The colors refer to the flower spathes.

SPATHODEA (Spatho'dea). Two or three tropical African evergreen trees, one of which, S. campanulata, is favored for growing as a street tree in many parts of the tropics and is cultivated in the southernmost parts of the United States. They belong to the Bignonia family, Bignoniaceae. The name means spathelike and refers to the calyx of the flower.

Spathodea campanulata, the African Tulip Tree, attains an ultimate height of about 70 ft., but mature specimens are often smaller. This tree is of upright growth; in winter and late spring it bears showy clusters of bright red flowers. It is easily damaged by cold and suffers breakage by wind storms rather readily. However, it grows quickly and soon recovers from any damages which may have been caused by wind or weather.

Propagation is by means of seeds and cuttings. For the best results this tree requires a fertile, well-drained soil but it will succeed under widely varying conditions.

S. nilotica is a smaller tree of a much-branched habit of growth.

SPATHOGLOTTIS (Spathoglott'is). Orchids which are widely distributed in the Oriental tropics, being found wild from India to the Philippines, as well as in Australia and Hong Kong. All are terrestrial, with tall, evergreen or deciduous leaves, and comparatively small, rounded, cormlike pseudobulbs set closely together. The flowers, on tall, slender spikes, vary in size; the lip is three-lobed. These Orchids bloom freely in summer and autumn and the inflorescences last a considerable time. The name is derived from *spathe,* a spatula or spathe, and *glottis,* a tongue.

Orchids for a Warm Greenhouse. Those kinds from very warm countries enjoy a greater degree of heat than others—those from northern India, for example. Generally, however, all require a greenhouse with a tropical atmosphere in the summer and a winter temperature of not less than 60 degrees. The leaf-losing kinds are not watered when dormant, and may be grown in a slightly lower temperature. The compost should consist of fibrous loam, with a little chopped sphagnum moss, sand, finely broken crocks or osmunda fiber. A small proportion of leaf mold is also beneficial.

Repotting is done when fresh growth appears, usually in early spring. Drainage must be ample, as abundance of water should be given when the roots are active. In winter much less water is required. Shading should be removed early in the autumn.

The Chief Kinds. S. aurea grows 2-3 ft. in height, and has golden-yellow flowers about 3 in. across, the lip having a few red spots. S. plicata is very variable, the flowers, which are smaller but more numerous than those of S. aurea, being deep-rose, although deep rose-purple and white forms are known. S. Vieillardii has spikes and leaves often more than 3 ft. in height, the flowers being white flushed with rose. Other worthwhile kinds are S. Lobbii, S. Petri, S. Fortunei, and S. rosea.

SPATTERDOCK. Nuphar, which see.

SPAWN. A term used to describe the vegetative portion of the Mushroom. This consists of thin, white, threadlike structures or mycelium. See Mushroom.

The small corms which are found clustering around the old corms of Gladioli are also known as spawn. These, if detached and planted, will develop into flowering corms in twelve months.

SPEAR LILY. See Doryanthes.

SPEARMINT. See Mint and Mentha.

SPECIES. A plant species is a kind of plant which is distinct from all other kinds in fundamental characteristics or characters by which it may be identified, and it propagates its kind through successive generations. All members of a species resemble each other more than they resemble members of any other group or population of plants. Even though they may vary from each other in characters of minor significance, such as flower color, size of parts, degrees of hardiness, etc., such variations are not normally greater than those that may occur among seedlings originating from a single plant.

Minor, but constant, natural variants within a species are given various subordinate designations by botanists, such as subspecies, forms, and varieties, but in garden practice it is general to refer to all such as varieties. The term varieties is also used to refer to distinct variations of species, as well as of hybrids, that have arisen under cultivation. Many botanists and horticulturists now use the technical term cultivars for variants of garden origin.

Species are usually grouped to form genera (see Genus), which are normally larger groups of related plants, although sometimes a genus consists of only one species which is not very closely related to any other species. Genera, in turn, are usually combined to form still larger groups, or botanical families, although a few families consist of only one genus, which is not very closely related to other genera.

In 1753, Linnaeus' *Species Plantarum (Species of Plants)* set the pattern of the so-called binomial (two-name) system that is still used for naming plants. Since Linnaeus' day, each species has been given a scientific name consisting of two words in Latin form. The first is a genus name, the second a specific or species epithet which, when used with the genus name, forms the species name of the plant. For example, the two words that form such a name as Rosa Hugonis, Iris gracilipes, or Rhododendron catawbiense form the complete species name in each case and indicate one particular kind of Rose, Iris or Rhododendron. These specific names cannot, correctly, be applied to any other plants. See Classification of Plants.

For practical purposes, a species of plant includes all of the individuals that are considered by competent botanists to belong together under the same species or specific name. Since species are not always sharply defined and thus not always easily recognizable by the amateur, the sensible course for gardeners to follow, and for those not trained in classification, is to accept the interpretations of botanical authorities who have made a study of this field. Such specialists have been consulted during the preparation of this Encyclopedia.

SPECULARIA—*Venus's Looking-Glass* (Specular′ia; Spec′ularia). Of the several kinds of Specularia which are known, only one is in fairly common cultivation, Specularia Speculum-Veneris. This is an attractive annual which is a native of various parts of southern Europe. It belongs to the Bellflower family, Campanulaceae. The name is an ancient one.

This dainty little plant, which reaches a height of 9 or 10 in., is in full beauty in summer; the bell-shaped flowers are purple; there is a variety with white flowers.

Specularia needs a sunny position in the garden and well-drained soil. Seeds are sown early in spring where the plants are to bloom, the seedlings being thinned out until they are about 3 in. apart. On light land in moderately mild climates a sowing may be made in September to provide flowers in early summer; seedlings raised in autumn should not be thinned finally until March.

SPEEDWELL. Veronica, which see.

SPENCERIA RAMALANA (Spencer'ia). A perennial herb from western China, closely related to Spiraea and belonging to the family Rosaceae. The name commemorates a British botanist, Spencer L. Marchant Moore.

Spenceria ramalana is suitable for the rock garden, or a sunny flower border. It thrives in any well-drained soil, forming rosettes of ferny leaves, and producing spikes of comparatively large, light yellow flowers in early summer. It is easily increased by division, or by seeds sown in pans of light soil in a cold frame in spring.

SPHAERALCEA—*Globe Mallow* (Sphaeral'cea). Mostly tender herbaceous and shrubby plants, rarely cultivated except in botanical collections. They are found wild in the warmer parts of the Americas and Africa and belong to the Mallow family, Malvaceae. The name Sphaeralcea is derived from *sphaira,* a globe, and *Alcea,* the generic name of the Mallow.

A Hardy Plant with Mallow-like Flowers. The principal herbaceous kind, S. Munroana, a native of western North America, is a perennial, 18 in. to 2 ft. in height, with three-lobed, cordate (heart-shaped) leaves and axillary and terminal clusters of five-petaled, mallow-like, scarlet and rose flowers in summer. This plant requires a sunny position and well-drained or light soil. The roots may be planted in autumn or spring; it is increased by division.

For the Greenhouse, and Outdoors in Mild Climates. The shrubby kinds are only suitable for a greenhouse with a minimum temperature of 40 degrees and for planting outdoors in frost-free or nearly frost-free regions.

Pruning and Propagation. Pruning consists of trimming the plants into shape as soon as the flowers have faded. Very little shading is required, and the soil is kept moist at all times, but less water is required in winter than in summer. Propagation is by inserting small, firm shoots in spring. They are placed under a bell jar until rooted.

The chief kinds are S. Munroana, scarlet, August, hardy perennial, and S. abutiloides, rose, 4 ft., August, a tender shrub. Others sometimes grown are S. rosea, a shrub about 12 ft. tall that has clusters of pink flowers and is a native of Guatemala, and S. umbellata, a Mexican shrub, 15 ft. tall, with red and white flowers.

SPHAGNUM MOSS. This grows in large, spongy masses in the wetter parts of bogs. The plants have no anchor roots and it is possible to rake them out easily.

The leaves of sphagnum have the power of absorbing water and retaining it for a great length of time. For this reason it is used as a moist, protective covering for the roots of plants during shipment, and for covering pots of newly planted bulbs, such as Freesias. It is also sometimes used for mixing in potting composts, and in the propagation technique called Air Layering, which see.

In recent years dried sphagnum moss, finely sifted, milled or ground has been effectively used as a soil substitute in which to grow pot plants. It has the advantages of being light in weight (important when plants have to be shipped considerable distances) and of not falling away from the roots when the plants are removed from their pots.

Because sphagnum provides essentially no plant nutrients, it is necessary to supply these by watering periodically with a fertilizer solution. Any of the soluble complete plant fertilizers that are prepared especially for house plants are likely to give satisfaction.

Seeds that are difficult to germinate, such as those of Palms, are often planted in sphagnum moss, and many other seeds, such as Snapdragons, that are much subject to damping-off disease, can often be raised more successfully when planted in finely sifted sphagnum than in soil. This is because the sphagnum is sterile.

SPHENOGYNE. An old name for Ursinea.

SPICE-BUSH. See Lindera.

SPIDERFLOWER. Cleome spinosa, which see.

SPIDERFLOWER, BRAZILIAN. See Tibouchina.

SPIDER LILY. Hymenocallis, which see.

SPIDER ORCHID. Brassia, which see.
SPIDER ORCHIS. See Ophrys.
SPIDER PLANT. Chlorophytum, which see.
SPIDERWORT. See Tradescantia.
SPIGELIA—*Pinkroot* (Spigel'ia). Herbaceous perennial plants, natives of North America, which belong to the family Loganiaceae. There are over thirty kinds, but only one, S. marilandica, is at all commonly grown. This is a perennial which forms a dense tuft of slender stems, 12 in. or more in height, and in summer bears

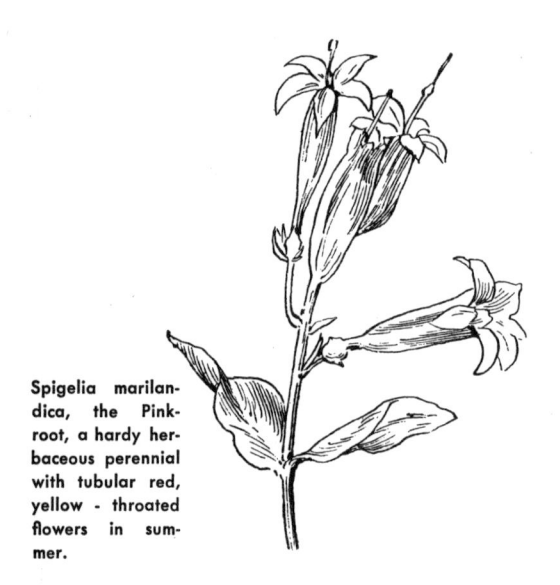

Spigelia marilandica, the Pinkroot, a hardy herbaceous perennial with tubular red, yellow-throated flowers in summer.

terminal clusters of tubular red flowers with yellow throats. The name Spigelia commemorates Adrian Spigel, a physician.

Difficult to Cultivate. S. marilandica is rather difficult to cultivate, so that its site needs careful selection, and it must be planted in a suitable soil. A location sheltered from the midday sun is best; the site is prepared by digging a hole 2 ft. in depth and filling it with a mixture of equal parts of loam, leaf mold and peat. The soil must be kept moist in summer. Propagation is by dividing the rootstock in spring.

SPIKE. A botanical term denoting a compact inflorescence ("flower cluster") in which sessile (stalkless) flowers are arranged on a single stem, as in Gladiolus.

Spike is also a term used to describe the puncturing of a lawn with a suitable tool or implement to produce slender holes a few inches apart and a few inches deep in order to improve aeration and drainage.

SPIKE HEATH. See Bruckenthalia.
SPIKENARD, AMERICAN. Aralia racemosa, which see.
SPILANTHES OLERACEA—*Para Cress, Brazil Cress* (Spilan'thes). A tropical herbaceous plant grown as a flower garden annual and for its pungent leaves which are used in salads. The name is derived from *spilos,* a spot and *anthos,* a flower and refers to the brown disc flowers of some kinds. Spilanthes belong in the Daisy family, the Compositae. It thrives in any fertile soil in a sunny location. It is raised from seeds sown in spring.

SPINACH. The common Spinach (Spinacia oleracea) is a favorite vegetable which is grown for the sake of its edible leaves in summer and in winter. Both the Winter and Summer Spinach are varieties of the same species or wild plant. They are distinguished by gardeners as Round-seeded and Prickly-seeded, the latter being generally grown to supply leaves in winter.

Summer Spinach is very easily managed, if suitable conditions are provided. It does not prosper in hot weather. It needs rich, moist soil; in dry, poor land the plants will "run to seed," that is, they will produce flowering stems instead of leaves, and are then useless.

For its best development Spinach needs a fertile, rather moist soil.

The first sowing is usually made in early spring as soon as the ground is in a fit condition, and the weather is mild. The ground should be dug over and decayed manure or compost and fertilizer mixed in. The surface soil is broken down to a fine tilth by forking and raking, and the seeds are sown in drills ½ in. or so deep and 12 in. apart. The seedlings must be thinned out until they are about 4 in. from each other. Plants which begin to produce flowering stems should be pulled up, for they are useless.

When to Sow Seeds. It is a mistake to sow much Spinach seed at one time; frequent small sowings should be made throughout the spring if a succession of produce is required. The later sowings may be made between rows of Peas and Beans, for there a certain amount of shade is provided, greatly to the benefit of the Spinach in warm weather. Copious watering is necessary during prolonged dry weather in early summer; if this detail is neglected, many of the plants may run to seed instead of continuing to produce large leaves.

The Prickly-Seeded or Winter Spinach is raised from seeds sown in August and early September, in drills ½ in. or so deep, and 12 in. apart, the seedlings being thinned out until they are about 6 in. from each other. As with the Summer Spinach, it is unwise to make one large sowing; two or three sowings should be made between the middle of August and the end of the second week in September; if the plants from one sowing should run to seed, the others are likely to develop normally.

A sheltered sunny place must be chosen for the Winter Spinach, and in severe weather it may be necessary to provide some protection to ensure the growth of leaves and so provide a continuous supply. This kind is hardy if sown in well-drained soil as far north as New York. In cold climates a light winter covering of salt hay, leaves or straw provides protection.

SPINACH BEET. Another name for Swiss Chard, which see.

SPINACH, MOUNTAIN. A name given to a plant which is occasionally cultivated as a vegetable, but is valued chiefly for its red-leaved variety used in summer flower beds. See Atriplex.

SPINACH, NEW ZEALAND. This tender plant can be grown to supply produce out of doors during the warm months only. For full details, see New Zealand Spinach.

SPINACH, PERPETUAL. Another name for Swiss Chard, which see.

SPINACIA. The botanical name of a number of annuals, the chief of which is the common Spinach, Spinacia oleracea. For cultivation, see Spinach.

SPINDLE PALM. See Hyophorbe.

SPINDLE TREE. A name applied to a group of shrubs valued for their ornamental fruits and rich autumn foliage tints. They are described under the name Euonymus.

SPIRAEA. This genus now consists solely of deciduous shrubs, the herbaceous plants formerly named Spiraea having been transferred to Astilbe, Aruncus and Filipendula. Spiraea belongs to the family Rosaceae. The name is derived from *speiraia,* and refers to the flexible branches, which were at one time twisted into garlands.

Spiraea nipponica bears a profusion of pure white flowers in late spring. Its foliage is gray-green.

Free-flowering Shrubs. Spiraeas are found wild in North America, northern Asia and Europe. One of the loveliest for spring bloom is S. arguta, which forms a dense bush, 6 ft. in height, of twiggy branches. The leaves are lanceolate, 1½ in. long, and the white flowers are formed in small clusters at the ends of the branches in April and May. When in full bloom it is clothed in a mantle of white. It is of easy cultivation and, being of compact growth, is suitable for small gardens. S. arguta is a hybrid kind; its parents are S. Thunbergii and S. multiflora.

S. Thunbergii, a native of China and Japan,

One of the best of hardy shrubs is Spiraea trichocarpa, the Korean Bridal Wreath. Its stems are covered with clusters of pure white flowers in June.

is an attractive shrub, 3-5 ft. high, of compact habit with slender, wiry branchlets, small, bright green leaves and pure white, star-like flowers borne during late March and April. It is one of the parents of the free-flowering S. arguta. The other parent is S. multiflora.

Another very attractive shrub is S. nipponica (bracteata). It grows 4-8 ft. high and bears clusters of crowded pure white flowers freely in June. S. canesceus is a rather loose-habited but vigorous shrub, with small, gray-green leaves, bearing white flower clusters with great freedom in long, arching branches in June. It is a native of the Himalayas. S. nipponica is a native of Japan.

S. Henryi, from China, was introduced in 1900 and quickly became popular by reason of its free-flowering qualities. It grows 6-9 ft. high and bears large clusters of white flowers in June.

S. Vanhouttei is a vigorous hybrid raised about 1862 in a nursery garden near Paris. Growing at least 6 ft. high, it has long, arching branches wreathed with clusters of white flowers in June.

S. Menziesii, a shrub 3-5 ft. tall, and S. salicifolia, of similar height, are two kinds that flower from the tips of the current year's wood during late summer. Both sucker freely and form large, dense masses, which require annual thinning. There are numerous varieties of each. Of S. Menziesii, one named triumphans is specially worthy of note; the flowers are bright purplish-rose in long, erect, dense panicles. Of S. salicifolia, the variety paniculata is very attractive by reason of its large, spreading heads of white or pink-tinged flowers.

S. prunifolia, Bridal Wreath, a native of Korea and China, is one of the most attractive of the spring-blooming kinds; this is especially true of its double-flowered variety named plena. Both this species and its variety have numerous pure white flowers in few-flowered clusters along stems of the previous year's growth. The shrub attains a height of about 6 ft. and is of graceful, slender appearance. S. Vanhouttei is also sometimes called Bridal Wreath.

S. trichocarpa, the Korean Bridal Wreath, grows 4-6 ft. tall, is an erect shrub and has very numerous white flowers in June. It is very decorative.

S. Douglasii, a native of the Pacific coast region, grows to a height of about 8 ft. and is very beautiful. Its flowers are deep rose-red in color.

S. Billiardii, a hybrid between S. Douglasii and S. salicifolia, is an attractive kind that grows 5-6 ft. tall and bears bright pink flowers in

The hybrid Spiraea Vanhouttei blooms profusely in June. It is a vigorous kind and easy to grow.

abundance during the months of July and August.

S. tomentosa, Hardhack or Steeplebush, is a stiff, upright shrub of minor garden importance although sometimes it can be used effectively in wild gardens and similar places. It has rosy-purplish flowers in densely packed conical heads, July to September.

S. japonica (the herbaceous plant commonly called by this name is Astilbe japonica, which see) is a dwarf shrub with erect stems, 5 ft. in height, clothed with small oval leaves, 2-3 in. long. The small pink flowers are produced in flat-topped heads (corymbs) in July and August. S. Bumalda, a hybrid between S. japonica and S. albiflora, has white to deep pink flowers. The variety Anthony Waterer is of richer color, and its leaves are often variegated.

Planting and Pruning. The shrubby Spiraeas are planted in fall or spring. They may be grouped in beds on the lawn, or in sunny or semishaded shrubberies. The methods of pruning differ with the various kinds. Those which flower from the buds made the previous year, such as S. Veitchii, are pruned after flowering by thinning out the older shoots only, while S. Aitchisonii, and others which bloom on the ends of the current year's wood, are pruned to within a few buds of the base of the flowering shoots in spring.

Propagation is by inserting cuttings made of leafy shoots in a cold frame in summer.

For the Rock Garden. S. bullata, which does not exceed 12 in. in height, is suitable for the rock garden. It has small, ovate leaves and flat-topped bunches of rose-colored flowers in July. S. decumbens is a miniature kind, 6 in. in height, with tiny ovate-oblong leaves and white flowers. Both kinds are very dainty and free flowering, and are easily grown in a sunny position in the rock garden.

SPIRANTHES—*Ladies' Tresses* (Spiranth'es). A large group of terrestrial, leaf-losing Orchids found wild in nearly all parts of the world. They vary greatly in appearance, but all have erect, flowering stems, usually leafy, and often the basal leaves assume the form of a rosette. The roots of some kinds are tuberous. Some are only a few inches high, while others reach a height of 3 ft. The flowers are often arranged spirally on the stems and some kinds are fragrant. Generally the individual flowers are very small, with nearly equal segments, the upper sepal and petals forming a hood.

The name Spiranthes is derived from *speiros,* a spiral or screw, and *anthos,* a flower, in reference to the form which the inflorescence assumes in some kinds.

Some Spiranthes are found wild in North America. When grown in gardens, they should be planted in slight shade and in moist soil or bog conditions or in somewhat drier soil, according to the needs of the individual kinds as mentioned under their species names below. The native American Spiranthes may also be successfully grown in pots in cool greenhouses.

The exotic (foreign) kinds require a compost of loam, leaf mold and sand, and a winter temperature of 45-55 degrees. They may be grown in cool greenhouses.

The Chief Kinds. In American and Canadian gardens the kinds of Spiranthes most likely to be cultivated are the native ones. Of these, S. cernua, Nodding Ladies' Tresses, and more particularly its variety odorata, are especially worthy of notice. These grow as wild plants in damp open woods, fields and meadows from Newfoundland and Quebec to Minnesota and South Dakota and southwards to Florida and Texas. The variety differs chiefly from the type plant in being taller and more robust and in having larger leaves and flowers.

S. cernua is 1-3 ft. tall and produces fragrant creamy white flowers, arranged in three spiraling rows along its stems, in late summer or fall.

S. gracilis, 6-24 in. high, grows in dryish soil from Nova Scotia to Minnesota and southward to Florida and Texas. Its white and greenish flowers are arranged in one spiraling row on its slender stems. They appear in late summer and fall.

S. ovalis, 8-18 in. high, grows in woods and hills from Virginia to Ohio, Missouri and Oklahoma and southward to Georgia and Louisiana. Its white flowers are arranged in three spiraling rows on the stems and appear in September.

S. Romanzoffiana, 8-18 in. high, grows in swamps, bogs and other wet places from Labrador and Newfoundland to Alaska and southward to Pennsylvania, Michigan, South Dakota, Colorado and California. The cream-colored or white flowers are in three spiraling rows along the stems. This kind blooms from July until frost.

Other American kinds include S. lucida, 6-12 in. high, white and yellow, May–July, found in wet places from Nova Scotia to Wisconsin and southwards to Virginia, Kentucky and Missouri; S. vernalis, 8-24 in. high, white, growing in dry or moist soil, from Massachusetts to Missouri, Florida and Texas; S. praecox, 8-24 in. high, white, August to September, a native of bogs and marshes from New Jersey to Florida and Texas; S. tuberosa, 4-8 in. high, white, August to September, in dryish soils from Massachusetts to Florida and Texas.

The exotic kinds most likely to be grown are natives of South America and the West Indies and include S. albescens, greenish, Colombia; S. bicolor, greenish with a white lip, Brazil; S. elata, West Indies and Brazil; S. Lindleyana, greenish white, Venezuela; S. metallica, light green with whitish lip, Brazil; S. picta, greenish white, West Indies; S. Sauroglossum, green with white lip, Brazil; S. Smithii, yellow or brownish with lip veined or striped green; S. uliginosa, greenish yellow, Brazil.

SPIREA. See Spiraea, also Astilbe.

SPIREA, BLUE. Caryopteris incana, which see.

SPIREA, FALSE. Sorbaria, which see.

SPIREA, ROCK. Holodiscus discolor, which see.

SPIRONEMA FRAGRANS (Spironem'a). A tender, Mexican perennial of herbaceous growth that may be cultivated outdoors in frost-free climates and also in pots and hanging baskets in greenhouses and window gardens. It belongs in the Spiderwort family, the Commelinaceae, and is sometimes grown under the name of Tradescantia dracaenoides. The name Spironema is derived from *speiros,* spiral, and *nemos,* a thread, and refers to the anther stalks or filaments. By some botanists this plant is now named Callisia fragrans.

The cultivation of this plant presents no difficulty. It thrives in any rich, rather loose, well-drained soil where a minimum temperature of 55-60 degrees is maintained and where the atmosphere is fairly humid. Repotting should receive attention in spring. Propagation is very easily carried out by means of cuttings inserted in sand, peat moss and sand or other propagating medium. Plants can also be increased by division.

Many stamens protrude from the fragrant white flowers of Spironema fragrans.

The plants thrive in light shade. At all seasons the soil should be kept moderately moist and especially so in summer. Feeding with dilute liquid fertilizer at weekly intervals benefits specimens that have filled their containers with healthy roots.

Spironema fragrans produces intensely fragrant, thin-petaled, white flowers in clusters arranged in terminal panicles. Its leaves are oblong-lanceolate and they sheath the stems with their bases. It produces long, hanging, runner-like stems. S. fragrans variety Melnickoff (sometimes listed as S. Melnickoffii) has its young leaves striped with pale yellow, brown or white.

SPIT. This is a term used by gardeners to denote the depth which is reached by thrusting a spade in the ground. Digging one spit deep means turning over the soil to the depth of the spade blade.

SPLEENWORT. Asplenium, which see.

SPONDIAS — *Golden Apple, Hog Plum* (Spond'ias). Tender trees, with edible fruits, which may be cultivated outdoors in southern Florida. They are natives of tropical countries, especially tropical Asia and Brazil, and belong to the Cashew family, Anacardiaceae. Spondias is the Greek name for Plum.

In their native habitat these plants grow 60 ft. in height, have pinnate leaves and bear panicles of white, purplish or yellow flowers, which give rise to plum-shaped, yellow or purplish, edible fruits. In Central America, S. Mombin and other kinds are grown for their fruits, which have an acid flavor and are principally eaten raw.

The chief kinds are S. cytherea (Otaheite Apple), 60 ft., flowers whitish, fruits golden-yellow; S. Mombin (Golden Apple, Hog Plum), 60 ft., flowers yellowish-white, fruits yellow; S. purpurea (Spanish Plum), flowers purple or greenish, fruits yellow to deep red.

SPONGE, VEGETABLE. The popular name of a number of climbing plants with fruits, which furnish bath sponges. See Luffa.

SPORE. Spores are special kinds of reproductive bodies. They are very simple in structure and much smaller than seeds. Whereas a seed consists of a seed coat inside which is the embryo plant, and the cotyledons or seed leaves, a spore consists simply of a spore coat enclosing a minute amount of protoplasm. Spores are produced by nearly all flowerless plants; Fungi, Algae, Lycopodiums, Ferns and Equisetums produce spores.

Ferns produce an enormous number of spores; they are formed in small bodies called sori, on the undersides of the fronds. Over forty-five thousand spores may be contained in a single sorus, so that a large Fern plant is capable of bearing thirty million spores in one season.

When the ripe spores of Ferns come into contact with moisture, they give rise to flat, green, heart-shaped bodies called prothallia (which see). The prothallia bear the sexual reproductive organs and, when fertilization has taken place, young Fern plants are produced.

In Lycopodium and Selanginella, the spores are produced in special spikes. Two kinds of spores are formed by the Selaginella, the micro or male kind, and the mega or female spore. These give rise to two kinds of porthallia, male and female.

Two kinds of spores are also found in Equisetum. The spores of Mosses and Liverworts are in special spore capsules.

SPORT. This word, as used by gardeners, means a sudden variation from type in habit of growth or color of flower. Thus, if a yellow flower appears on a shoot of a pink variety of Chrysanthemum, it is said to be a sport of that variety. Similarly, bush Roses often give rise to climbing "sports." The botanist calls such sports mutants.

SPOTTED LAUREL. See Aucuba.

SPRAGUEA UMBELLATA. (Spra'guea). An herbaceous perennial flowering plant of little horticultural importance. This plant, which grows about 12 in. in height, has radical (springing from the root), spatulate (spoon-shaped) leaves, and small dense umbels of white or light pink flowers in summer. It is a native of mountainous regions from British Columbia to California and belongs to the Purslane family, Portulacaceae. The name commemorates Isaac Sprague, an American botanical artist.

This plant is sometimes grown in the rock garden, and may be treated as an annual. The seeds are sown in a well-drained pan of sandy soil in a greenhouse in March; the seedlings are transplanted, 1½ in. apart, in seed flats. When well established, they are gradually hardened off and planted out of doors in May. Ordinary well-drained or light garden soil is suitable and a sunny position is required.

If desired, the plants can be propagated by taking cuttings in summer.

S. multiceps is similar to S. umbellata but is smaller (about 6 in. tall) and has rose-purple flowers. It is native from Washington to Wyoming.

SPRAY DAMAGE. When spraying plants with fungicides to control disease, insecticides to control pests, and fertilizers used for foliar (leaf) feeding, there is always a danger of damaging the leaves with the spray fluid. This may occur if the spray is not sufficiently diluted, if the plants are in a soft condition, or if the weather and atmosphere are unfavorable. For example, Potato and Tomato foliage may be scorched when sprayed with Bordeaux mixture to control blight. Also, plants growing in a smoky atmosphere may be damaged owing to the liberation of copper by the acids in the atmosphere.

Proprietary insecticides and fungicides should always be used by very carefully following the manufacturers' instructions, so as to avoid "scorching" and other forms of damage.

SPRAYERS. Sprayers are instruments designed for the application of sprays to plants. There is a wide range of types, from simple ones to the high-pressure outfits in use on large fruit plantations and for the application of sprays to shade trees; the larger machines are usually driven by means of gasoline engines.

A sprayer typically consists of a compartment or tank to hold the liquid spray, a pump to provide pressure to force the spray out, and one or more nozzles designed to break the spray into a fine mist before it reaches the plant. In a simple syringe-type sprayer the container and pump are one and the same and the nozzle is fixed at one end of the container; but in most sprayers there are hose connections between the pump and the nozzle and sometimes between the pump and the tank.

Many types of sprayers are available, including the bucket-pump type, the knapsack type and the wheelbarrow type. Some have reservoirs which, when pumped full of compressed air, are sufficient to empty the tank without further pumping; with other types the operator pumps continuously to eject the spray.

SPRAYS. Sprays, in the horticultural sense, are chemical substances in suspension or solution in a liquid. They are applied to plants in the form of a fine mist for the purposes of controlling insects, diseases caused by fungi and other organisms, and weeds, and to fertilize plants through their leaves. See Foliar Feeding.

Sprays are applied through special devices known as sprayers (see Sprayers) in such a way that all parts of the plants that are treated are covered with an even coating of the spray.

The objective when spraying is to obtain complete coverage with the use of a minimum amount of spray and without wastage. To ensure this, the liquid must be applied in a finely divided state; it should consist of fine drops, not large ones. Whenever possible, a still day should be chosen for spraying, so that the spray material may be directed where it is needed without drifting in the wind and being wasted, and without danger to other plants upon which it may fall and cause possible harm. This is of special importance when weed-killing sprays such as 2, 4-D and Ammate are being used, and when certain sprays such as lime sulphur are used near painted surfaces, which they may discolor.

The materials from which the sprays are prepared are usually purchased in concentrated form and must be diluted before use. It is of great importance that the dilution be correct; too weak a spray will fail to achieve the results desired; too strong a one may seriously harm the plants to which it is applied. See Pests and Diseases for further information.

SPREKELIA FORMOSISSIMA — *Jacobean Lily* (Spreke′lia). A tender bulbous plant which closely resembles Hippeastrum and belongs to the same family, Amaryllidaceae. It has a globose (roundish) bulb, 2 in. in diameter, strap-shaped leaves, 12-18 in. in length, and on the end of a stout stalk bears a cluster of large crimson flowers, 3 in. in diameter. The flowers are six-petaled; the uppermost petal stands upright, two are stretched out horizontally and the three lower ones form a tube around the stamens. Sprekelia flowers in June and July. The name commemorates J. H. Von Sprekelsen, of Hamburg, Germany, who sent this plant to Linnaeus. This plant is a native of Mexico.

Bulbous Plants for the Greenhouse. When grown in a greenhouse, the bulbs are potted in February or March in a compost of two parts of loam, one part of leaf mold, with a little well-decayed manure, sand, and bone meal. They are set in a greenhouse with a minimum

The Jacobean Lily, Sprekelia formosissima, may be grown outdoors in the South. It is also a good bulb for growing in greenhouses. Its flowers are deep crimson.

temperature of 45 degrees. Very little water is needed until they are well rooted; then the soil is kept moist throughout the summer and liquid fertilizer is applied when the flower spikes are developing and at weekly intervals until the foliage dies naturally. During summer they are shaded from the hottest rays of the sun only.

While in flower the plants are kept in a cool greenhouse and shaded from sunlight to prolong the life of the flowers.

When the flowers have faded the plants are again exposed to all but the fiercest rays of the sun, until the leaves start to wither. Less water is then given, and they are exposed to full sunlight to ripen the bulbs. When completely dried off, they are stored under the greenhouse benches until potting time in spring. Old bulbs are not repotted each year. It is sufficient to top-dress them with fresh soil in spring and repot once in three years.

Planting Out of Doors. In mild localities in the South this plant can be grown entirely out of doors. Good drainage and rich soil are provided and the bulbs are planted 6 in. deep in April. Where winters tend to be severe, they should be protected in winter by a thick layer of ashes or other mulch material placed on the soil.

Propagation is by detaching and potting the offsets, or by seeds. The seeds are sown in a deep, well-drained pan of light soil in spring. They are set in a warm greenhouse, and the seedlings, when they have formed two leaves, are potted separately in 3-in. pots and subsequently in larger pots. Six or seven years elapse before the seedlings produce flowers.

SPRIGS AND SPRIGGING. When planting Bermuda Grass (Cynodon Dactylon) to form lawns, as is commonly done in the South, individual stolons (pieces of underground stems) are often planted by hand 6-10 in. apart over the area to be transformed into lawns. The individual stolons are called sprigs and the process is known as sprigging. Sprigs of Bermuda Grass do not start into growth until the soil becomes warm.

SPRING BEAUTY. See Claytonia.
SPRING MEADOW SAFFRON. See Bulbocodium vernum.
SPRING SNOWFLAKE. See Leucojum vernum.
SPRING STARFLOWER. Brodiaea (Triteleia) uniflora, which see.
SPRINGTAILS. See Pests and Diseases.
SPROUTING KALE. See Kale.
SPRUCE. See Picea.
SPRUCE, HEMLOCK. See Tsuga.
SPUR. This term is used to designate the slender, tubular projections of the petals or sepals of certain flowers such as Columbines, Delphiniums and Dutchman's Breeches. The same term is used to describe short woody side shoots that develop

The short side shoots along the branch of this Apple tree are called spurs.

naturally, or that are induced to develop by pruning, along the branches of certain trees and shrubs, including Apples, Pears and others.

SPURGE. Euphorbia, which see.
SPURGE, ALLEGHENY. Pachysandra procumbens, which see.
SPURGE, JAPANESE. Pachysandra terminalis, which see.
SPURGE LAUREL. Daphne Laureola, which see.

SQUASH. The name Squash, as used in North America, refers to various varieties of Cucurbita maxima, Cucurbita moschata and Cucurbita Pepo. The terms Squash and Pumpkin (which see) are, however, confused and not applied with precision. The summer and the early

A hill of young bush Squash plants.

The same hill, with the plants nearing maturity.

autumn bush Squashes and Vegetable Marrows are derivatives of C. Pepo; the Cushaw and winter crookneck Squashes are derived from C. moschata; and the autumn and winter Squashes, such as Hubbard and the Turban varieties, from C. maxima.

Squashes are frost-tender annuals that make rapid growth in warm weather and produce fruits that are edible when cooked. In some kinds, the summer bush varieties and the Vegetable Marrows, the fruits are eaten when young and immature; in others they are allowed to ripen before they are harvested. Certain kinds may be kept well into the winter if they are allowed to ripen, are handled carefully to prevent injury and are stored under suitable conditions.

Soil and Site. Squash need a sunny location. The soil must be well drained and of a fairly light character; these plants do not thrive in heavy, clayey, wet earth. It should be made very fertile but, as the hills are spaced widely, the manure or compost and fertilizer used should be concentrated in the hills and their immediate vicinities rather than distributed evenly through the entire area.

For vining or running varieties the hills should be spaced 8 by 8 ft. apart; for bush Squashes 3 ft. apart each way is sufficient. A good way of preparing hills is to dig out about two bushels of soil and fill the hole with a half-and-half mixture of sandy soil and well-rotted manure or with equal parts of rich compost and soil to which a complete fertilizer of about a 5-10-5 analysis has been added at the rate of half a pound to each hill. Unless the soil is heavy, do not make mounds of the hills but leave the surface of each site prepared for sowing level with the surrounding ground.

Sowing the Seed. It is usual to sow the seeds of Squash directly in the hills after the ground has warmed and the weather is settled; however, where the season is short, or if for any other reason an early start is desired, the seeds may be sown indoors 3-4 weeks before the plants are to

Summer bush Squash, such as this Zucchini, are harvested when young before the fruits reach a large size.

Summer Crookneck is a popular Squash that is bright yellow in color.

be planted outdoors. When sowing indoors, plant 5-6 seeds in a 5-in. pot or in a berry basket, thin the seedlings out to 3 or 4, and later transplant outdoors without disturbing the roots.

When sowing directly outdoors, plant 6-8 seeds in each hill and cover them with soil to a depth of about one inch. When the young plants begin to crowd each other, gradually thin them out until three remain at each hill.

Summer Care. From their first appearance above ground, Squash plants outdoors must be kept dusted with a rotenone or other effective dust until at least the middle of July, to avoid damage from the squash bug and cucumber beetle, both troublesome pests. To reduce the danger of harm from vine borers, encourage the vines to root at the nodes (joints from which the leaves arise) by covering them with soil at those points.

Weeds must be kept down by regular cultivation or by mulching, and during dry weather the hills must be watered copiously. Provided the soil is not very fertile, an application of a complete fertilizer when the plants are about half grown is beneficial. However, care should be taken not to overfertilize, otherwise the plants are likely to run to vine instead of fruiting well. Fruits on summer Squash plants that develop past the stage when they are tender enough to harvest and use should be cut off promptly and thrown away; this encourages the formation of more fruits.

Harvesting and Storage. Summer Squashes should be used while they are young and the skin is easily penetrated if pressed with the thumbnail. Fall and winter Squashes may be used before they are mature, but are at their best when they are fully grown and when the skin has hardened to such an extent that it cannot be penetrated by the thumbnail.

All Squashes should be harvested and placed in storage before hard frost. The first light frost of the season does no harm to the fruits but it is a warning to cut them and get them under cover without delay. Squash should be stored in a shed, attic, garage or any dry place where the temperature is as cool as possible without actually freezing.

Varieties. Among the best varieties of summer Squash are Summer Crookneck, Summer Straightneck, Table Queen (Acorn), Patty Pan (White Bush Scallop), Yankee Hybrid, Caserta and the Italian Vegetable Marrows, Zucchini and Cocozelle.

Winter Squash varieties include Hubbard, Warted Hubbard, Golden Hubbard, Blue Hubbard, Boston Marrow, Delicious, Golden Delicious, Buttercup and Butternut.

SQUAWBERRY. Mitchella repens, which see.
SQUILL. See Scilla.
SQUILL, STRIPED. See Puschkinia.

The Butternut Squash is distinctive in its shape and is a favorite variety.

SQUIRREL. See Pests and Diseases.

SQUIRREL CORN. Dicentra canadensis, which see.

SQUIRREL'S-FOOT FERN. Davallia bullata, which see.

SQUIRREL-TAIL GRASS. Hordeum jubatum, which see.

SQUIRTING CUCUMBER. See Ecballium.

STACHYS—*Woundwort, Lamb's-Ear, Chinese Artichoke* (Stach'ys). Hardy and tender perennial, flowering plants and tuberous-rooted vegetables belonging to the Mint family, Labiatae. The name is an ancient Greek one for another kind of plant. Although this is a very extensive group, numbering over two hundred kinds, very few are worth cultivating. They are widely distributed throughout Europe and other north temperate regions, and several are found wild in North America. S. Sieboldii, the Chinese Artichoke, is grown in vegetable gardens for its curiously shaped tuberous roots (see Artichoke).

Tender Kinds. Most cultivated kinds of Stachys are hardy outdoors in the North but one of the most attractive, S. saxicola, is distinctly tender and will not withstand freezing. This kind is splendid for growing in window gardens and greenhouses and for planting outdoors in warm, dry climates such as that of southern California. S. saxicola is a native of Morocco. It attains a height of 8-10 in. and branches and spreads freely. Its stems are densely covered with white hairs, as also, to a lesser extent, are its heart-shaped or rounded leaves, each of which measures 1 in. or so across. The flowers are white with purple stamens and are in terminal spikes, but they are not very showy, the foliage being the most attractive feature of this plant.

S. saxicola thrives in any moderately fertile, porous soil. The pots in which it is grown should be well drained and care should be taken, when watering, not to wet the foliage. A sunny location and a minimum temperature of about 45 degrees

The gray, woolly-leaved Stachys lanata or Lamb's-Ear, which produces spikes of small purplish flowers in summer.

suit this plant well. Propagation is easily accomplished by cuttings planted in sand or vermiculite.

S. coccinea, a native of Texas, Mexico and Arizona, is another tender kind that may be grown in pots for flowering indoors in winter. It attains a height of 2-3 ft., and has red or orange-scarlet flowers in rather distantly spaced whorls. It requires the same culture as S. saxicola.

The Gray-leaved Lamb's-Ear. S. lanata is one of the most popular kinds. This is popularly known as Lamb's-Ear or Lamb's-Tongue, on account of its whitish, woolly leaves. It forms dense tufts of foliage which are attractive at all times of the year, and during summer it produces spikes, about 12 in. high, of small, purplish flowers.

A sunny location and well-drained, rather

Stachys saxicola is an attractive pot plant.

Stachys grandiflora bears a profusion of rich violet or rosy-purple flowers in summer. It is suitable for the perennial border.

Stachys nivea is a low-growing kind suitable for rock gardens.

poor, sandy soil suit it best. It may be planted in an irregular clump in the front of the herbaceous border, as an edging for the border or shrubberies, or as an edging or carpeting for spring flower beds. To increase this plant it is simply necessary to tear off rooted offsets in autumn and insert them in the positions in which they are to grow.

S. discolor, sometimes known as S. nivea, grows 6-10 in. high and has pink or creamy white flowers. It is suitable for rock gardens.

Taller kinds suitable for the herbaceous border are S. coccinea, with slender stems 2 ft. in height, clothed with ovate, lanceolate leaves, heart-shaped at the base, and bearing spikes of scarlet flowers in summer.

S. (Betonica) grandiflora is 12 in. high and has violet flowers in summer. A particularly good form is the rich rosy-purple variety superba. The variety robusta, bright rose-pink, is also worth growing. These plants flourish in ordinary garden soil and require a semishaded position. They may be planted at any time when the ground is in a workable condition, in fall or spring.

Very little attention is needed except to prevent them from spreading beyond their allotted space. Most of the Stachys run underground by means of their rhizomes, and therefore spread very rapidly. All are easily increased by division of the rootstocks at planting time.

STACHYURUS PRAECOX (Stachyu'rus). A somewhat tender, deciduous (leaf-losing) flowering shrub from Japan, especially valuable because it flowers in early spring. It grows about 3 ft. in height, has ovate leaves, 6 in. in length, toothed at the margins. The pale-yellow flowers are produced in pendent racemes. Stachyurus belongs to the family Stachyuraceae; the name is derived from *stachys,* a spike, and *oura,* a tail, and refers to the pendent flower spikes.

This plant is hardy in sheltered places about as far north as Philadelphia and requires an open position. It should be planted in October or November in a soil compost of loam and peat moss or leaf mold. No pruning is required. Young plants are obtained by detaching small side shoots in July and August; these are inserted in a propagating bed in a cold frame. Subsequently they are potted separately, hardened off in a cold frame and planted out of doors in their permanent positions.

Another kind is S. chinensis, which also bears pale yellow flowers in racemes up to 4 in. long, opening a week or two later than S. praecox. This kind is less hardy.

STAFF TREE. A name sometimes applied to Celastrus.

STAGGERBUSH. Lyonia mariana, which see.

STAG-HEADED. A term applied to old trees when the extremities of the branches are dead. The condition is often noticeable among old Oak trees and generally occurs when the roots have penetrated unsuitable subsoil, or an insufficient water supply is conducted from roots to leaves.

The condition often arises from a sudden lowering of the natural water level, such as may be brought about by deep drainage, or by a very dry year, but it may not be noticed immediately. There is a gradual diminution of the water supply to the higher parts of the tree, and it is first noticed by the leaves becoming smaller and the shoots shorter. After a time the tips of the branchlets die, and gradually the branches die back to the point to which the water can be raised.

A similar condition may be brought about in old trees when heartwood forms at a faster rate than sapwood, by which water is conducted from roots to leaves.

When trees are otherwise healthy, some good can be done by cutting away the branches at a point 9-12 inches below where they are dead, at the junction with a living branchlet. The ground beneath the branches should be well watered in dry weather. It is also helpful to loosen the surface of the soil, and apply a surface dressing of compost and fertilizer or manure.

Stag-headed trees may also be caused when the ground becomes abnormally wet and excludes air, thus preventing the roots from functioning properly. In such a case the ground should be drained.

The exclusion of adequate supplies of air, which often results from raising the grade around trees by filling soil over the roots, is also a frequent cause of stag-headed trees.

STAGHORN FERN. Platycerium, which see.

STAGHORN SUMACH. See Rhus typhina.

STAKING. Many plants grown in gardens need support to protect them from breakage and other damage by wind, rain and hail storms and to ensure that they develop as well-shaped specimens with straight stems. The need for support may be temporary, as is often the case following

Soft string is a suitable material with which to tie plants to stakes. The tie should be made in such a way that when the stem expands with growth the string will not cut into it.

the transplanting of trees and shrubs, or it may last throughout all or most of the life of the plant, as it does with weak-stemmed kinds such as Raspberries, Clematis, Sweet Peas, Morning Glories, and many annual and perennial herbaceous plants, such as Chrysanthemums, Dahlias, Asters and Gladioli, where neatness of appearance and straightness of stems are important.

There are many ways of providing plants with support. For example, they may be trained to walls, pergolas, fences or trellises or over large

Stems, such as those of Delphinium, which are likely to grow crooked, should be staked early.

[12—8]
Standard-trained Lantanas planted among Heliotropes and Petunias

[12—8a]
Steps are attractive garden features

[12–9]
Stewartia

[12–9a]
*Mountain Ash
(Sorbus Aucuparia)*

A row of Gladioli may be supported by pushing bamboo canes into the ground along the row and stretching string from stake to stake.

rocks or tree stumps. They may be tied to wires stretched between posts, or beneath the inside of a greenhouse roof or they may be aided to resist wind by hilling soil about their bases as is done with Corn, Beans and Potatoes.

A favorite method of supporting garden plants is by staking. This consists of pushing more or less slender lengths of bamboo canes, wooden stakes, stout wires or pieces of twiggy brushwood into the soil near the plant to be supported, or sometimes, in the case of clump-forming specimens, among the stems of an individual plant. Usually, but not always, the stems are tied to the stakes. Poles and single posts used to support such crops as Pole Beans and Climbing Roses are, in effect, extra-large stakes, although they are not generally thought of as such.

When staking, the main objective is to provide adequate support. The next most important point is to do the job in such a way that the stakes are not unsightly and will not be conspicuous when the plant has reached its maximum development for the season. To achieve this it is essential that the stakes be of a kind suitable for the particular plant and purpose for which they are used, that they be of appropriate length and thickness and unobtrusive in color. It is also important that minimum damage be done to roots and other underground plant parts in the process of staking. In some cases, as with Dahlias and young trees, it is advantageous to drive the stakes into position before setting the plant, thus avoiding danger of damage to the below-ground plant parts. In all cases stakes should be in position well before there is danger of the plant stems falling over or breaking.

In most cases plant stems are secured to the stakes with twine, raffia or other suitable tying material. Ties should be as inconspicuous as possible and should permit natural thickening of the stems without danger that the tying material will strangle them or cut into them.

Annuals and Herbaceous Perennials. Methods of staking of annuals and herbaceous perennials are basically similar. Support is needed only on a temporary basis—during the growing season. At the end of that season the annuals die and the perennials die down to the ground. With some annuals, for example Larkspurs and African Marigolds, and certain perennials, for example Chrysanthemums and Boltonias, the entire plant needs support. In other cases, as for instance with Carnations and Sea Lavender, only the flower stems need support.

For plants with fairly stout stems, bamboo canes or round or square wooden stakes (those

Pot plants such as Freesias may be given support by placing three or four stakes around the outside rim of the pot and tying strings around them to support the shoots.

but for slender-stemmed plants such as Christmas Begonias short lengths of stout wire may be substituted. Usually a single central stake is placed in position first and then, if needed, additional ones are inserted around it out towards the rim of the pot. The additional stakes generally number three or more according to the needs of the plant.

When placing stakes, care should be taken to locate them so that they will be hidden by the foliage so far as practicable. Great care must be exercised not to damage bulbs, tubers or other thick underground plant parts by pushing stakes through them.

To support such slender plants as Freesias, Tritonias and Ixias when several are grown in one pot, slender pieces of twiggy brushwood made of redwood or cypress are especially good because when in contact with moist soil they do not rot quickly but will remain serviceable for several seasons) are well adapted. The bamboos may be slenderer than a pencil or as much as ¾ in. in diameter depending upon their length and the stoutness of the stems they are to support. Wooden stakes may be from ½ in. to 1½ in. in diameter. Wooden stakes should be pointed at their bases and treated there with cuprinol, asphaltum paint or other wood preservative that is not toxic to plants. Under no circumstances should creosote be used. Wooden stakes are usually painted green, brown or some other color that is not conspicuous among foliage and flowers.

Pieces of twiggy brushwood (branches of Cherry and Birch are especially suitable) sharpened at their lower ends and pushed well into the soil around clumps of perennial Asters, Chrysanthemums, Phlox and other plants that have fairly slender stems give effective support. Peonies are often supported by a ring of stout wire that encircles the foliage mass and is held above the ground by three wooden or metal stakes.

Pot Plants. Many kinds of plants grown in pots need staking. Bamboo canes, either natural colored or dyed green, are most commonly used,

Bamboo canes are among the most effective plant supports. Here Chrysanthemums are being tied to such canes.

When a tree is close against a stake, contact between trunk and stake, which may damage the bark by rubbing, may be prevented by wrapping the trunk in burlap or other soft cloth.

(well-branched leafless pieces of Birch are excellent) may be pushed in among them when they are about half grown. The plant stems will push up between the interlacing brushwood and from it will receive ample support. An alternative method of staking such plants is to insert four or five pieces of wire, slender bamboo stakes or straight pieces of Willow twigs just inside the rim of the pot and then to encircle these in one or two places with a tie of raffia, strong thread or soft string.

Trees and Shrubs. Shrubs normally need no staking. Even newly planted specimens are likely to be quite secure without artificial support. If aid is deemed necessary it may be provided by driving wooden or metal (pieces of galvanized iron pipe are sometimes useful) stakes of appropriate length into the ground and securing the stems or branches to them.

The staking of trees, especially newly transplanted ones, is often of very great importance. Small specimens may be tied securely to a single stake. This method is appropriate only for trees that are planted bare-rooted, that is, without a ball of soil surrounding their roots. It is important to drive the stake into the ground first and then to set the tree in the planting hole with the base of its trunk close to the stake. Care must be taken when securing the tree to the stake to wrap wads of burlap or other soft material around the trunk at the points where ties are made, to prevent the bark of the tree from damage by being

A young Plane tree secured to three tall stakes.

The tree is secured to the stakes by wires which are threaded through rubber hose where they encircle the trunk. The trunk has been wrapped with burlap strips to prevent excessive drying.

rubbed against the stake. Trees should be well secured.

Balled and burlaped trees (those dug with a ball of soil around their roots) may be staked immediately after planting by driving three cedar poles or other suitable stakes of appropriate length into the ground to form a triangle just outside the perimeter of the root ball; the trunk is secured to these with horizontal wires stretched

Low-branched trees such as this are also easily made secure by the three-stake method.

Large trees may be secured by wires attached to deadmen (anchors) buried in the ground. Where they go around the trunk, the wires are threaded through rubber hose.

In wind-swept locations, such as sites near the sea, it is often necessary to stake newly planted evergreens. These Red Cedars have each been secured to two Cedar poles with wires threaded through rubber hose where they circle the trunks.

The wire from the tree and that from the deadman (anchor) are fastened to a turn-buckle. This permits the wire to be tightened until it is quite taut.

taut and threaded through pieces of rubber hose where they encircle the trunk.

An alternative method, especially suitable for large trees, is to secure around the trunk at a suitable height 3 or 4 guy wires (they should be threaded through rubber hose where they loop the trunk) and to stretch these towards the ground at an angle of approximately 45 degrees and secure them to either three stakes or three deadmen (pieces of concrete, wood or other material buried in the ground to serve as anchors) set to form an equilateral triangle outside the limits of the root ball. If stakes are used they should be driven well into the ground with their tops protruding only a foot or so above the surface. They should be angled so that their lower ends are driven inward toward the tree.

STAMEN. The male organ of a flower. Normally a stamen consists of an anther or sac, which produces and discharges dustlike male cells called pollen, and a supporting stalk or filament. Sometimes there are no filaments and the anther is then said to be sessile.

STAND. A growth or population of plants. The term is often used in reference to young seedlings in such phrases as "a good stand of Corn" and "a poor stand of Turnips." It is also in common use in respect to trees in such phrases as "a stand of evergreens" and "a stand of Birch."

STANDARD. This term denotes a tree, shrub or any other plant having a stem clear of branches for several feet from the ground. In a standard Rose, for example, the lowest branches are usually about 4 ft. from the ground; in a standard fruit tree they may be 5 or 6 ft. from the ground. Weeping standard Roses are on stems 5, 6 or even 7 ft. high. Half-standard Roses are on stems 2 or $2\frac{1}{2}$ ft. high. Half-standard fruit trees are on stems about 4 ft. high.

Other plants that are often grown in standard form include Geraniums (Pelargoniums), Fuchsias, Lantanas, Hibiscus, Chrysanthemums, Catalpas and Oleanders. Many other kinds of plants can be so trained.

The word standard is also applied to the uppermost and usually erect, broad petals of flowers such as Peas and Sweet Peas, as well as to each of the three erect petals of Iris flowers to differentiate between them and the spreading or drooping petals, which are termed the falls.

STANGERIA (Stanger′ia). A South African genus that consists of only one species, S. eriopus, and belongs in the Cycad family, the Cycadaceae.

A Lantana trained as a standard (tree form) and underplanted with Geraniums and Ageratums.

Stangeria was named in honor of William Stanger, a former surveyor-general of Natal, South Africa.

S. eriopus forms a short, thick, stem or trunk from the top of which grow a few spreading, pinnate dark green leaves. The individual leaflets are toothed along their margins. This is a rare plant in cultivation. It is closely related to the genus Zamia and requires the same culture. See Zamia.

STANHOPEA (Stanho'pea). A group of epiphytal (tree-inhabiting) evergreen Orchids, many of which are remarkable for the shape, color and scent of the flowers. All are found wild in tropical America, from Mexico to Brazil. They have ovoid pseudobulbs, 2 or 3 in. high, each with a single broad evergreen leaf. In nearly all kinds the flowers are borne on drooping stems; they are large and last for only four or five days, sometimes less, but they are produced freely, in summer chiefly.

These Orchids are of curious shape. The sepals are larger than the petals, the latter being often reflexed. The lips are thick and waxlike. Some kinds have as many as eight or more flowers on a spike, and are strongly scented. Stanhopea commemorates a former Earl Stanhope of England.

Orchids for a Warm Greenhouse. These Orchids should be grown in a warm moist greenhouse. In winter a temperature of 60 degrees by night is sufficient, as the plants are then dormant and only occasional waterings are required. In summer, many produce quantities of roots which revel in moist, warm air, but usually die as winter advances. Water should be given freely in the summer.

Orchid baskets are used for these plants; they should be suspended so that the leaf tips are about 12 in. from the glass. The potting compost may be cut osmunda fiber, Tree Fern fiber or Fir bark or Redwood bark. It should be replenished about March, but unless the compost is badly decayed or the plants are in a starved condition, transference to another basket should be avoided.

The Chief Kinds. S. tigrina, the Lynx Flower, has up to four large flowers, dark red and yellow. S. oculata bears four to eight flowers, light yellow with reddish spots or marks. S. Wardii, S. Bucephalus and S. insignis are yellow. S. devoniensis is light yellow, sometimes almost white, marked and spotted with crimson. S. ecornuta is ivory-white. Other handsome kinds are S. Ruckeri, S. platyceras, S. peruviana, S. Martiana, S. Lowii, and S. graveolens.

STANLEYA PINNATA (Stan'leya). A herbaceous perennial flowering plant related to Arabis. It grows wild in western North America and belongs to the Mustard family, Cruciferae. This plant is rarely met with in gardens, as it is not sufficiently showy to merit extensive cultivation. It grows about 5 ft. high, has entire, or divided glaucous (gray-blue), glabrous (smooth) leaves, and bears racemes of golden-yellow flowers in midsummer. The name Stanleya was given in honor of Edward Stanley, Earl of Derby.

A sunny position is necessary and any ordinary garden soil is suitable. Plants are raised by sowing seed in a flower pan filled with finely sifted soil in April. They germinate quickly in a cold frame and the seedlings are transplanted, ½ in. apart, in a box filled with light soil. When established, they are hardened off, and planted out, 6 in. apart, in a reserve bed. In the autumn or spring they are planted in their permanent positions. New plants can also be obtained by division of the roots at planting time.

STAPELIA—*Carrion Flower* (Stape'lia). These tender, succulent-stemmed plants are mostly

Stanhopea Orchids are best grown in baskets in a warm, moist greenhouse. This is Stanhopea eburnea.

Stapelia variegata is one of the commonest kinds of these curious succulents.

more curious than beautiful, and are therefore not widely grown, although a few kinds are generally included in collections of succulent plants. They are all natives of South Africa and belong to the Asclepias family, Asclepiadaceae. The name Stapelia commemorates J. Van Stapel, a Dutch physician of the seventeenth century. It is called the Carrion Flower on account of the fetid smell emitted by the flowers of many kinds.

There are upwards of ninety kinds, most of which are of low-growing, tufted habit. The stems are fleshy, leafless, more or less four-angled, and covered with irregular protuberances. They are either green or reddish-purple. The flowers, which appear from near the bases of the shoots, are star-shaped, five-petaled, 1-6 in. or more in diameter. They are purplish in color and mostly blotched or striped with yellow.

For House or Greenhouse. Stapelia is easy to grow and can be successfully cultivated in a window or greenhouse with a minimum temperature of 45 degrees. The plants are potted in rather small, well-drained pots, and are given full sunlight and free ventilation at all seasons of the year. No syringing or damping is required. For potting, a compost of two parts of loam, and one part of broken bricks, limestone rubble and sand is used.

Watering must be done carefully; during the summer months the soil is moistened when it becomes dry, but throughout the winter sufficient moisture only is needed to prevent the stems from shriveling. Repotting is rarely necessary and should only be done when the plants are not making satisfactory growth, for they flower best when pot-bound.

Propagation by Division and Cuttings. New plants may be obtained by seeds, cuttings or division. Division is the method usually adopted, as it is the simplest. A few roots are usually to be found at the base of the shoots, and if the latter are detached they can be at once repotted in small pots. When cuttings are made, the cut surfaces should be exposed to the air for twenty-four hours to allow a corky skin to form at the base; they are then inserted in sand or sandy soil and placed on a shelf, bench or window sill to form roots. The rooting medium is not watered until it becomes quite dry, then it is well moistened, and this method of watering is continued until roots are formed.

Raising Seedlings. To raise plants from seeds it is necessary to fill the lower half of a flowerpot with crocks and the remainder of the space with

Stapelia Leendertziae has dull purplish bell-shaped flowers.

sandy compost. The seeds are scattered thinly on the surface and lightly covered with soil. They will germinate in a warm room if a piece of glass is laid over the pot or in a greenhouse with a minimum temperature of 55 degrees.

When the seedlings are large enough to handle, they are set 1 in. apart in a pan of sandy soil and, later on, potted separately in small pots.

The chief kinds are S. Asterias, the Starfish Flower, 10 in., purple, violet and yellow; S. gigantea, 12 in., yellow and brown flowers up to 12 in. across; S. grandiflora, 12 in., purple, hairy; S. Leendertziae, 3-4 in., dark black-purple; and S. variegata, 6 in., purple and yellow. Many other kinds are grown by fanciers.

These plants are sometimes called Toadflowers.

STAPHYLEA — *Bladdernut* (Staphyl'ea). Hardy leaf-losing shrubs, often of large size, native to Europe, Asia and North America. Their brown seeds are produced in inflated, hard and attractive bladder-like coverings, hence the common name. They have striped bark, opposite, pinnate leaves and attractive white flowers. Staphylea gives its name to the family Staphyleaceae; the name is taken from the Greek *staphyle,* a cluster, and refers to the clusters of flowers.

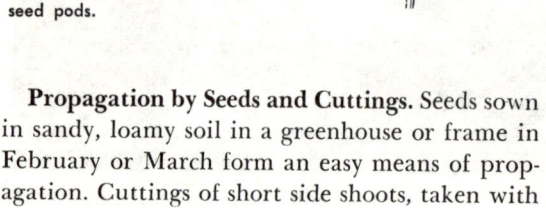

The Caucasian Bladder Nut, Staphylea colchica, is a handsome deciduous shrub. It bears clusters of white flowers in May, followed by large, inflated seed pods.

Propagation by Seeds and Cuttings. Seeds sown in sandy, loamy soil in a greenhouse or frame in February or March form an easy means of propagation. Cuttings of short side shoots, taken with a slight heel of old wood and inserted in a sand bench in a propagating house in July, can be rooted without much trouble. Young plants should be planted in a reserve border and the tips of the shoots removed occasionally to induce a sturdy, bushy habit.

When about 1½ ft. high, the plants should be set permanently in deep, loamy soil that is moderately moist. They appreciate light shade. Allow plenty of space for their development because they are wide-spreading. Except during their early years, when the plants are being trained to shape, no regular pruning is required.

Excellent for Forcing. One kind, S. colchica, is an excellent shrub for forcing into bloom in the greenhouse. For this purpose it is usual to cultivate it in pots plunged out of doors in summer, and to keep it in good condition by frequent feeding. The root restriction tends towards the production of flowering wood.

The Best Kinds. S. colchica, a Caucasian shrub, 12-15 ft. high, bears large, handsome clusters of white flowers in May; these are followed by inflated seed pods 2 in. long. S. colchica variety Coulombieri is regarded as being a hybrid between S. colchica and S. pinnata. It is quite as vigorous as S. colchica, and is as beautiful in flower. The seed cases are larger. Variety grandiflora is larger-flowered than the type.

S. pinnata, the European Bladdernut, is a large shrub, 12-15 ft. high, with leaves made up of five to seven leaflets, small clusters of white flowers, and rounded bladder-like fruits 1 in. or so in diameter. It grows wild in central and southern Europe. S. trifolia, the American Bladdernut, is a shrub 12-14 ft. high, native to eastern North America. It has three-parted leaves and white flowers.

S. holocarpa, from central China, sometimes forms a tree 30 ft. high. It has three-parted leaves and white or pink-flushed flowers. The variety rosea has rose-colored flowers. Two other kinds are S. Bolanderi, a native of California, and S. Bumalda, from Japan. They are not so hardy as the others listed.

STAR ANISE. Illicium verum, which see.

STARCH HYACINTH. Muscari racemosum, which see.

STARFISH FLOWER. Stapelia Asterias, which see.

STARFLOWER. Trientalis and Aletris, which see.

STARFLOWER, SPRING. Brodiaea uniflora, which see.

STAR GRASS. See Hypoxis and Aletris.

STAR JASMINE. Trachelospermum jasminoides, which see.

STAR MAGNOLIA. See Magnolia stellata.

STAR-OF-BETHLEHEM. See Ornithogalum umbellatum and Campanula isophylla.

STAR-OF-THE-VELDT. See Dimorphotheca.

STARTER SOLUTION. A weak dilution of liquid fertilizer that is poured around newly set-out plants to encourage them to recover from the shock of transplanting and make new roots rapidly.

STAR TULIP. Calochortus, which see.

STARWORT. See Aster.

STATE AGRICULTURAL EXPERIMENT STATIONS. At least one Agricultural Experiment Station, supported by funds received from the United States Government and from the state, is located in each state. Most frequently the stations are connected with State Agricultural Colleges and thus come under the general supervision of the Office of Experiment Stations of the United States Department of Agriculture, Washington, D. C.

These stations carry out a great deal of research and educational work and serve the gardener and the agriculturist well. They offer many free services, such as seed testing, soil testing, recommendations regarding disease and pest control, the use of fertilizers, consultation and advice. They issue bulletins, circulars and other publications of interest to the gardener and horticulturist.

It is important for every gardener to know of the help that can be obtained from the Agricultural Experiment Stations and to make use of the splendid assistance and facilities they provide. The following list indicates where each station is located:

Alabama: Auburn
Alaska: College
Arizona: Tucson
Arkansas: Fayetteville
California: Berkeley
Colorado: Fort Collins
Connecticut: New Haven
 Storrs
Delaware: Newark
Florida: Gainesville
Georgia: Coastal Plain Station, Tifton
Hawaii: Honolulu
Idaho: Moscow
Illinois: Urbana
Indiana: Lafayette
Iowa: Ames
Kansas: Manhattan
Kentucky: Lexington
Louisiana: Baton Rouge
Maine: Orono
Maryland: College Park
Massachusetts: Amherst
Michigan: East Lansing
Minnesota: St. Paul
Mississippi: State College
Missouri: College Station, Columbia
 Fruit Station, Mountain Grove
Montana: Bozeman
Nebraska: Lincoln
Nevada: Reno
New Hampshire: Durham
New Jersey: New Brunswick
New Mexico: State College
New York: State Station, Geneva
 Cornell Station, Ithaca
North Carolina: Raleigh
North Dakota: Fargo
Ohio: Wooster
Oklahoma: Stillwater
Oregon: Corvallis
Pennsylvania: State College
Puerto Rico: Federal Station, Mayaguez
 Insular Station, Rio Piedras
Rhode Island: Kingston
South Carolina: Clemson
South Dakota: Brookings
Tennessee: Knoxville
Texas: College Station
Utah: Logan
Vermont: Burlington
Virginia: College Station, Blacksburgh
 Truck Station, Norfolk
Washington: College Station, Pullman
 Western Station, Puyallup
West Virginia: Morgantown
Wisconsin: Madison
Wyoming: Laramie

Experimental Stations in Canada. The Canadian Government maintains stations similar to the State Agricultural Experiment Stations in the United States. The Canadian stations are called Experimental Farms, Experimental Stations and Experimental Substations. One or more is located in Newfoundland, Prince Edward Island, Nova Scotia, New Brunswick, Quebec, Ontario, Manitoba, Saskatchewan, Alberta, British Columbia and Yukon and Northwest Territories. All are administered from the Central Experimental Farm at Ottawa and are concerned largely with special local problems concerning forestry, farming, animal husbandry, horticulture, etc.

For publications and information concerning gardening in Canada, communications should be addressed to the Division of Horticulture, Department of Agriculture, Ottawa, Canada.

STATE FLOWERS. State flowers have been officially designated as such by the legislatures of most states: in Mississippi, New York, Rhode Island and Wisconsin they have been chosen by vote of school children. Not always is the state flower a native of the state it represents, and some, such as American Beauty Rose, Purple Lilac and Scarlet Carnation, are neither natives nor part of the naturalized flora of North America. In all cases, however, state flowers may be cultivated in the areas they represent.

Alabama: Goldenrod (Solidago)
Alaska: Forget-Me-Not (Myosotis alpestris)
Arizona: Giant Cactus or Sahuaro (Carnegiea gigantea)
Arkansas: Apple Blossom (Malus sylvestris)
California: California Poppy (Eschscholzia californica)
Colorado: Columbine (Aquilegia caerulea)
Connecticut: Mountain Laurel (Kalmia latifolia)
Delaware: Peach Blossom (Prunus Persica)
District of Columbia: American Beauty Rose
Florida: Orange Blossom (Citrus sinensis)
Georgia: Cherokee Rose (Rosa laevigata)
Hawaii: Hibiscus or Pua Aloa (Hibiscus Rosa-sinensis)
Idaho: Mock Orange (Philadelphus Lewisii)
Illinois: Native Violet (Viola)
Indiana: Zinnia (Zinnia elegans)
Iowa: Wild Rose (Rosa suffulta)
Kansas: Sunflower (Helianthus annuus)
Kentucky: Goldenrod (Solidago)
Louisiana: Magnolia (Magnolia grandiflora)
Maine: Pine Cone and Tassel (Pinus Strobus)
Maryland: Black-eyed-Susan (Rudbeckia hirta)
Massachusetts: Trailing Arbutus (Epigaea repens)
Michigan: Apple Blossom (Malus sylvestris)
Minnesota: Showy Lady's-Slipper (Cypripedium Reginae)
Mississippi: Magnolia (Magnolia grandiflora)
Missouri: Red Haw (Crataegus mollis)
Montana: Bitterroot (Lewisia rediviva)
Nebraska: Goldenrod (Solidago serotina)
Nevada: Sagebrush (Artemisia tridentata)
New Hampshire: Purple Lilac (Syringa vulgaris)
New Jersey: Violet (Viola)
New Mexico: Yucca (Yucca)
New York: Rose (Rosa)
North Carolina: Flowering Dogwood (Cornus florida)
North Dakota: Wild Prairie Rose (Rosa arkansana)
Ohio: Scarlet Carnation (Dianthus Caryophyllus)
Oklahoma: Mistletoe (Phoradendron flavescens)
Oregon: Oregon Grape (Mahonia Aquifolium)
Pennsylvania: Mountain Laurel (Kalmia latifolia)
Rhode Island: Violet (Viola)
South Carolina: Yellow Jessamine (Gelsemium sempervirens)
South Dakota: Pasque Flower (Anemone patens)
Tennessee: Iris (Iris)
Texas: Bluebonnet (Lupinus subcarnosus)
Utah: Sego Lily (Calochortus Nuttallii)
Vermont: Red Clover (Trifolium pratense)
Virginia: Flowering Dogwood (Cornus florida)
Washington: Rhododendron (Rhododendron macrophyllum)
West Virginia: Rhododendron (Rhododendron maximum)
Wisconsin: Violet (Viola)
Wyoming: Indian Paintbrush (Castilleja lineariaefolia)

STATE TREES. Most states have chosen, by action of the legislature or other means, official state trees, as indicated in the following list. Not all states recognize an official tree.

Alabama: Slash Pine (Pinus caribaea)
Arizona: Honey Mesquite (Prosopis glandulosa)
Arkansas: Shortleaf Pine (Pinus echinata)
California: Redwood (Sequoia sempervirens)
Colorado: Blue Spruce (Picea pungens)
Connecticut: White Oak (Quercus alba)
Delaware: American Holly (Ilex opaca)
Florida: Cabbage Palm (Sabal Palmetto)
Georgia: Pine (Pinus)
Idaho: Pine (Pinus monticola)
Illinois: Native Oak (Quercus)
Indiana: Lodgepole Pine (Pinus contorta latifolia)
Kansas: Cottonwood (Populus)
Kentucky: Tulip Poplar (Liriodendron Tulipifera)
Louisiana: Magnolia (Magnolia grandiflora)
Maine: White Pine (Pinus Strobus)
Maryland: White Oak (Quercus alba)
Massachusetts: Elm (Ulmus americana)
Michigan: Apple (Malus sylvestris)
Minnesota: White Pine (Pinus Strobus)
Mississippi: Magnolia (Magnolia grandiflora)
Missouri: Red Haw (Crataegus mollis)
Montana: Ponderosa Pine (Pinus ponderosa)
Nebraska: Cottonwood (Populus)
Nevada: Single-leaf Pinyon Pine (Pinus cembroides monophylla)

STATE TREES

The Redwood, Sequoia sempervirens, is the state tree of California. This is a young specimen.

Connecticut, Maryland and West Virginia have all selected the White Oak, Quercus alba, as their state tree.

The Tulip tree, Liriodendron Tulipifera, is the official state tree of Kentucky.

The White Pine, Pinus Strobus, is officially recognized as the state tree of Maine and Minnesota.

New York, Vermont and Wisconsin have designated the Sugar Maple, Acer saccharum, as their official tree.

New Hampshire: Yellow Birch (Betula lutea)
New Jersey: White Cedar (Chamaecyparis thyoides)
New Mexico: Pinyon Pine (Pinus cembroides)
New York: Sugar Maple (Acer saccharum)
North Carolina: Flowering Dogwood (Cornus florida)
North Dakota: Green Ash (Fraxinus pennsylvanica lanceolata)
Ohio: Buckeye (Aesculus glabra)
Oklahoma: Redbud (Cercis canadensis)
Oregon: Douglas Fir (Pseudotsuga taxifolia)
Pennsylvania: Eastern Hemlock (Tsuga canadensis)
South Carolina: Cabbage Palmetto (Sabal Palmetto)
South Dakota: Black Hills Spruce (Picea glauca densata)
Tennessee: Red Cedar (Juniperus virginiana)
Texas: Pecan (Carya Pecan)
Utah: Blue Spruce (Picea pungens)
Vermont: Sugar Maple (Acer saccharum)
Virginia: Flowering Dogwood (Cornus florida)
Washington: Western Hemlock (Tsuga heterophylla)
West Virginia: White Oak (Quercus alba)
Wisconsin: Sugar Maple (Acer saccharum)
Wyoming: Cottonwood (Populus)

STATICE. The plants formerly known by this name are now correctly named Armeria and Limonium, which see. Statice is still commonly used as a garden name for many of these plants.

STAUNTONIA HEXAPHYLLA (Staunton'ia). A climbing shrub closely allied to Holboellia, which it resembles. It has stout, woody stems clothed with compound leaves with three to seven leaflets, which are smooth and leathery. The flowers, which are six-petaled and half an inch in diameter, are white tinged with violet, and are produced in small clusters in spring. It is a native of Japan and belongs to the Lardizabala family, Lardizabalaceae. The name commemorates Sir G. L. Staunton, a physician of the late eighteenth century.

This beautiful climbing shrub is only suitable for growing out of doors in warm localities. In other parts of the United States it must be planted in a greenhouse or conservatory. It requires deep, rich loam in which leaf mold is freely incorporated. The soil must be kept moist in summer by copious waterings when required, and an occasional application of liquid fertilizer is necessary. Wires or a trellis should be fixed to the wall as support for the twining shoots.

Pruning and Propagation. Any pruning of the shoots which becomes necessary to keep the plants within bounds should be done when the flowers have faded. To obtain new plants firm young shoots are removed, trimmed and inserted in a propagating bench in a greenhouse or in a cold frame in summer. When well rooted, they are potted separately in small pots and grown in a frame or greenhouse until large enough to plant out.

The berries which succeed the flowers are about 3 in. long. They are edible and are much appreciated in Japan.

STEEPLEBUSH. Spiraea tomentosa, which see.

STEIRONEMA — *Loosestrife* (Steirone'ma). Hardy, perennial, yellow-flowered herbaceous plants that are closely related to Lysimachia and belong to the Primrose family, Primulaceae. They are natives of North America. The name is derived from *steiros*, sterile, and *nema*, a thread, and refers to the infertile stamens (staminodia).

These plants are of no great horticultural value although they are sometimes grown in wild gardens and flower borders and are useful for decorating damp, shady or sunny locations according to kind. They are easy to grow and may be propagated by division in spring or early fall and by seeds sown as soon as they are ripe. The seed soil should be kept always fairly moist.

Kinds include S. ciliatum, 4 ft., a native of wet,

sunny locations; S. lanceolatum, 2 ft., a native of moist or wet woods; S. intermedium, 4 ft., a native of dryish woods and S. pumilum, 4 ft., a native of moist, sunny locations.

STELIS (Stel'is). A large group of epiphytal Orchids (Orchids that grow on trees) containing about 150 kinds, which are found wild throughout tropical America from the West Indies to Brazil. A few are cultivated because they are free-blooming, although the flowers are not showy. All are of more or less tufted growth, and, in place of pseudobulbs, have stems, each with one leaf. The flowers are produced from the junction of the stem and leaf, usually on tall, many-flowered, erect spikes. The different kinds vary considerably in size and many bloom in the autumn and winter months. Stelis is said to be an old word for a parasitical plant, a kind of Mistletoe.

Orchids for a Warm Greenhouse. All these Orchids require a greenhouse with a winter temperature of about 55 degrees at night. In summer a minimum temperature of 60 degrees at night is high enough. A moist atmosphere is necessary at all times, together with shading in summer.

Repotting should be carried out, if required, in early or late spring, according to the state of the plants; a compost of osmunda fiber, Tree Fern fiber or of Fir bark or Redwood bark is suitable. Drainage must be free, as the plants require water throughout the year. Some of the small-growing kinds may be attached to blocks of wood, but pots are preferable.

The chief kinds are S. micrantha, with small, whitish flowers; S. grandiflora, brownish; S. gigas, with greenish-white sepals and dark brown petals; S. smaragdina, green; and S. sesquipedale, yellowish.

STELLARIA—*Stitchwort* (Stella'ria). A large genus of hardy herbaceous plants, widely distributed all over the world, but chiefly found in temperate countries. Some are common garden weeds, the best known of which is S. media, the common Chickweed.

Only one of these plants is of any horticultural value. This is S. graminea aurea, a slender-stemmed plant with narrow, pale yellow, linear leaves, 1 in. in length, and small, white, star-shaped flowers in summer. It is sometimes used as an edging for summer flower beds. The plants are raised by dividing them into small pieces in autumn. These pieces are planted 1 in. apart in flats of light, sandy soil and are kept in a cold frame during the winter. In late spring they are hardened off and planted as an edging to flower beds.

Stellaria belongs to the Pink family, Caryophyllaceae. The name is derived from *stella,* a star, and refers to the star-shaped flowers.

STENANDRIUM LINDENII (Stenand'rium). A tropical ornamental foliage plant, from Brazil, which belongs to the Acanthus family, Acanthaceae. This low-growing, compact plant is chiefly used as an edging for the benches in a hothouse. It grows about 6 in. in height, has broad-elliptic leaves, rounded at the tips and narrowing at the leafstalks; they are velvety, dark green, and yellowish-white along the veins and purplish beneath. The flowers, which are inconspicuous, are yellow, ¾ in. in diameter and are produced on short spikes in summer. The name Stenandrium is derived from *stenos,* narrow, and *aner,* man, and refers to the narrow anthers.

A minimum winter temperature of 55 degrees is required. The plants are repotted in spring in a compost of equal parts of peat, loam and leaf mold to which sufficient sand is added to make it porous. During the winter they are watered moderately, but at all other times the soil is kept moist. A light position in the hothouse is required in winter; during the summer a minimum temperature of 60 degrees is high enough. Very little damping and syringing are required; the atmosphere need only be kept moderately moist.

Propagation by Cuttings. After flowering, the shoots are pruned back to about 1 in. Cuttings are taken annually, in spring, to maintain a constant supply of young, vigorous plants. Small side shoots are taken off, trimmed, and inserted in a sand bed in a warm greenhouse. They are kept covered with a bell jar until roots are formed, when they are set in separate small pots. When established in these, they are repotted in 5-in. pots and the points of the shoots are pinched out to ensure bushy plants.

STENANTHIUM (Stenanth'ium). Hardy, summer-flowering, tuberous-rooted plants of great beauty, found wild in North America, and belonging to the Lily family, Liliaceae. They grow up to 6 ft. in height, have long, grasslike leaves, and produce feathery spikes of white or purple flowers. The name Stenanthium is derived from *stenos,* narrow, and *anthos,* a flower, and refers to the small, narrow flowers.

Plants for a Sheltered Position. These plants are suitable for the edge of the woodland, for the herbaceous border, or nooks in the shrubbery. In the North they need a sheltered, semi-shaded location and the site must be well drained. When preparing the ground, plenty of peat moss or leaf mold should be incorporated and a layer spread around the bulbs. They are acid-soil plants.

Stenanthiums should be disturbed as little as possible, as established plants flower more freely. A top-dressing of leaf mold or peat moss is beneficial in spring. To increase the plants it is necessary to lift them in spring and separate the offsets, which are then planted promptly.

The chief kinds are S. robustum, Feather Fleece, white, fragrant, 6 ft., late summer; S. gramineum, greenish-white, 3-4 ft., June; and S. occidentale, 2 ft., purple, summer.

STENIA (Ste'nia). Only a few kinds of this Orchid are known. All are tufted, epiphytal plants (growing on trees), with or without small pseudobulbs and evergreen leaves. They are found wild in tropical South America.

The name Stenia is from *stenos,* narrow, and alludes to the shape of the pollen masses. The best-known kind is S. fimbriata, which has slender stems shorter than the leaves, each bearing a single flower about 2 in. across, pale yellow except for a few reddish marks at the base of the lip, the margin of which is beautifully fringed. This plant, which is often called Chondrorhyncha fimbriata, usually flowers in the summer.

Orchids for a Hothouse. These Orchids need a greenhouse with a minimum winter temperature of 60 degrees at night. A moist, rather shady position, free from drafts, is desirable. Shade from strong sunlight is necessary and water must be given throughout the year. The compost used for potting may consist of osmunda fiber cut into pieces, of Tree Fern fiber, or of Fir bark or Redwood bark. It is important that the container used be very adequately drained. Repotting should be done in about March.

Other kinds are S. pallida and S. guttata, in both of which pale yellow is the prevailing color.

STENOCACTUS (Stenocac'tus). A group of Mexican Cacti closely related to Echinocactus and requiring the same culture. They belong to the Cactus family, Cactaceae. The name is derived from *stenos,* narrow, and Cactus.

Among the many kinds that are sometimes cultivated by fanciers are the following: S. albatus, 5 in., flowers white; S. crispatus, 5-6 in., flowers purple or purple and white; S. grandicornis, 5 in., flowers white; S. lamellosus, 5 in., flowers red; S. Lloydii, 6 in., flowers pink; S. Ochoterenaus, 3 in., flowers white or pink; S. pentacanthus, 3 in., flowers pale yellow; and S. tricuspidatus, 3-4 in., flowers yellowish-green.

STENOCARPUS (Stenocarp'us). A group of tender evergreen trees and shrubs that are natives of Australia and New Caledonia and belong to the Protea family, Proteaceae. Some are grown out of doors in southern California. The name is derived from *stenos,* narrow, and *karpos,* fruit, and alludes to the narrow follicles.

These plants prefer a peaty soil. They are propagated by seeds and cuttings. The kinds most commonly grown are S. salignus, 20-50 ft., with fragrant, yellowish flowers, and S. sinuatus, 30-90 ft., flowers bright red.

STENOGLOTTIS (Stenoglott'is). Terrestrial Orchids from South Africa, which have fleshy roots and are leaf-losing in the sense that the foliage dies after flowering, although the new leaves soon appear. Erect, leafy spikes, 12 or 18 in. high, develop from the center of a number of narrow basal leaves and bear numerous flowers in September and October. The flowers are not large, but very attractive. The name is derived from *stenos,* narrow, and *glotta,* a tongue.

Orchids for Amateurs. These Orchids may be grown with Odontoglossums and Masdevallias, but, as they are dormant during winter, the temperature need not be so closely regulated, a winter minimum of 50 degrees at night being quite safe. In summer the temperature will naturally rise higher, and shading is then necessary. The pots should be well drained and a compost used of fibrous loam with an addition of leaf mold and sand; a little chopped sphagnum moss may be added. Drainage must be free, as abundance of

Stenoglottis fimbriata is a native terrestrial Orchid of South Africa. It bears spikes of rosy-mauve flowers.

water is needed in the summer to insure success.

In winter, after flowering, water may be withheld for a time. Repotting should be done annually, about February, and if more than one growth is present the plants may be carefully divided, if necessary.

The two chief kinds are S. fimbriata and S. longifolia; both have rose-mauve flowers. A white variety of S. longifolia is known and there are slight color variations in both kinds.

STENOLOBIUM (Stenolob'ium). Tender shrubs or small trees that belong to the Bignonia family, Bignoniaceae. They are native from Florida to Mexico and South America and one species, S. stans, Yellow Bells or Yellow Elder, is much planted in tropical countries and in the southernmost parts of the United States. The name Stenolobium is derived from *stenos,* narrow, and *lobos,* a pod, and refers to the shape of the fruits.

Stenolobium stans is often grown under the names of Tecoma stans and Bignonia stans. It is a rapid grower and in tropical countries assumes the proportions of a small tree, but in the United States it is usually a large shrub. The showy, funnel-shaped flowers are borne in profusion and are bright yellow. It is readily propagated by seeds, cuttings and layering, and grows well in any reasonably good soil.

STENOTAPHRUM — *St. Augustine Grass* (Stenotaph'rum). Stenotaphrum belongs to the Grass family, Gramineae. Its name is derived from *stenos,* narrow, and *taphros,* a trench, and refers to the cavities in which the bases of the flowers are embedded in the stalks.

The St. Augustine Grass, S. secundatum, is native from South Carolina to Texas and into tropical America. It is a coarse, creeping kind that attains a height of about 1 ft. In the South, where superior lawn grasses do not thrive, it is much used as a lawn grass.

As Ornamental Pot Plants. S. secundatum variegatum is sometimes grown as a pot plant. It is about 12 in. in height, and has narrow leaves which are green and white. The flowers are inconspicuous. It spreads by means of a thin, creeping rhizome. For potting, the best compost consists of one part each of loam, peat moss or leaf mold, and sand.

As the plants are most serviceable in 5-in. pots, they are not repotted annually. Each spring the plants are removed from their pots and divided into three or four sections. Each portion is then repotted separately in a 5-in. pot and "grown on" until the following spring, when the same process of division is repeated. The soil is kept moist at all times, but during the summer water is required more frequently.

STEPHANANDRA (Stephanand'ra). Tender and hardy leaf-losing shrubs, natives of eastern Asia, with bright brown slender stems, small white or greenish-white flowers, and attractive leaves with finely cut margins. They are very closely allied to the shrubby Spiraeas, but are less showy in flower.

Four kinds are grown in our gardens: S. incisa, a graceful, spreading shrub 3-6 ft. high, with dainty, finely cut leaves, native to Japan and Korea; S. incisa "crispa nana," dwarfer and with crimped, fernlike foliage; S. Tanakae, a Japanese shrub more vigorous than S. incisa, with stronger and more erect branches; and S. chinensis, an eastern Chinese kind. All of these

An informal hedge of Stephanandra incisa.

are hardy in the North, although they may require some protection in severe winters. The leaves become rich reddish and orange in fall.

Stephanandra belongs to the Rose family, Rosaceae. The name, taken from the Greek *stephanos,* a crown, and *andros,* a man, refers to the dominant character of the stamens.

Propagation. These shrubs can be increased by seeds sown under glass in sandy soil, either as soon as ripe or during the following spring. They can also be propagated by cuttings, 3-4 in. long, made from young shoots inserted in a propagating bench in a greenhouse in July and by hardwood cuttings made after the leaves drop in fall.

Pruning, which is carried out in spring, consists of thinning out the oldest shoots to the ground line. If this pruning is neglected the bushes become a dense mass of growth and the graceful outline, which is a definite feature of well-developed specimens, is lost. They succeed in any good garden soil and make good hedge shrubs.

STEPHANOTIS—*Madagascar Jasmine* (Stephano'tis). Tropical evergreen climbing plants with woody stems. Only one kind, S. floribunda, is in general cultivation. This is a quick-growing climbing plant, with twining stems and opposite, smooth, shiny, elliptic, deep green leaves, 3 in. in length. It is free-blooming and produces large clusters of deliciously scented flowers throughout the summer. The flowers are white, of waxy texture, 1½ in. long, tubular and spread out at the tips into five petals. The flowers remain fresh for a long time, both on the plants and when cut and placed in water.

The Stephanotis, which are natives of the tropics of the Old World, belong to the Asclepias family, Asclepiadaceae. The botanical name is derived from *stephanos,* a crown, and *otos,* ear, and refers to the ear-shaped appearance of the stamens.

A Free-flowering Hothouse Climber. S. floribunda is of rampant growth and will fill a large space in the hothouse if allowed to develop to its fullest extent. It may be grown in a large pot or tub, but the best results are obtained by planting

The fragrant, white-flowered Stephanotis floribunda, the Clustered Wax Flower, an evergreen climber for the warm greenhouse.

it in a prepared bed of soil. A hole 3 ft. wide and 2 ft. 6 in. deep is taken out, and a 6-in. layer of broken bricks or stones is placed in the bottom for drainage. These are covered with a layer of grass turfs and the remainder of the space is filled with prepared compost consisting of equal parts of turfy loam, peat moss and leaf mold; to this should be added half a part of

[12–10]
Streptosolen Jamesonii

[12–10a]
Stanhopea Bucephalus

[12–10b]
Stanhopea tigrina

[12–10c]
Bird of Paradise Flower
(Strelitzia Reginae)

[12–11]
Strawberries

[12–11a]
*Alpine Strawberry
Baron Solenmacher*

well-decayed manure and a liberal quantity of coarse sand.

After the soil mixture has been allowed to settle, a well-rooted plant from a 5-in. pot is set in the center of the bed, and the shoots, as they develop, are trained to wires fixed to the roof of the greenhouse.

Summer and Winter Management. During the summer months well-established plants are watered copiously, but only a moderate amount of water is required during the winter. The foliage should be syringed twice daily from March to September, except when the plants are in bloom; at other times a light syringing once daily, on warm days only, is sufficient. To keep the plants in bounds and shapely, the straggling weak shoots are cut right out and the vigorous ones are shortened in February.

Young plants can be flowered in 5-7-in. pots; a few fresh plants should be raised annually for this purpose. The old plants should be discarded after three years unless required for planting out in a prepared bed of soil.

Propagation Is by Cuttings in Spring. Short side shoots, 2-3 in. in length, are taken off and inserted in a warm propagating case with a bottom heat of 70-75 degrees. When rooted, they are potted singly in 3-in. pots, using the compost that has been suggested for them, but without manure.

The potted plants are returned to the propagating case and kept there until well rooted. They are then gradually hardened off and set on the open benches. The shoots are pinched back to the second joint, and when new shoots are forming repotting is done in 6-in. pots. When the plants are well rooted in these, the side shoots are cut back to two joints, and the next shift is into 7-in. pots, unless the plants are required for planting in a bed of soil from 5-in. pots.

STEPS, GARDEN. Varying levels add charm to gardens and are often inevitable. Where grades are steep or changes of level sudden, steps frequently provide the simplest and most effective means of making walking progress easy.

Garden steps may be constructed of masonry or various other materials; they may be architectural and formal or very informal. In general, they should blend with the surroundings.

In wild gardens, rock gardens and other naturalistic areas, rustic steps built of wood or somewhat rough slabs of stone are often most suitable, but in the formal garden steps of dressed stone, brick or even concrete are most effective. The simplicity and clean lines of these provide a contrasting setting for the flowers. Such steps are strong and safe in all weathers,

Stone steps provide easy access between different levels of this garden.

A path up this steep slope is provided by these informally laid steps.

are easily kept clean and, once built, need little or no attention.

Wooden steps should be constructed of a wood resistant to decay, such as locust, redwood or cedar. On gentle and moderate slopes suitable logs may be laid to serve as risers (vertical parts of steps) with their ends embedded in the earth and the treads or horizontal parts surfaced with gravel, cinders, tan bark, pine needles or other suitable material.

Steps formed of turf are very effective when well located and well cared for, but they do not withstand much wear, and call for considerable upkeep.

Stone steps in a grass bank look well. A low stone wall built "dry"—that is, without the stones being cemented together—may well be made at each side of the steps; the crevices between the stones can be filled with flowering plants.

Whenever possible, garden steps should be comparatively less steep than indoor ones. The

Logs of Locust form the risers for these steps; the treads are soil, surfaced with tan bark.

height of each riser should not be greater than half the width of the step, and should not exceed 6 in. Excellent effects are often obtained by having risers 4 or 5 in. high and the width of each step considerably more than 12 in.

Like all other garden construction, steps should be well made. Those of masonry must be provided with substantial, well-drained foundations carried below the frost line.

STERCULIA (Stercu'lia; Ster'culia). Tropical and subtropical trees of little horticultural value. They are found wild in various parts of the world, including Australia, India, tropical Asia, tropical America, China and Japan. These evergreen trees grow up to 60 ft. in height and have lobed leaves, which in some kinds resemble those of the Plane Tree. The inflorescences or clusters of flowers are axillary (produced in the axils of the leaves), and consist of panicles of purple, red or yellow flowers. The flowers are remarkable as they have no petals, the colored sepals forming the attractive feature.

Sterculia belongs to the family Sterculiaceae. The name is derived from *stercus,* manure, and refers to the odor of the leaves of some kinds.

Several kinds yield fibrous bark which is made into ropes. From the fruit of S. scapigera, jellies, sweetmeats, and drinks are made by the Chinese.

Sterculias are grown to some extent in southern Florida. S. apetala, 45 ft., has yellow flowers spotted pink or purple. In S. foetida, 60 ft., the flowers are red or purplish-red and have an offensive odor. This last-named is a clean-limbed, smooth-barked tree well worth planting in frost-free regions.

STERILIZATION OF SOIL. This subject is dealt with under the heading of Soil Sterilization, which see.

STERNBERGIA—*Yellow Starflower* (Stern-ber'gia). Hardy bulbs suitable for the rock garden or an alpine greenhouse. They are natives chiefly of southern Europe and belong to the Amaryllis family, Amaryllidaceae. The name honors Count K. M. von Sternberg, a botanist of Prague. The bulbs average 1½ in. in diameter, and the linear or narrow, strap-shaped leaves are about 12 in. in length. The yellow crocus-like flowers are funnel-shaped, 2 in. in length and erect on short stalks. Only a few kinds are in cultivation. They are sometimes called Winter Daffodils.

Sternbergia lutea, a hardy bulbous plant which produces yellow flowers in early autumn.

Bulbs for the Rock Garden. These bulbs need a sunny well-drained position in the rock garden. Sandy loam with a little leaf mold and limestone rubble form the best soil mixture. The bulbs are planted 3 in. deep and 4 in. apart. The early-flowering kind, S. Fischeriana, is planted in August or September, and the late-flowering kinds in spring.

During the winter months the ground should be mulched with a layer of ashes, peat moss, salt hay or other suitable material to protect the bulbs from frost. They should not be disturbed for several years, or until they show signs of deterioration in growth, when they should be lifted and replanted in fresh soil. The largest bulbs are selected for replanting and the small offsets are utilized for increasing the stock.

For the Cool Greenhouse. The bulbs are potted in September or April, according to the kind. Deep, well-drained pans are used and they are filled with a soil mixture of sandy loam, lightened with a little leaf mold or peat moss and sand, and a small quantity of crushed limestone is added.

The bulbs are set 1 in. deep and 1½ in. apart; the pans are placed in a cold frame until the flowers appear, when they are taken into the greenhouse. Those kinds which are potted in the autumn should be protected with mats placed over the cold-frame sash during cold weather. When they are growing freely the soil is kept moist; at other times the soil is only watered when it becomes fairly dry. After flowering, less water is given and the bulbs are gradually dried off and repotted in the autumn or spring.

Propagation is by removing the small offsets at planting or potting time, and growing them until flowering size is reached.

The chief kinds are S. lutea, yellow, August and September; S. Fischeriana, yellow, early spring; S. colchiciflora, yellow, August. S. Fischeriana and S. lutea produce leaves and flowers at the same time, but S. colchiciflora sends up its leaves in the spring, and the flowers do not appear until late summer.

STEVENSONIA GRANDIFLORA (Stevenson'ia). This Palm, from the Seychelles Islands, forms a slender trunk, 30-40 ft. high, covered in its young state with stout prickles. On the apex it bears a large tuft of leaves averaging 6 ft. in length and 4 ft. in width. A distinguishing feature of this Palm is the yellowish blotching on the leaves. The name Stevensonia commemorates a former Governor of Mauritius. This plant is the only member of its genus.

Palm for a Lofty Conservatory. This Palm is probably tender in the United States, except possibly in southernmost Florida. Because it grows to a great height, it is only suitable for lofty conservatories. A minimum winter temperature of 55 degrees is required. Small plants are repotted annually into larger pots in March; eventually they are set in large pots or wooden tubs and kept growing vigorously by top-dressing them with rich compost in spring and by watering them in summer with liquid fertilizer. The best soil consists of equal parts of peat moss and loam to which sand is added, together with a sprinkling of crushed charcoal and some rotted manure.

Summer and Winter Management. A moist, semishaded location is required and the soil is kept moist during the summer. During the winter less watering and damping are needed, but the soil ought not to be allowed to remain dry for long periods.

Raising Seedlings. Propagation is by seeds. Freshly imported seeds must be used, as they will quickly lose their powers of germination.

The seeds are soaked in tepid water for several days; the vessel of water is placed on or near the hotwater pipes. They are then sown in a pan of sandy soil and plunged in fiber in a propagating case with a bottom heat of 75-80 degrees. The seedlings are potted separately in small pots and returned to the glass case. When well established, they are set on the open bench and subsequently are repotted.

STEVIA (Stev'ia). Tender, mostly subshrubby plants of little horticultural value. They are native from Texas to Arizona and down to South America and belong to the Daisy family, Compositae. Their name commemorates Dr. P. J. Esteve, a professor of botany at Valencia. They

Stevia rhombifolia variety stephanocoma glandulifera is a native of Mexico.

are little cultivated except in botanical collections. The plant commonly grown as Stevia is Piqueria, which see.

Stevias average 2 ft. in height, have woody stems, and entire (undivided) or three-cleft leaves, and bear terminal heads of small white, pink or purple flowers, resembling those of the Eupatorium. They will grow in ordinary garden soil in a sunny or semishaded location in mild climates. Propagation is by division in spring or by inserting cuttings of small side shoots in pots of sandy soil in summer.

STEWARTIA (Stewart'ia). Hardy leaf-losing flowering shrubs which are found wild in the United States and Japan. They belong to the Tea family, Theaceae. The name commemorates John Stuart, Lord Bute, who lived in the eighteenth century.

These beautiful trees or shrubs, which reach a height of 20-50 ft. or more, bear large white or cream-white five-petaled flowers in late summer.

They thrive in ordinary well-drained loamy garden soil; if the ground is clayey, compost, peat moss or leaf mold and sand should be mixed with it. They will thrive in sandy soil if loam and thoroughly decayed manure or compost are mixed in. They need little pruning, but any necessary trimming or thinning should be done in March.

The simplest method of propagation is by layering a few of the lowest branches in August. Cuttings, which are rather difficult to root, may be inserted in July in a frame kept close; or seeds may be sown in a slightly heated greenhouse or frame in spring. Seedling plants should be repotted as often as necessary, and grown in pots until they are large enough to be planted out of doors, for it is difficult to transplant them from the open ground; they should have the shelter of a cold frame until they are well established.

The chief kinds are Stewartia ovata (pentagyna), 10-15 ft., and its splendid variety grandiflora, which has conspicuous purple stamens; S. Pseudo-Camellia, 20-50 ft.; S. Malachodendron (S. virginica), 8-12 ft.; S. koreana, 40-50 ft.; S. sinensis, 20-30 ft.; and S. serrata, 30-40 ft. They flower in July and August.

STIGMA. This botanical term denotes that portion of the pistil of a flower, usually the upper portion, which receives the pollen in the process of pollination, leading to fertilization of the flower.

STIGMAPHYLLON—*Golden Vine* (Stigmaphyl'lon). Tropical evergreen climbing plants which are cultivated for their ornamental foliage and attractive flowers. They are found wild in the West Indies and South America and belong to the family Malpighiaceae. The name Stigmaphyllon is derived from *stigma* and *phyllon*, a leaf, and refers to the leaflike appendages on the stigmas.

The principal kind in cultivation, S. ciliatum, has slender woody twining stems up to 10 ft. in length. They are clothed with ovate, evergreen, slightly hairy leaves which are heart-shaped at the base and taper off to fine points at the tips. During early summer this plant produces small axillary clusters of yellow, conspicuous flowers.

A Hothouse Climbing Plant. Stigmaphyllon does not do well in pots and is therefore planted out in a bed of prepared soil in the hothouse. A hole is dug 30 in. in depth and 24 in. in diameter, and a 6-in. layer of stones or broken bricks is placed in the bottom for drainage. These are covered with the rough siftings from the compost, and the remainder of the space is filled with a mixture of equal parts of loam and leaf mold or peat moss with a scattering of sand.

The plant is then set in the center, and the soil made firm around the roots. Wires or a trellis is fixed to the roof to support the twining shoots. After planting, the soil is not moistened until it becomes moderately dry, then it is thoroughly saturated. The soil is afterwards kept moist throughout the year, but much less watering is required in winter. During the summer months the foliage is syringed daily (except when the plant is in flower), but throughout the winter syringing is only done on sunny days.

Pruning and Propagation. Pruning consists of cutting out weak shoots and shortening extra vigorous ones in February.

Propagation is by cuttings. Firm side shoots are taken off in April, the leaves are removed

Stewartia Pseudo-Camellia, a small Japanese tree, bears white flowers in summer.

from the lower half of the stem and a cut is made below the bottom joint.

The cuttings are inserted in small, well-drained pots filled with sandy, finely sifted compost. After being moistened, the pots of cuttings are set in a warm propagating case kept close until roots are formed.

The chief kind is S. ciliatum, 10 ft., yellow, June. Another kind sometimes cultivated is S. littorale, 8 ft., yellow, June.

STINKING CEDAR. Torreya taxifolia, which see.

STIPA—*Feather Grass, Spear Grass* (Sti'pa). Hardy and tender Grasses, a few of which are of value in gardens. They are found wild in many parts of the world and belong to the family Gramineae. The name refers to the feather-like inflorescence.

The two kinds cultivated in gardens are Stipa elegantissima and S. pennata; both are perennials and their management presents no difficulty in ordinary well-drained garden soil, if they are planted in a sunny position. Planting may be done in autumn or in spring. If left undisturbed for several years, they grow into attractive clumps and are ornamental when in bloom in summer. Propagation is by lifting and separating the clumps into rooted pieces in early autumn or in spring for immediate replanting where they are to remain. Another way is to sow seeds in flats of sandy soil in a greenhouse or frame in March, or out of doors in a reserve border in April or May, the seedling plants, when large enough, being planted out where they are to remain.

The favorite kind is S. pennata, a hardy species, which grows 3-4 ft. high. S. elegantissima is less hardy, thrives in sandy soils and attains a height of 3 ft. The inflorescences of these kinds may be cut and dried for use in flower arrangements for attractive winter decoration indoors.

STIZOLOBIUM—*Velvet Bean* (Stizolob'ium). Tropical and subtropical annual twining plants of vigorous growth and rambling habit. They do not stand frost, require a long growing season, and are adaptable for cultivation in the warmest parts of the United States only. Stizolobium belongs to the Pea family, the Leguminosae. The name is derived from two Greek words meaning stinging pods and refers to the fact that the hairs on the pods of some kinds are extremely irritating.

These plants are grown for winter forage and for ornament in the far South. Often they are planted among crops of Corn, the stalks of the Corn affording support for the stems of the Velvet Beans. They thrive in any ordinary soil.

Kinds include S. Deeringianum, Florida Velvet Bean, a native of tropical Asia which produces stems 50-100 ft. long and has large clusters of purple flowers. Several varieties of this kind are grown; S. Hassjoo, Yokohama Bean, flowers dark purple, probably a native of Japan; S. niveum, Lyon Bean, flowers white, probably a native of southern Asia and the Philippines; and S. pruritum, Cowage or Cowitch, flowers dark purple, pods covered with irritating hairs. The latter is naturalized in the West Indies and is not ordinarily cultivated.

STOCK. The plant which forms the rooted and hence lower part of a grafted or budded plant is called the stock or understock to differentiate it from the scion or part of another plant which is budded or grafted on and caused to unite with the stock.

The word stock is also used to refer to plants that are retained for propagation purposes; often such plants are termed stock plants.

STOCK, NIGHT-SCENTED. Mathiola bicornis. For details of cultivation, see Stocks.

STOCKS: DELICIOUSLY FRAGRANT FLOWERS
How to Grow Them in Garden and Greenhouse

The genus Mathiola contains several plants which have long been favorites in gardens, and are known collectively as Stocks. All are notable for their delicious fragrance, and the large-flowered types, like the Ten-Weeks, East Lothian and Brompton Stocks, in modern seedsmen's strains, are showy subjects for spring bedding, and for cool greenhouse cultivation. By far the

Modern varieties of Ten-Weeks Stocks are favorites for cutting and garden decoration.

most popular are the Ten-Weeks Stocks. These, despite their name, take 14-15 weeks from seed sowing to flower. Virginia Stock is a quite different plant and belongs to a different genus. For an account of it, see Malcomia.

The name Mathiola, sometimes spelled Matthiola, commemorates an Italian botanist and physician, Pierandrea Mattioli. The genus belongs to the Mustard family, the Cruciferae.

Night-scented Stock (Mathiola bicornis). This hardy annual grows about 12 in. in height, has rather slender stems, and bears small, purplish-white flowers which are inconspicuous by day but open in the evening, and then give off a delicious perfume. It is usual to grow these plants near the house so that the air, scented by their fragrance, is wafted through the open windows or on to a porch or terrace. Because the Night-scented Stock is rather drab-looking by day, it is a good plan to mix an equal quantity of the seeds of Virginian Stock (Malcomia maritima) with it, when sowing, to ensure color by day.

Night-scented Stock likes a sunny position and will thrive in ordinary garden soil. The site should be dug deeply, and some decayed manure or compost should then be added to the soil.

When to Sow Seeds. Early in spring the surface of the soil is raked over; the seeds are sown thinly on the surface and are covered by drawing the rake gently backwards and forwards over the soil. If the ground is dry, it should be watered before sowing. When the seedlings are an inch high they ought to be thinned out to 3 in. apart. Very little subsequent attention is required, except that the soil must be regularly stirred with a cultivator and kept moist in dry weather.

Ten-Weeks Stocks. These have been evolved from Mathiola incana variety annua. The double kinds, which form bushy plants about 1-2 ft. in height, can be obtained in many distinct colors, including purple, blue, mauve, crimson, copper, rose, pink, and yellow as well as white. They are invaluable as summer bedding plants where nights are fairly cool; they do not bloom satisfactorily in hot weather.

The seeds are sown in pans or flats in a greenhouse with a minimum temperature of 45 degrees, 6-7 weeks before the plants are to be set in the garden. The flats or pans are well drained and filled with a compost of two parts loam or good garden soil, one part peat moss, and one part of sand. This is passed through

Ten-Weeks Stock are the most popular kinds. These fragrant annuals are useful both for garden decoration and for cutting.

a sieve with a ½-in. mesh and pressed firmly into the seed pans or flats. By watering with a fine spray the soil is moistened, and then the receptacles are allowed to drain for 10-15 minutes before the seeds are sown.

Raising Ten-Weeks Stocks. The seeds are scattered thinly on the surface and covered by sifting a little fine soil over them. A pane of glass or sheet of paper is laid over the seed container, but this covering must be removed as soon as the seedlings appear above the surface. By placing the seedlings near the light (on a shelf near the glass) and admitting air on warm days, they are encouraged to make sturdy growth. When an inch in height, they should be transplanted into flats filled with a compost similar to that used for seed sowing, but in a slightly rougher state. They are set 2-3 in. apart, well watered, and shaded until established; they are grown in a cool, sunny greenhouse.

Before the young plants are set in the garden, the plants are placed in a cold frame for a week or two and finally are planted out of doors as soon as danger from frost has passed.

Seedlings of Ten-Weeks Stocks may also be raised by sowing the seeds in a cold frame 2-3 weeks before it is safe to sow them outdoors, or they can be sown out of doors when the trees begin to expand their buds in spring. By sowing in the greenhouse early, the blooms are produced much earlier. This is almost a necessary procedure in the North.

East Lothian or Intermediate Stocks. These are more robust than the Ten-Weeks Stocks and are of bushier habit of growth. They can be obtained in various colors, including scarlet, pink, purple and mauve as well as white. By sowing the seeds in spring, and treating the plants as advised for the Ten-Weeks Stocks, they can be grown for summer display to provide a succession of bloom after the latter have lost their freshness. The flowering period is thus extended well into the autumn. These plants are only useful where summers are fairly cool.

In fairly mild climates these Stocks develop into stronger plants and bloom earlier if they are grown as biennials, the seeds being sown in pots or flats filled with light soil in August. They are set in a cold frame and the seedlings are pricked off into deep flats when they are 1 in. in height. Later, they are potted singly in 3-in. pots and are sheltered in a sunny cold frame during the winter. This must be ventilated freely in mild weather, and water should be carefully applied to the soil to prevent damping off. A little lime should be mixed with the potting compost.

In spring, the plants are "hardened off" and planted out in the beds or borders. For early blooms, in the greenhouse, a few of the plants may be potted in 5-in. pots.

Brompton and Spring-flowering Stocks. These come into bloom before the Ten-Weeks Stocks, and are much hardier. The Brompton Stocks are of shades of pink, purple, mauve, scarlet and white, and average 2 ft. in height.

The spring bedding kinds, which grow about 12 in. in height and branch freely from the base, are obtainable in pink, scarlet, purple, blue or white. The Queen Stocks grow 18 in. in height, and the colors range from crimson and pink to purple and scarlet. They are invaluable for cutting.

When to Sow Brompton Stocks. All the kinds in this section should be treated as biennials by sowing the seeds in July–August to produce flowering plants the following spring and early summer. The seeds are sown in a cold frame. The seedlings are transplanted into flats and sheltered in a cold frame or they may be planted out of doors, 6 in. apart, in nursery rows, and set in their final locations 12-15 in. apart, in early autumn. They require a sunny position and well-drained soil. No fresh manure is required, as this causes sappy growth.

Greenhouse Culture. Ten-Weeks Stocks are excellent subjects for growing in greenhouses to supply cut flowers and as decorative pot plants. They may be flowered from January to June north of latitude 35 degrees north, and further south at high elevations. To supply cut flowers the column or nonbranching type is grown almost exclusively; for use as pot plants the branching types are generally preferred.

The seeds are sown from September to March, the plants from later sowings being smaller and shorter-stemmed than those from fall sowings. The soil should be well-drained and must be kept moderately moist but not constantly saturated. The temperature should be held at 50 degrees at night and slightly warmer in the daytime.

When the young seedlings have developed their second set of leaves, they are potted individually into 2½-inch pots or are transplanted to flats, in which they are spaced 3 in. apart. The plants need full exposure to sunshine and an airy, rather dry atmosphere for the best results; excessive humidity of the air or soil is decidedly harmful.

If the plants are to be grown in pots, they should be transferred to successively larger sizes as the roots become pot-bound, until they occupy containers that measure 5, 6, or even 7 in. in diameter. When these final pots are reasonably well filled with roots a regular program of feeding with dilute liquid fertilizer at weekly or semiweekly intervals should be initiated.

When grown for cut flowers, Stocks are most frequently planted out in soil-filled benches or beds in the greenhouse. A planting distance from 6 by 8 in. to 8 by 10 in., depending upon the vigor of the variety and the time of the year when planting is done, will prove to be about right; the wider spacing is given to vigorous-growing varieties and plants set in the benches in fall rather than in winter or spring.

For the best results in the production of cut flowers it is usual to pick off any side shoots that form and allow each plant to develop but one spike of flowers. If a branching spike is preferred, the tips of the young plants should be pinched out when the plants are about 4 in. tall.

Whether they are grown in pots or are planted out in beds or benches, Stocks require a moderately heavy and fairly rich soil. One that contains an appreciable amount of lime is favored and it should be fairly rough, rather than in a fine sifted condition, at planting time. A dressing of unleached wood ashes or other potash fertilizer applied to the soil before planting, or when the plants are partly grown, is particularly beneficial to Stocks.

Temperature is all important in the production of good greenhouse Stocks. At night this should not exceed 45-50 degrees and during the day should not be more than 5-10 degrees higher, whenever the weather permits it to be held down to those levels.

STOCK, VIRGINIA. Malcomia, which see.

STOKESIA—*Stokes' Aster* (Stoke'sia). A genus of one hardy herbaceous perennial plant, Stokesia laevis, belonging to the Daisy family, Compositae, and named in honor of Jonathan Stokes, M.D., 1755–1831.

The beautiful blue flowers of Stokesia laevis, a choice perennial for the front of the perennial border.

This plant is native to North America from South Carolina to Louisiana, growing 12-18 in. tall, and bearing, in summer and autumn, large blue flowers like those of a refined China Aster. The variety called superba is superior to the type. It grows taller and has larger, richer colored flowers. The plant enjoys well-drained, loamy soil in a fully sunny position and is admirable for the front of the flower border or for the rock garden. It is increased by division in spring and may also be raised from seeds sown in a greenhouse in late winter or in a cold frame or a sheltered bed outdoors in April or May. In the North Stokesia requires some winter protection in the form of a covering of salt hay, evergreen branches or some other suitable material.

There are varieties with pinkish, creamy white and lilac flowers.

STOLON. A botanical term which denotes a horizontal stem, at or just below the ground level, that develops a new plant at its tip. The runners of Sweet Violets and Strawberries are stolons. The term is also applied to a shoot that bends to the ground and puts forth roots, as do some kinds of Rubus.

STOMA, STOMATA. A stoma (plural, stomata) is a tiny opening or pore in the epidermal layer or outer skin of a leaf. Stomata usually occur chiefly on the lower surface of leaves but in some cases—for example, Water Lilies—they are on the upper surface. The stomata make possible the interchange of gases between the air and the interior of the leaf and they regulate the giving off of water vapor.

STOMATIUM (Stoma′tium). A group of small succulent plants that belong to the family Aizoaceae and were at one time included in the genus Mesembryanthemum. They are grown chiefly by fanciers of succulent plants and require the same culture as Mesembryanthemum, which see. One of the most commonly cultivated kinds is S. Fulleri which is about 1 in. high; has crowded branches and leaves covered with silvery warts and toothed at their edges. Its flowers are yellow.

STONE CHIPS. Stone, crushed so that it will pass through a half-inch or three-quarter-inch mesh, with all dust and smaller particles removed, constitutes the stone chips or stone chippings of the gardener. The stone may be sandstone, millstone, grit, limestone, bluestone or any other kind deemed suitable for the purpose. Stone chips are much used by rock gardeners both for mixing with the soil and for using as a surface covering.

STONE CRESS. See Aethionema.

STONECROP. Sedum, which see.

STONE FRUITS. A term used collectively for the tree fruits in which the seed is enclosed by a hard, stony layer (the stone), surrounded by a soft fleshy portion; for example, Plums, Peaches, Nectarines, Cherries, etc.

STONE PINE. Pinus Pinea, which see.

STONE PLANTS. See Argyroderma and Lithops.

STONES IN SOIL. Soils often contain stones; sometimes stones are present in excessive quantity and may interfere with cultivation. Their presence causes diminished evaporation from the surface; they tend to raise the mean temperature of soils; they result in an increase in the normal moisture content.

Experiment has proved that stones may actually increase the cropping power of soils if they are not excessively numerous. Their worst fault is that they are a hindrance to tillage. Stones help to break up stiff, clayey soil and their beneficial action often far outweighs any inconvenience they may cause.

STOOL. This term is used by gardeners to denote the root crowns or clumps of plants, particularly those of Raspberry, Chrysanthemum and other kinds which give rise to numerous shoots.

STOPPING. A term which means pinching off or cutting off the soft tips or ends of the shoots of plants to ensure the development of other shoots, thus providing well-branched plants. It is synonymous with pinching.

STORAX. See Styrax.

STOVE. A word at one time used by gardeners to denote a hothouse, a greenhouse in which the minimum temperature does not fall below 60 degrees. Stove plants, referred to in old books, are tropical plants.

STRAIGHTEDGE. An instrument which is used in the work of grading plots of land; it consists of a piece of wood 6-10 ft. in length with a perfectly straight edge and the opposite side, or part of it, strictly parallel with the straight edge. One edge is rested on pegs driven into the ground and on the upper edge a level

Using a straight edge and level to determine a grade.

is placed; the position of the straightedge is altered by raising or lowering the pegs which support it until a true level is shown.

STRAIN. This word is used to describe a particular type of plant which has been raised by careful selection within a variety. There are various strains or types of many familiar flowers and vegetables, some of which are superior to others, although the variety name may be the same. For example, there are many strains of hybrid Gloxinias, Tuberous Begonias, Hippeastrums and Delphiniums, and their value depends on the care taken in the cultivation of the plants for seeds so that they breed true. For this reason it is wise to buy seeds from seedsmen of good repute.

STRANVAESIA (Stranvae'sia). A small group of evergreen shrubs, few of which are in cultivation. The two chief kinds are S. Nussia (glaucescens), a native of the Himalayas, and S. Davidiana, a native of China. Two varieties of S. Davidiana are salicifolia and undulata. Stranvaesia belongs to the Rose family, Rosaceae. The name commemorates a botanist, W. Fox Strangways, Earl of Ilchester.

These shrubs are not very hardy and are suitable for cultivation in the open garden only in mild climates. In summer they bear corymbs (flattish bunches) of white flowers, and these are followed in autumn by small, reddish fruits.

Stranvaesia should be planted in spring in well-drained soil with which compost or other decayed organic material has been mixed. Little pruning is needed, but the branches may be trimmed or shortened as may be necessary to keep the shrubs shapely; this work is done in spring, before new growth begins. An increased stock is obtained by layering a few of the lowest branches, or by seeds when procurable. The seeds are sown in sandy soil in a frame in spring, and the seedlings are grown in pots and given the shelter of a frame until large enough to be planted out of doors.

STRATIFICATION. Stratification is a method of carrying seeds through the period from the time they ripen until they are ready to germinate, with minimum trouble and occupying minimum space. Some seeds, especially those of certain trees and shrubs, will not germinate soon after they ripen, yet perish if they are permitted to dry. They need a storage period of several weeks or even months at low temperatures and in a moist, dark place before they are ready to grow. In nature these conditions are provided for by the seeds' falling to the ground in autumn or early winter and soon being covered by forest debris, which assures darkness and prevents drying. Winter provides the necessary low temperatures.

Gardeners often find it convenient to stratify such seeds rather than to sow them immediately. Stratification provides the conditions the seeds must have without their taking up as much space or requiring as much attention as would be the case if they were sown immediately after they were gathered.

Stratification consists of mixing the seeds with sand or sand and peat moss that is just moist and storing them where they will remain moist and cool. A favorite way is to place layers of sand, or sand and peat moss, alternately with layers of seeds in wooden boxes, then bury the boxes 6 in. deep outdoors in a shaded place where the soil is well drained. It is a good plan to surround the boxes, before burial, with wire netting or screening to foil the attempts of rodents to dig up the seeds. If fine seeds are being stratified, they may be spread between layers of cheesecloth as they are buried in the sand, or sand and peat moss. The cheesecloth makes it easy to find the seeds when they are needed for sowing.

Yet another method of stratifying seeds is to mix them with slightly moist sand, or sand and peat moss, place the mixture in jars, and store these in a refrigerator.

Whichever means of stratification is employed, the seeds should be picked or sifted from the sand or sand and peat moss mixture and should be sown in the regular way in pots, flats, cold frames or outdoors when it is time for them to germinate.

The majority of seeds needing stratification germinate the spring following the summer or autumn in which they ripen, but some kinds will not germinate until one year later than that. All seeds that are handled in this manner can be germinated by sowing in a cold frame or outdoors as soon as they are ripe, provided the seedbed is kept evenly moist and always favorable to the needs of the seeds.

STRATIOTES ALOIDES — *Water Soldier, Crab's-Claw* (Stratio′tes). A hardy perennial aquatic plant which is found wild in various parts of Europe. It belongs to the Frog's Bit family, Hydrocharitaceae. The name is from *stratiotes,* a soldier, and refers to the somewhat sword-shaped leaves.

The plant is of low, creeping growth with small, fleshy leaves and greenish-white flowers. It spreads quickly and may become a nuisance in garden pools. It is propagated by offshoots or side growths taken from the bases of the leaves.

STRAW. This, the dry stems of cereals, such as Wheat, Oats and Rye, has many uses in gardening. It is especially good for protecting tender plants from frost damage, for mulching Strawberries, Raspberries, etc., and as a valuable source of organic matter after it has been used as bedding for animals or mixed with waste vegetable matter and composted.

STRAWBERRIES: MOST POPULAR FRUIT
Full Details about Their Planting and Care

The Strawberry is our most widely cultivated small fruit. In suitable varieties it is grown in every state, much of Canada, except the coldest regions, and even in the milder parts of Alaska. It is grown extensively commercially in widely separated parts of the United States and Canada and is the most popular and easily grown garden fruit.

The common cultivated Strawberry, Fragaria chiloensis variety ananassa, is descended from the wild species, F. chiloensis, of the Pacific coasts of North and South America, and F. virginiana, a native of eastern North America. These were taken to Europe by early travelers, where they soon became hybridized, and some of the resulting varieties were returned to North America. From them, other varieties, especially suitable for culture in the United States and Canada, were developed, and commercial planting started about the year 1800. A rapid expansion of Strawberry planting took place after the Civil War, when varieties having fruits suitable for shipping became available.

The Strawberry is suited to a wider range of climatic conditions than any other Temperate Zone fruit. Over the years varieties have been developed for such extremes as are found in Florida, with its hot, humid climate and short summer days, and the prairie provinces of Canada, with their long, hot, dry summer days and cold winters, often without much snow cover. There are even varieties that will stand the winters of Wyoming without protection. The Strawberry, with its many varieties, is a very adaptable plant.

Varieties of the common Strawberry are classified as June-bearing and everbearing, according to whether they produce one crop of fruit (in June in the North, earlier in the year in the South) each year and no more, or bear a succession of fruits from late July or August until frost. The June-fruiting varieties are divided into early varieties and late varieties, there being a week or more difference between the dates of ripening of these kinds. In addition to varieties of the common Strawberry, other kinds called Alpine and Hautbois Strawberries are sometimes cultivated.

Soil and Site. Strawberries will grow on a wide range of soils, provided the plants are in good

A mulch of salt hay or straw protects ripening Strawberries from dirt.

No fruit garden is complete without its Strawberry bed. The plants will grow in any well-drained soil that contains organic matter. Early spring is the best time to plant a new bed.

physical condition and are managed properly. Soil texture, if not extreme, is secondary in importance to good drainage, freedom from soil-borne diseases, a satisfactory moisture supply, sufficient organic matter in the soil and freedom from perennial weeds. The ideal soil is a deep, sandy or gravelly loam, overlying a subsoil that is retentive of moisture but is well-drained. Coarse sands and gravels are subject to drought and compact clay soils are poorly drained and difficult to manage; for these reasons they are less satisfactory.

A soil well-supplied with organic matter is not only less subject to drought, but also is easily worked, and its mellow condition is favorable for the rooting of the Strawberry runners.

Good drainage, surface as well as internal, is important because Strawberry roots are easily injured if the soil is saturated. Soils that are nearly saturated in winter heave readily, causing damage to the roots. The red stele root rot disease is a disease of poorly drained soils. A gentle slope and a porous subsoil favor good drainage.

In gardens where Tomatoes, Potatoes, Peppers and Eggplants are grown, the crop rotation should be planned so that Strawberries will not be planted on land which has grown these crops within the previous 3 years. These crops may infect the soil with verticillium wilt, a troublesome root disease of Strawberries.

Good air circulation is desirable as a partial protection against frost, which is usually worse in low spots surrounded by higher ground. Fungus diseases of the foliage are less severe where there is good air movement, as on a slope. The direction of the slope influences the time of ripening of the fruits. Strawberries on a south-facing slope ripen several days earlier than those on a north-facing slope. This difference should be considered, as it may give one an advantage on early or late markets or of a longer season of home picking if early varieties are planted on a south slope and late varieties on a north slope. Strawberries require a sunny location.

Harvesting Strawberries—one of the most pleasurable of garden chores.

Preparation for planting depends upon the previous management of the soil for several years. Organic matter in quantity is desirable and may be supplied by the generous application of rich compost, or by the addition of stable manure at the rate of about 20 tons to the acre; this amount may be increased or decreased, according to the needs of the soil and the supply of manure.

If manure or rich compost in sufficient amounts is not to be had, then the soil should be managed so that the ground is occupied by a grass, or legume sod, preferably the latter, for at least two years before the Strawberries are planted. The sod crop should be heavily fertilized to stimulate the production of as much plant material as possible to be plowed under in preparation for the Strawberries. A hoed crop should be grown for one year before the Strawberries are planted.

Many growers fertilize their fields with a complete fertilizer such as a 5-10-5 at the rate of 1,000 pounds to the acre when making the land ready for planting; or they apply the same amount as a dressing sprinkled alongside the rows of plants at the first hoeing after the plants are set out. A fertilizer supplying nitrogen alone at this time would probably be sufficient in most good soils.

The land should be plowed in the fall if possible, but spring plowing is satisfactory on light soils that permit early working. The making ready of the soil should be as thorough as for vegetables. Strawberry plants are set out more easily, and start better in a loose, mellow soil that is free from lumps.

Strawberries are usually planted in early spring as soon as the soil can be had in suitable condition. Late planting, if followed by hot, dry weather, may result in a poor stand of plants. Late fall planting, even in late October or early November, is successful if the plants are well-mulched before severe weather arrives. The mulch must be removed in the spring and the planting managed like a spring-planted bed. The principal advantage of fall planting is the early start the plants get in the spring.

The plants to be set out should be purchased from nurseries specializing in the production of Strawberry plants. Virus-free plants should be specified, as these are much superior to the older stocks, which are often virus-infected and do not grow vigorously.

The young plants should have vigorous roots, straw-colored or nearly white and fibrous. Plants with black and sparse roots are not suitable for planting.

Cold-storage plants are being used for planting in increasing numbers. These come mostly from Maryland, where they are dug during the winter while fully dormant and are kept in cold storage at a temperature of about 32 degrees F. until the shipping season. These plants, because they are fully dormant at planting time, prove superior to plants that are dug after growth has started.

When the plants are received from the nursery the bundle should be opened and the plants heeled in (planted temporarily) in a shallow trench in a moist, shady place until they are to be permanently planted. If they are dry on arrival, the roots should be soaked in water for an hour.

Planting Systems. Strawberries may be grown in matted rows or in hills. With the matted row system all of the runner plants that develop are usually allowed to grow and the result is most often an overcrowded fruiting row. Much better results are secured if many of the runners are eliminated so that the plants are spaced at the best distance for maximum production. If the runner plants in a matted row system are spaced about the mother plants about 6-8 in. apart until the row is filled out to a width of 18 in. and all later runners are removed, overcrowding is prevented and superior results obtained. The spacing is done when the bed is hoed.

When the plants are grown in hills, all of the runners are removed as they appear, leaving only the plants that were planted to produce the crop. The hill system usually produces the best fruits, but because the plants are set more closely together at planting time the costs for plants are higher.

Strawberries planted to produce a matted row bed are usually set 1½-2½ ft. apart in the row, depending on the runner-making ability of the variety and the fertility of the soil. The distance between the rows is 3-3½ ft.

In the hill system the plants are set 1-1½ ft. apart in the row and 2-3 ft. between rows. Sometimes they are set in beds of 2 or 3 rows with an alley between for the pickers. A variation of this is to set the plants in hills and allow a runner to take root in the row, on each side of the mother plant, or sometimes on each side of the row to make a triple row. The essential thing, whatever system is followed, is to prevent the excessive crowding that often results when too many

Strawberries planted in hills.

It is important to set Strawberry plants at the correct depth. In this picture the horizontal line represents the soil surface, and the middle plant is properly set. The plant at the left is not set deep enough, the plant at the right is set too deep.

runners are allowed to take root and establish themselves.

Method of Planting. The plants may be set out with a trowel, or with a spade. The spade requires two persons. One inserts the spade in the soil vertically and pushes it back and forth to make a V-shaped hole into which the roots are placed, spread apart and not crowded together in a lump. The top of the crown of the Strawberry plant should be even with the surface of

Planting Strawberries with a spade.

the ground. As the spade is removed, the soil should be firmed about the roots by pressing it with the foot. A properly set plant should resist a strong tug without becoming loosened in the soil. During planting, the roots should not be allowed to dry out.

Removing Blossoms. Amateur gardeners are often so anxious to obtain fruits from the Strawberry plants they set out that they permit them to bear fruit the first season. This is a mistake. The plants should not be allowed to fruit until their second season; all blossoms should be removed the first year to prevent fruiting. Plants that fruit the first year are not able to make a good start at becoming well established.

Controlling weeds is the principal job during the growing season. The field should be cultivated and hoed often enough to eliminate all weeds while they are yet small. They are much easier to control while small and it is important to eradicate them before they have competed with the Strawberries for nutrients and moisture.

Chemical weed control is used by some growers and if it is done properly it can greatly reduce the number of cultivations needed. Special herbicides (weed killers) that kill germinating weed seeds may be used. These weed killers, such as Crag No. 1, are not effective on seedlings over a quarter inch in height. To use them effectively the field is cultivated and hoed to eliminate all sizable weeds, and is then sprayed with the herbicide in dilutions recommended by the manufacturer. For a few weeks the herbicide kills the germinating weed seeds, then loses its effectiveness, and the process is repeated. It does not injure the plants, but may stunt the roots temporarily as they begin to develop on the runner plants.

Weed killers containing 2,4-D may be used to control broad-leaved weeds, but this material is not effective on grasses. It should not be used later than mid-August, as it affects the fruit buds which develop after that, and many misshapen berries will result the following spring. It should not be used in the spring of the bearing year. 2,4-D is useful for cleaning up the weeds in a bed that is being renewed after harvest.

Other weed killers are sometimes used. The dinitro compounds are effective on Chickweed if properly used. New materials are being developed rapidly and Strawberry growers should secure the latest information on chemical weed killers from their State Agricultural Experiment Stations.

Geese have also been used to weed Strawberries. They do not eat Strawberry leaves and they do eat grasses and some, but not all, broad-leaved weeds. Young geese are better weeders than old geese and they must get the weeds while these are small as they do not do a good job on old weeds. The geese must be confined with a 30-inch fence, and water, some feed, and shade are necessary. These should be at least 25 feet from the Strawberries to prevent excessive trampling by the geese.

The Strawberry bed usually needs one weeding in the spring of the fruiting year. Unless this is done, it will be very weedy by the time the berries are ripe and the competition between the weeds and the berries for moisture will reduce the crop.

Irrigation is usually a profitable practice in

growing Strawberries. The plants are shallow-rooted, with the bulk of the roots in the top 6 in. of the soil, and the effects of dry weather are soon felt. The crop may be reduced one half or more by a water shortage when the berries are ripening. Strawberries need about an inch of rain a week and any deficiency should be made up by irrigation if a water supply is available. Portable pipe and revolving sprinklers are used on large plantings. In the garden, porous canvas hose (soil-soaker) is used.

The fertilizer requirements of Strawberries have been the subject of much experimentation, but the results are less clear-cut than with many other crops. Nitrogen is most apt to bring profitable results; and late summer and early fall applications when the fruit buds are being formed have sometimes resulted in increased yields. Nitrogen applied in the spring of the bearing year usually decreases yields and may result in soft berries and much rot in a wet season.

The phosphorus and potash requirements of Strawberries are usually met in most soils suitable for Strawberry growing. In the home garden there is no harm in using these elements in a complete fertilizer. On infertile soils complete fertilizers may be used. Strawberry growers should recognize that water, early planting, spacing of runner plants, winter mulching, weed control and the control of diseases and insects are much more effective in increasing yields than are fertilizers.

The best practice is probably to apply nitrogen in mid-August at the rate of 50-60 pounds per acre. This may be obtained by using 150-200 pounds of ammonium nitrate or twice as much nitrate of soda. Other materials that furnish the same amount of nitrogen may be used. The fertilizer is broadcast over the plants when dry and then brushed off with a broom, or piece of brush, to avoid burning the foliage.

Harvesting. The berries should be picked every other day because they are highly perishable. The pickers should handle them carefully to avoid bruising. As soon as possible the filled baskets should be removed to the shade or a cool cellar.

After harvest, the bed, if not too weedy and if in good vigor, may be renewed for another crop the following season. This is done by removing the tops (cutting off the old foliage), cleaning

When harvesting Strawberries, handle the berries carefully to avoid bruising them.

out the weeds, and fertilizing the bed. Some growers plow out the plants along the side of the row and renew it with the runner plants that grow in late summer from the center plants, but beds so renewed may be less productive than those where all the plants are left, if the row is not too crowded.

Winter Protection. Strawberries should be mulched for winter protection. The crowns and roots of the plants, if unprotected, are often severely injured by low winter temperatures. This injury appears the following spring and is evidenced by reduced growth, reddened foliage, and eventually, when the berries are ripening, by the wilting and collapse of the plants.

To prevent this injury the mulch should be applied before temperatures drop below 20 degrees F., but after two or three hard frosts have occurred. The plants should be covered to a depth of 2-3 in. with the mulch.

Wheat straw and marsh hay are excellent mulching materials. Rye and oat straws are also good. Leaves and sawdust are sometimes used if better materials are not available. Pine needles are much used in the South.

In the spring, part of the mulch is raked off the plants into the alley between the rows. The leaves and flower clusters push up through the thin covering of straw which is left to keep the berries clean, to conserve moisture and to check

Cutting the free end of a runner beyond the young Strawberry plant that is to be layered.

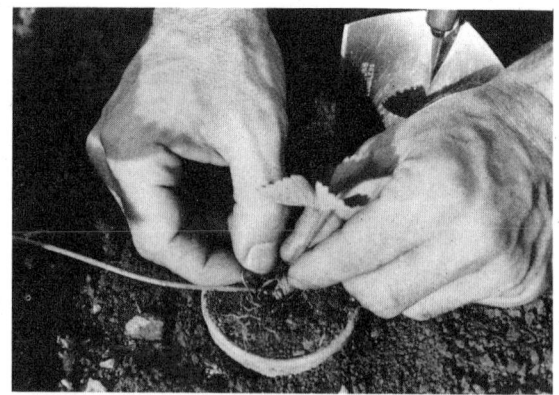

Layering a Strawberry by pinning a young plantlet into a pot filled with soil.

weed growth quickly to a considerable extent.

Propagation. The Strawberry may be propagated from seeds or by the division of plants in early spring, but by far the easiest and best way is by young plants formed on runners. Runners are slender, trailing stems which develop from the bases of mature plants in July. For the best results propagation should be done from parent plants which have not been allowed to fruit the year the young plants are taken.

The parent plants should be the most vigorous, disease-free plants with good flower trusses in their first year. Runners which fail to produce a flower truss in their first year should always be removed and destroyed. Having selected the parent plants, the next thing is to concentrate their energies into vegetative production. The flower stalks should be cut and no flowering or fruiting allowed. The plants may be marked ones in the ordinary bed or given a small nursery bed of their own. They should be hoed, fertilized and well watered.

Layering Runners. In July, the runners will form and should be restricted to four to six per plant. The runners should be trained to root either in 3-in. pots, filled with good soil, or in a prepared bed of equal parts, by bulk, loam and compost (or peat), liberally enriched with bone meal, between two boards or rows of bricks by the sides of the parent plants. Small plantlets form where the runners rest on the soil, and this can be encouraged by pegging the runners down, where the plantlets are rooting, in the pots or bed. Once the plantlets are growing and rooting, the free end of the runner should be cut at 2-3 inches beyond, but leaving the basal end still attached to the parent plant. Although more than one plantlet can be formed by a single runner, it is wise to propagate only one plantlet per runner in the interests of getting first-class stock, fully characteristic of the parent strain.

The young plantlets should be kept watered in dry weather, and an occasional feeding with a liquid fertilizer is helpful. In four to five weeks, the young plants are usually ready to be severed from the parent plant, and can be transplanted for the making of new beds, or grown on for forcing under glass. The parent plants may be allowed to grow on for fruiting, but should not be used for propagation again.

All this may seem a counsel of perfection, and many gardeners are tempted to propagate from their fruiting plants rooted with or without their attention in the ordinary soil. This may succeed for a few seasons, but in time is usually attended

Layering a Strawberry runner by weighting it down with a stone.

by a perceptible falling off in the performance of the plants and their fruiting vigor.

Strawberries from Seeds. Strawberries do not come true to variety from seeds, and seed-raising is chiefly of interest to the hybridist or those interested in raising Alpine and Hautbois Strawberries. The seeds are located on the outsides of the fruits and are separated by crushing, washing and drying fully ripe fruits. They should be sown very shallowly in pans or flats in a cold frame or greenhouse in March or in light soil out of doors in early spring. The plants are later transplanted to the beds where they are to grow and produce their fruits.

Growing Everbearing Varieties. The everbearing varieties of Strawberry require special treatment, as they produce very light crops when grown in the same way as the June-bearing varieties. They are less vigorous and produce fewer runners.

The soil should be highly fertile from the addition of stable manure or compost or commercial fertilizer, and irrigation will be necessary, as the berries ripen if the weather is dry.

Growers in Ohio have developed a method of growing the everbearing varieties in hills under a sawdust mulch. The plants are set out in the spring in hills, cultivated a few weeks and then mulched with an inch of sawdust all over the field. All runners are removed as soon as they appear. The blossoms are picked off until early July, after which they are left on the plants and the berries begin ripening a month later, continuing until frost. The costs of growing the everbearers by this method are high, but the returns from out-of-season Strawberries are also high if a market is available at luxury prices.

Strawberry-growing in Barrels. Strawberries may be grown in pots or boxes on window sills, and a good method for limited space is to grow them in a barrel. A sound, clean barrel is prepared by drilling with 1-in. drainage holes, 6 in. apart, in the bottom, and with rows of 2½-in. holes in the sides, about 12 in. apart, staggered so that the holes of one row lie between those of adjacent rows. The barrel is stood on bricks, and a 2-in. layer of broken bricks, stone or rubble placed in the bottom. A 6-in. drainpipe of earthenware, stout cardboard, or tile is placed centrally, filled with broken brick, and the barrel then filled with a rich soil mixture, such as equal parts by bulk of good loam and rotted manure or compost, plus 6 oz. bone meal per bushel. The soil should be well firmed as it is put in, and the young plants inserted in the holes as filling proceeds. The center pipe is lifted out to leave a core of porous brick, and half a dozen plants can be set on top of the barrel when filled.

The barrel should stand in a well-sunned but sheltered place, and may be watered through the central core. It is usually necessary to replace the plants annually, and only first-class stock should be used.

Varieties of Strawberries are very numerous and many are rather local in their suitability for different latitudes and soils. The varieties suited to New York are wholly unsuitable for Tennessee, Louisiana, California and other regions where conditions are very different from those where the varieties originated.

The varieties favored for planting are changing rapidly as many new ones are being developed by the experiment stations. Prospective planters should inquire of their State Agricultural Experiment Stations, or of their Strawberry-growing neighbors for information regarding the best varieties for local conditions. The catalogues of Strawberry nurseries offer the varieties currently in favor. The following are the better and more widely grown sorts at present.

For the northern states westward to the Mississippi valley, the principal varieties are Howard (Premier), Catskill, Sparkle, Temple, Fairland, Robinson, Fairfax, and Pathfinder. New and promising are the varieties Empire, Erie, Eden, Vermilion, and Armore. For the upper Mississippi valley Beaver and Senator Dunlap are among the hardiest.

For Washington, D. C., to the Carolinas, the varieties Blakemore, Klondike, Massey and Suwannee are recommended, the latter being a high-quality variety for home use. Dixieland and Pocahontas are new and promising for trial in this region.

For Kentucky and Tennessee, the varieties Tennessee Beauty, Tennessee Shipper and Aroma are important. In the Gulf coast states, Missionary, Blakemore, Klonmore and Klondike

The Alpine Strawberry, Baron Solemacher.

are important. These same kinds as well as the variety Ranger are suitable for Texas.

For Florida the recommended varieties are Florida Ninety and Missionary.

For the Pacific Northwest the varieties Marshall, Brightmore, Corvallis and Northwest are recommended.

Varieties suitable for cultivation in California are Marshall and several that were developed there, Shasta, Donner, Tahoe, Lassen and Sierra.

The everbearing varieties Gem, Superfection and Brilliant are all very similar, if not identical, and are good. Streamliner and Twentieth Century are other everbearing varieties worth growing.

For Canada the following varieties are recommended: In Alberta, British Sovereign, Senator Dunlap, Premier, Borden; in British Columbia, British Sovereign, Marshall, Senator Dunlap, Magoon; in Manitoba, Senator Dunlap, Glenmore; in New Brunswick, Premier, Senator

The variegated-leaved Strawberry is an attractive ornamental variety. It bears small edible fruits.

Dunlap, Catskill, Mackenzie; for Nova Scotia, Premier, Senator Dunlap, Catskill, Pathfinder; for Prince Edward Island, Senator Dunlap, Borden, Crimson Glow; for Quebec, Premier, Mackenzie, Senator Dunlap, Catskill, King; for Saskatchewan, Senator Dunlap, Dakota, Prairie Bell.

Alpine and Hautbois Strawberries are quite distinct from varieties of the common Strawberry. They represent species native to Europe. The Alpine kinds are derived from Fragaria vesca variety semperflorens; the Hautbois Strawberry is F. moschata. All bear small berries of delicious flavor over a long period during summer and fall.

These kinds of Strawberries are usually propagated by seeds sown in spring. The young plants are transplanted to flats of fertile, porous soil and later to outdoor beds or are

The Alpine Strawberry produces small flavorful fruits throughout the summer.

planted as edgings or borders to paths. Most varieties should be spaced about 12 in. apart, but one of the best and most commonly available, the Alpine Strawberry Baron Solemacher, needs 18 in. between individuals. Baron Solemacher is a vigorous grower; it does not form runners. The Alpine variety Cresta is a good runner-forming kind. Fragaria vesca variety variegata has leaves handsomely variegated with white.

STRAWBERRY, BARREN. Waldsteinia fragarioides, which see.

STRAWBERRY BEGONIA. Saxifraga sarmentosa, which see.

STRAWBERRY BUSH, RUNNING. Euonymus obovatus, which see.

STRAWBERRY GERANIUM. Saxifraga sarmentosa, which see.

STRAWBERRY GUAVA. Psidium Cattleianum, which see.

STRAWBERRY JAR. A type of ornamental pottery or ceramic container designed for the accommodation of growing plants and characterized by having a number of pocket-like openings in their sides as well as one large opening in the top. Strawberry jars are vase shaped. After they are filled with suitable soil, plants (Strawberries of purely decorative kinds) are set in the pockets and in the tops of the jars.

STRAWBERRY RASPBERRY. Rubus illecebrosus, which see.

STRAWBERRY TOMATO. Physalis pruinosa, which see.

STRAWBERRY TREE. See Arbutus Unedo.

STRAWFLOWER. Helichrysum bracteatum, which see. See also Everlasting Flowers.

STRELITZIA—*Bird-of-Paradise Flower* (Strelit′zia). A group of tender perennial plants, only one of which is commonly grown. This is Strelitzia Reginae, which has large ornamental leaves on long strong petioles (leafstalks), and bears brilliant orange and purple flowers, several together within a large bract, on stems 3 ft. or more high in spring. It is a native of South Africa and belongs to the Banana family, Musaceae. The name commemorates Charlotte of Mecklenburg-Strelitz.

A Remarkable Plant. This is one of the most remarkable of exotic flowering plants and is magnificent when in full bloom. It thrives in a greenhouse in which a minimum temperature of 50-55 degrees is maintained, and may either be grown in large flowerpots or in a prepared bed of soil on the floor of the greenhouse. The plants must be exposed to the sunshine and free ventilation is needed during warm summer weather. At that season the plants require a good deal of water and the soil must be kept moist; in winter the soil should be watered only when it is fairly dry.

Planting may be done in autumn or early spring. The most suitable soil consists of loam, two thirds, with one third of peat and leaf mold, and a free scattering of sand. If Strelitzia is grown in a bed of soil, care must be taken that it is well drained. If the plants are grown in pots, those 7-, 8- or 9-in. wide are suitable. Early spring is the best time to repot those plants which need this attention.

Outdoor Culture. In climates where little or no frost occurs, as in parts of California and Florida, Strelitzias may be grown outdoors. They thrive in any good soil and need liberal amounts of water during their season of active growth. Established plants benefit from an annual application of fertilizer. A mulch of compost or other organic material is of benefit.

Propagation and Kinds. The simplest way of increasing the stock of Strelitzia is to detach the small side shoots, or offsets, when the plants are repotted. If seeds can be obtained, they should be sown in a warm greenhouse in pots of sandy soil in February or March.

In addition to S. Reginae the following kinds are sometimes cultivated: S. augusta, which has a distinct trunk and attains a height of 18 ft., flowers white; S. kewensis, a hybrid between S. Reginae and S. augusta that is intermediate in appearance between its parents and has pale yellow flowers with lilac-pink markings at the bottoms of its petals; S. Nicolai, similar to S. augusta but usually larger and with the inner segments of the flowers blue instead of white; S. parvifolia, like S. Reginae a trunkless kind, 3-4 ft. tall, flowers purple and yellow. All, except the artificially produced hybrid, S. kewensis, are natives of South Africa.

STREPTOCARPUS—*Cape Primrose* (Streptocar′pus). A group of perennial plants suitable for

A nice plant of a modern hybrid Streptocarpus.

cultivation in a warm greenhouse. They are found wild chiefly in South Africa and belong to the Gesneria family, Gesneriaceae. The name is from *streptos,* twisted, and *karpos,* a fruit, an allusion to the shape of the seed vessel. These showy greenhouse plants have been greatly improved in recent years; the flowers are finer than those of the old varieties, and their color range, which has been much extended, includes pink-crimson, lavender-blue, purple, pale yellow and other shades. They flower during the summer months principally.

When to Sow Seeds. Seeds sown in January or early February, in a greenhouse having a minimum temperature of 55-60 degrees, will provide plants that will begin to bloom in July; to ensure plants that will furnish a succession of flowers during the early autumn months, seeds are sown under similar conditions in March.

The seeds are sown in pots of a finely sifted, sandy soil mixture consisting of loam, leaf mold and sand, and the pots are placed in a glass-covered case in a warm greenhouse. Care must be taken to keep the compost moist, but not saturated. When the seedlings show, the pots should be placed on the greenhouse bench; before the seedlings become crowded, they must be potted separately in 2½-in. pots in a mixture of loam, two thirds, and leaf mold, one third, the mixture being passed through a sieve and a generous sprinkling of coarse sand added to make the mixture porous.

Hints on Management. During the spring the plants will flourish in a temperature of about 55 degrees. When they are well rooted in the small pots they must be repotted in others 5 or 6 in. wide, in which they will bloom. The compost for the final potting should consist of loam, two thirds, leaf mold and decayed manure, one third, with a little sand and a scattering of bone meal added. They must be given rather close and moist conditions for a week or two after repotting, but in summer they should be grown under as cool conditions as practicable, with free ventilation and shade from bright sunshine. When the flower spikes show, the plants will benefit if fed once a fortnight with weak liquid fertilizer.

Making the Plants Bloom Again. When the plants raised from seeds sown in March have finished flowering, they should be kept in a greenhouse, temperature 55 degrees, for the winter, and if treated correctly they will furnish a second display of bloom in spring. The old flower stems must be cut off as soon as the blooms have faded, and a little of the old soil should be removed and replaced with fresh compost. When flower stems are seen in spring,

Streptocarpus Wendlandii

weak liquid fertilizer must be applied once every week or ten days.

Streptocarpus, although perennial, should not be kept for several years; it is better to raise fresh plants annually.

In addition to progagation by seeds, these plants may be increased by division and by leaf cuttings in the same way as Gloxinias. These vegetative methods are worth while only when an especially fine kind must be reproduced true to type; for general purposes, seed affords the best means of increase.

Kinds. The original species or wild types are rarely cultivated; preference is given to the numerous beautiful varieties and strains which are so easily raised from seeds.

An exception is found in Streptocarpus Wendlandii, a remarkable plant which produces one very large, ribbed leaf which may be 18 in. in length, and bears violet-blue flowers on a stem 15-18 in. high in spring. It is raised from seeds sown in a warm greenhouse in March and is treated in the same way as advised for the other kinds. Another species that is sometimes grown is S. saxorum which has erect, branching stems, small elliptic leaves and pale lilac and white flowers. This kind can be propagated by stem cuttings.

The flowers of the garden varieties are larger than those of the old sorts, and their coloring is more attractive and varied. The white, blush and rose-red shades are particularly pleasing and the lavender-blue is charming. The Streptocarpus is fairly easily managed, and amateurs with greenhouses might well devote more attention to its cultivation.

STREPTOPUS—*Twisted Stalk* (Strep'topus). A group of hardy, perennial, herbaceous plants that are natives of North America and eastern Asia. They belong to the Lily family, Liliaceae. The name is derived from the Greek *streptos,* twisted, and *pous,* foot, and refers to the twisted flower stalk of some kinds.

Streptopus are of minor horticultural importance but are occasionally planted in wild gardens, where they are likely to succeed with comparatively little care. They appreciate shaded woodland places and moist soil that contains goodly amounts of leaf mold or other decayed organic matter. They may be propagated by seeds and by division of the rootstocks in early spring or early fall.

Kinds include S. amplexifolius, 2-3 ft. tall, flowers greenish-white, berries red; S. roseus, 2-2½ ft. tall, flowers purple or pink, berries red; S. streptopoides, 1-1½ ft. tall, flowers red and yellowish-green, berries red (in the variety atrocarpus, black). The first two kinds mentioned are natives of North America. S. streptopoides and its variety atrocarpus are natives of Japan.

STREPTOSOLEN JAMESONII (Streptoso'-len). A tender, evergreen shrub of vigorous or climbing growth, which bears showy, orange-colored flowers in the summer months. It is a native of Colombia and Ecuador and belongs to the Nightshade family, Solanaceae. The name is derived from *streptos,* twisted, and *solen,* a tube, and alludes to the formation of the tube of the flower.

In Outdoor Gardens. In the far South and in California Streptosolens may be grown outdoors and are very fine garden plants. They are especially well suited for training against walls. They grow well in any reasonably good soil and need a sunny location.

Where not winter-hardy outdoors, these showy plants may be used with excellent effect during the summer months in outdoor flower beds and be taken indoors during the winter.

In the Greenhouse. Streptosolens are, perhaps, of chief value as greenhouse plants. They may be grown in large flowerpots or tubs, or planted in a bed of soil and trained to cover a pillar or other support. S. Jamesonii is often grown as a large specimen plant, its shoots supported on sticks or a wire trellis fixed in the pot. A winter temperature of 50 degrees suits this plant. At that season it needs comparatively little water, but the soil must not be allowed to get dry. In summer, the conditions of an ordinary, well-ventilated greenhouse are suitable. The best potting compost consists of loam, two thirds, and leaf mold and decayed manure, one third, with a scattering of sand.

This shrub should be pruned in early spring by shortening the side shoots on the main stems and by thinning out weak, crowded shoots. Propagation is by cuttings of firm shoots, 3-4 in. long, taken off in August and prepared by removing the lowest leaves and cutting just beneath a joint; the cuttings are planted in a propagating bench in a greenhouse, covered with a hand light or bell jar, and shaded from bright sunshine.

STRIKE. This word is sometimes used by gardeners as a verb meaning to treat the cuttings of plants in such a way that they will form roots. When a gardener "strikes cuttings" he inserts them in a suitable rooting medium and keeps them in a propagating frame or other place where conditions favor rooting. Strike is also sometimes used as a noun in such a phrase as "a good strike of cuttings," meaning a successful rooting of a batch of cuttings.

STRIPED SQUILL. Puschkinia, which see.

STROBILANTHES (Strobilanth'es). Tender, herbaceous perennial plants or shrubs which are suitable for cultivation in a warm greenhouse. They are natives of Malaya and other warm parts of Asia, and belong to the family Acanthaceae, the Acanthus family. The name is derived from *strobilos,* a cone, and *anthos,* a flower, and refers to the shape of the inflorescence or cluster of flowers.

These plants thrive best in a greenhouse having a minimum winter temperature of 60 degrees. They are propagated by cuttings of the young shoots inserted in spring in a greenhouse propagating case and kept warm and moderately moist until rooted. They are then set on the greenhouse benches and, shortly afterwards, are potted separately in 2½-in. pots, and subsequently in 5-in. pots. A suitable soil compost consists of loam, two thirds, and leaf mold, one third, with a scattering of sand. During the summer months the soil must be kept moist, but in winter it should be watered only when it is fairly dry.

Old plants may be grown through a second year; they are pruned into shape in February and are then repotted in larger pots. If kept warm and moist they will soon start into fresh growth.

The favorite kind is Strobilanthes Dyerianus, with purple and silver leaves, and violet-blue flowers. Others are S. anisophyllus (Goldfussia anisophylla), lavender; S. glomeratus (Goldfussia glomerata), purple; and S. isophyllus (Goldfussia isophylla), lavender.

STROMANTHE (Stroman'the). Tropical South American perennial herbaceous plants, closely related to Calathea and requiring the same culture. They belong to the Maranta family, Marantaceae. The name is derived from *stroma,* bed, and *anthos,* flower, and refers to the form of the inflorescence or flower cluster.

The only kind likely to be found in cultivation in North America is S. Porteana, which attains a height of 6 ft. and has leaves that on their upper surfaces are bright green with transverse bands of silvery white and beneath are colored rich purple. The flowers are blood-red. The plant sometimes cultivated as S. Porteana variety Oppenheimiana is Ctenanthe Oppenheimiana, which see.

STROMBOCACTUS (Strombocac'tus). Small, rounded Cacti of the family Cactaceae, from Mexico; they are of dwarf habit, and have flattened tubercles sparsely furnished with spines. The small flowers are produced from the crowns of the plant. The principal kinds are S. disciformis, flowers whitish; S. macrochele, 3 in., white; and S. Schmiedeckianus, pale pink. The name is derived from *strombos,* a top, and refers to the shape of the plant. For details of cultivation, see Cacti.

STRUTHIOPTERIS. Another botanical name for the Ferns described as Blechnum spicant and Pteretis Struthiopteris, which see.

STRYCHNOS (Strych'nos). A large group of tropical trees and shrubs that belong in the Logania family, the Loganiaceae. Only two are likely to be found in cultivation in North America, and those outdoors only in southern Florida. They are sometimes included in botanical collections of plants in greenhouses. The name Strychnos is an ancient Greek one used by Theophrastus for a quite different plant.

These plants thrive in any reasonably well-drained soil and appreciate high temperatures and a humid atmosphere. They may be propagated by seeds, cuttings, and air layering.

Strychnos Nux-vomica, Strychnine, is a tree about 40 ft. tall. It is a native of India. From its seeds, which are contained in berry-like fruits, the poison strychnine is obtained.

Strychnos spinosa, Natal Orange, is a spiny shrub that attains a height of about 10 ft. and bears edible fruit, the pulp of which is sweet and of a pleasant flavor. This species is a native of the tropics of South Africa and Madagascar.

Certain other species of Strychnos are used by South American Indians as sources of curare, a potent arrow poison.

STUARTIA. Stewartia, which see.

STYLE. A botanical term for the part of the pistil between the ovary and stigma.

STYLOMECON — *Flaming Poppy, Wind Poppy* (Stylome'con). A genus of one species, Stylomecon heterophylla, previously named Meconopsis and belonging to the Poppy family, Papaveraceae. The name is derived from *stylos*, style, and *mekon*, Poppy, and refers to the appearance of the flower and the fact that the pistil has a distinct style. The plant is a native of western North America. It grows up to 2 ft. tall, with deeply divided and toothed leaves and coppery orange, crimson-centered flowers, 1½ in. across, with the fragrance of Lily of the Valley. It is hardy and can be grown successfully in the same way as advised for the annual Meconopsis.

STYLOPHORUM DIPHYLLUM—*Celandine Poppy* (Styloph'orum). This hardy, herbaceous, perennial plant, which is found wild from Pennsylvania to Wisconsin and Missouri, belongs to the Poppy family, Papaveraceae; the name is derived from *stylos*, a style, and *phero*, to bear. The plant grows 10-12 in. high, has deeply cut ornamental leaves, and bears yellow, poppy-like flowers in summer. It thrives best in well-drained or light sandy, loamy soil, and should be located in light shade towards the edge of the flower border or in the rock garden or wild garden. Spring is the best time to plant.

If an increased stock is desired it is obtained by lifting the old plants carefully in spring and separating them into rooted pieces for immediate replanting or, preferably, by sowing seeds in sifted, sandy, loamy soil in a frame or greenhouse in March, or outdoors as soon as the soil is in suitable condition. The young plants should be grown in pots in a cold frame until they are large enough to be planted out of doors. If they are well developed by autumn they may be planted in September or October; otherwise planting should be deferred until spring.

STYLOSUS. A botanical term meaning having a prominent or protruding style.

STYRAX—*Storax* (Sty'rax). Evergreen and leaf-losing trees and shrubs, natives of North

Styrax Obassia is a splendid small tree which has an abundance of fragrant white flowers in June.

America, Asia and Europe. Numerous kinds have been described, but only a few are in cultivation, and those lose their leaves in autumn. They are very ornamental, with attractive white flowers produced in summer after the majority of shrubs have ceased to bloom. In some kinds the leaves are large and handsome. A few have been in cultivation for a long period but others have only become known during the present century.

Certain kinds of Styrax are the sources of the

Stromanthes are tropical decorative flowering plants.

balsamic resin called benzoin. This is a pathologic product that results from wounding the trunks and branches of the trees. It is very fragrant, with the scent of vanilla, and is used in perfumery, in the preparation of lotions, toilet waters, tooth powders, incense and for similar purposes; medicinally it is used as an expectorant, an inhalant and an antiseptic for external application.

Sumatra benzoin is obtained from Styrax Benzoin, Siam benzoin from S. tonkinensis and possibly other species. From Bolivia comes a variety of benzoin called estoraque or benjui which is derived from S. Pearcei variety boliviensis. In all probability other species of Styrax also yield benzoin. Styrax gives its name to the family Styracaceae, and the name is the ancient Greek name for Styrax officinalis.

Propagation is best effected by seeds sown as soon as possible after they are gathered. They may be sown in pots or flats placed out of doors for the winter and taken into a warm greenhouse in spring, when germination should soon follow. Now and then seeds may lie longer in the soil, and it is not wise to destroy them as worthless until the second spring after sowing has passed. Some kinds can be rooted from cuttings of short shoots in summer; they are placed in a sandy bed in a cold frame kept close, but they do not root very readily.

It is also possible to raise plants by layering the lower branches, but no other method of propagation equals seeds.

The best soil for Styrax is well-drained loam in which peat or compost has been mixed. These shrubs are impatient of root disturbance, therefore they should be planted in permanent places while quite small and not be moved afterwards. When planting, it is wise to mix peat moss or leaf mold with the soil placed immediately about the roots. This will encourage the formation of young roots.

Planting may be carried out during autumn or spring, taking care to choose a place sheltered from cold winds where the shrubs will not be crowded by less choice kinds as they grow. No regular pruning is necessary; just a little may be needed now and then to encourage the plants to form shapely specimens.

The Best Kinds. Of the several kinds, one of the best known and most easily grown is S. japonica, a leaf-losing tree 10-20 ft. high with a spreading head of twiggy branches, bearing bright-green, oval leaves 1-3½ in. long, and ½-1½ in. wide, and an abundance of pure white pendulous flowers, each one about ¾ in. across, in June. The flowers are followed by hard seeds, which ripen in autumn. This plant is a native of China and Japan and was introduced into cultivation in 1862. It is hardy in the North and is a very showy shrub or small tree.

S. Obassia, also from Japan, has been known since 1879 but has never been common. It may grow 20-30 ft. high, either as a shrub or a small tree. It is conspicuous by reason of its large, oval or rounded leaves, which are 4-8 in. long and at least half as wide, and by its clusters, 6-8 in. long, of pure white fragrant flowers, which open in June. This is a most desirable kind and is hardy in the North.

S. Hemsleyana was introduced from central and western China in 1900. It forms a tree or large shrub, 20-30 ft. high, and its more or less ovate leaves are 3-5½ in. long and up to 3½ in. wide. The pure white flowers are borne in terminal clusters, 4-6 in. long, in June. This kind is not hardy in the North.

S. Wilsonii is a shrub 8-10 ft. high, introduced from western China in 1908. It has small leaves, rarely more than 1 in. long, and bears its pure white drooping flowers singly on short stalks from the leaf axils in June. It is very attractive when in flower, but is not hardy in the North.

S. Veitchiorum, a native of central China, is related to S. Hemsleyana. It grows 12-15 ft. high and bears large white flowers in terminal clusters in June. It is not hardy in the North.

S. dasyantha is a very rare tree. It was introduced from central China in 1800. The white flowers are produced in slender clusters from near the tips of the shoots in July. It is hardy in the North.

S. Shiraiana is a Japanese tree of small dimensions introduced to North America in 1915. The white flowers are borne in July from the tips of short side shoots. It differs from most of the other kinds by its long corolla tubes. It is hardy in the North where winters are not very severe.

S. langhongensis and S. shweliensis are two of the newer and less-known kinds from Yunnan, introduced in 1910 and 1913 respectively. Like the other kinds, they are attractive and well worth attention.

Two of the earlier-known kinds are S. americana, the American Storax, a bush 3-9 ft. high, native to the southeastern United States, and S. officinalis, the European Storax, a large bush 12-20 ft. high, native to southern Europe and Asia Minor.

The European Storax is not hardy in the North; the American Storax is hardy as far north as New York.

SUBSOIL. A term used in gardening to indicate the soil which lies below that part which is cultivated. It is often hard and infertile. When fresh ground is being cultivated to form a garden, it is important that the subsoil should not be brought to the surface and the upper soil buried. The work of grading should be carried out in such a way that the layers of soil remain in their respective positions.

The subsoil can be improved by extra deep plowing, by double digging and similar deep cultural operations and by mixing with it compost, manure and other organic materials and soil amendments. Growing deep-rooting crops such as Clover also improves subsoil.

SUBTROPICAL. A term once much used in temperate regions to describe summer flower beds which were filled with tender plants of graceful growth, or possessing ornamental leaves, which imparted a tropical or subtropical aspect to the garden. Among those used for this purpose were Banana, various Palms, Tree Ferns, Eucalyptus, Grevillea, Acacia lophantha, and others which need the shelter of a greenhouse during the winter months. They were set out of doors in June and lifted and replaced in the greenhouse at the end of September or early in October.

Subtropical gardening of the type described above is now rarely carried out on a lavish scale in temperate regions but sometimes examples are seen in public parks and botanic gardens.

In the truly subtropical areas of North America, such as Florida and southern California, permanent subtropical gardening is practiced and spectacular effects are obtained by the use of many plants that cannot be grown outdoors in severer climates. Subtropical plants are those that withstand somewhat lower temperatures than truly tropical kinds; most will survive an occasional frost but not hard freezing.

SUCCESSION CROP. A crop, planted immediately after an earlier one is harvested, in the expectation of harvesting the second from the same piece of ground in the same growing season. Succession cropping is generally practiced in the vegetable garden and makes it possible to obtain large total yields from fertile soil. Examples are: Beets and Carrots sown immediately after early Peas are removed, and a late crop of Snap Beans planted to succeed an earlier crop of the same kind.

SUCCORY. Another name for Chicory. See Cichorium Intybus.

SUCCULENT PLANTS. A term used to denote those plants which have thick succulent leaves or stems; for instance, Echeveria, Rochea,

A group of succulent plants.

Sempervivum, Sedum, Aloe, Gasteria, Agave, as well as nearly all kinds of Cacti.

SUCKER. Suckers are similar to runners except that the horizontal parts of their stems are below the surface of the soil. On the underground parts of suckers true leaves are replaced by scale-leaves. Rooted suckers may be dug up and planted elsewhere to increase stocks of the desirable plants. Garden Mint and Perennial Asters are well-known examples of plants that spread by suckers, and the Goutweed (Aegopodium) is a persistent weedy plant which spreads rapidly by this means.

Sucker shoots growing from the base of a Magnolia tree. These should be removed close to the trunk.

Shoots which grow from the understock on which a tree or shrub is budded or grafted are also called suckers. Such shoots from understocks often develop on Roses. Suckers also often develop freely from the bases of certain trees and shrubs. It is most necessary that suckers which grow from understocks be cut off as low down as possible, otherwise they may weaken the named varieties grafted or budded on them and eventually kill them.

SUGARBERRY. Celtis laevigata, which see.
SUGAR CANE. See Saccharum.
SUGAR MAPLE. Acer saccharum, which see.
SUGAR PALM. Arenga pinnata, which see.
SULPHATE OF AMMONIA. See Fertilizers.
SULPHATE OF COPPER. See Fungicides, under Pests and Diseases.
SULPHATE OF LIME. Gypsum, which see.
SULPHATE OF POTASH. See Fertilizers.
SULPHUR. See Fungicides, under Pests and Diseases.
SUMAC. See Rhus.
SUMMER BEDDING. See Bedding Plants for Spring and Summer Display.
SUMMER CYPRESS. Kochia scoparia, which see.
SUMMER FIR. Artemisia sacrorum viridis, which see.
SUMMERHOUSES. Structures built in

This summer house provides a cool and shady retreat—as well as a feature of interest in a formal flower garden.

A summer house in the Japanese style.

In a garden of informal character a summer house of simple design is most appropriate.

Located over a lake, this pretty summer house is a cool retreat in hot weather.

gardens for shelter and as centers for rest and entertainment have been popular through the centuries. Such summerhouses are built with a roof and a floor but are usually open on one or more sides and, ideally, look out on a pleasant garden view.

With today's emphasis on outdoor living the modern summerhouse is often furnished with a fireplace for preparing picnic meals and with furniture and other appurtenances for entertaining the family and guests and adding to their comfort. It may be installed in connection with a terrace or swimming pool and is ordinarily of simple construction to harmonize with the house and garden. This type of summerhouse is very different from the overelaborate examples that were popular half a century and more ago. The Victorian summerhouse was cumbersome and overdecorated and usually was put to very little practical use.

SUMMER HYACINTH. Galtonia candicans, which see.

SUMMER SAVORY. See Satureia.

SUMMER SNOWFLAKE. See Leucojum aestivum.

SUMMER SWEET. Clethra alnifolia, which see.

SUNDEW. See Drosera.

SUNDEW, PORTUGUESE. See Drosophyllum.

SUNDIALS. The use of sundials in modern gardens is primarily as ornaments and they may therefore be considered simply as garden furniture. If a sundial is to be set with expectation that it will record time, certain of its limitations in this respect should be understood.

In the first place only a dial especially made for the exact longitude and latitude of the location in which it is set will accurately denote the time there. Commercially made sundials are approximately true for the general areas for which the dials have been prepared. It must not be expected, however, that a dial made for one place will be even approximately true for a place a great distance away; for example, a dial designed to tell the time in England would be useless for that purpose in Texas.

This sundial forms a center of interest in an herb garden.

When properly installed, a dial accurately made for the location in which it is set will give correct sun time for that precise place four times a year, approximately on December 25th, April

A simple sundial set on top of a stone pillar at Williamsburg, Virginia.

16th, June 15th, and September 1st. On all other days there will be a modest variation from true sun time. At no period will the dial record daylight saving time, of course.

It is important to remember that correct sun time coincides with standard time in North America only exactly on the lines of longitude of the 75th, 90th, 105th and 120th meridians; to the east or west of these, sun time is earlier or later than standard time.

Sundials designed to be set horizontally (as most are) must stand on a solid foundation or pier that has a perfectly level top. A level should be used to determine this. To set a sundial with close accuracy, select one of the few days mentioned above on which it will record correct sun time; stand the dial temporarily on its stand and, when the shadow it casts points due north, turn the dial until that shadow records noon and appears as a slender pointer only, then fix the dial in that position.

SUNDROP. See Oenothera.
SUNFLOWER. See Helianthus.
SUNFLOWER, ORANGE. See Heliopsis.
SUNKEN GARDEN. A garden on a level site may be improved if part of it is sunk below the natural ground level. In seaside gardens which are exposed to strong winds, it is a great advantage to plant below the normal ground level, for the protection thus afforded to the shrubs and plants makes a great difference to their progress.

If the sides of a sunken garden are transformed into low, stone-built, dry walls, they provide a home for many charming flowering plants—for example, Aubrieta, Pinks, Bellflower, Stonecrop or Sedum, Houseleek or Sempervivum, yellow Alyssum, Arabis, and many more. Plants may be set in the crevices between the stones, or seeds, mixed with a little fine soil, may be sown there.

A sunken garden may be planted with Roses, or, in autumn, the beds can be filled with spring flowering bulbs and plants, and, in spring, with summer bedding plants. Or it may be a garden of annuals—hardy annuals raised from seeds sown in April where the plants are to bloom, or of half-hardy annuals raised under glass and planted out of doors in May.

Still another way of planting a sunken garden is to fill it with old-fashioned flowers (flowers that were typical of gardens during past centuries—Musk, Heliotrope, Tiger Lilies, Pansies, etc.) or with fragrant flowers.

SUN PLANT. See Portulaca.
SUN ROSE. Helianthemum, which see.
SUN SCALD. Injury caused to plants by exposure to excessive sunshine is termed sun scald. It may affect the foliage or bark and may be due to excessively high temperatures as well as to too intense light. See Sun Scald, under Some Specific Physiological Diseases in the section Pests and Diseases.
SUPERPHOSPHATE. See Fertilizers.
SUPPLEJACK. Berchemia scandens, which see.
SURINAM CHERRY. Eugenia uniflora, which see.
SUTHERLANDIA FRUTESCENS — *Cape Bladder Senna* (Sutherland'ia). A tender evergreen shrub which is suitable only for cultivation out of doors in the mildest parts of the United States; elsewhere it must be grown in a frostproof greenhouse. This shrub is found wild in South Africa and belongs to the Pea family, Leguminosae. The name commemorates James Sutherland, a former superintendent of the botanical gardens at Edinburgh, Scotland.

Sutherlandia frutescens, which reaches a height of 3-4 ft., has red, pea-shaped flowers which are borne in racemes from the axils of the leaves in June; these are followed by inflated or bladder-like pods, from which the popular name is derived. Planting or potting should be done in spring; if the soil is of a loamy character it will be suitable if a little peat is mixed with it; on light or clayey ground a hole should be dug and filled with a mixture of peat and good topsoil.

Very little pruning is needed, but in order to keep the shrub shapely the branches may be trimmed in spring, and thin, weakly shoots may then be cut out.

Propagation is by means of cuttings, taken in July and inserted in a cold frame kept close and shaded until roots have formed. Seedlings may also be raised by sowing the seeds in a slightly heated greenhouse in spring; the plants should be grown in pots until they are large enough to be planted out of doors.

SWAINSONA—*Darling River Pea* (Swainson'a). Evergreen shrubs of slender growth which are suitable for cultivation out of doors in California and the far South and, elsewhere, in a greenhouse in which a minimum temperature of 40 degrees is maintained in winter. They belong to the Pea family, Leguminosae, and are natives of Australia and New Zealand. All bear small, pea-shaped flowers of various colors in summer. The name commemorates Isaac Swainson, a noted horticulturist of the eighteenth century.

These shrubs are not difficult to manage if grown in pots in a compost of loam, two thirds, and peat moss, one third, with a free scattering of sand. During the summer months the plants must have cool, airy conditions if they are kept in the greenhouse; it is usual to place them out of doors or in a cold frame for the summer months, from the end of May until about the middle of September.

These plants need careful watering; if the soil becomes sodden they will prove unsatisfactory. Good drainage is necessary. In summer the soil must be kept moist but in winter it should not be watered until it is fairly dry. When it becomes necessary to repot the plants this should be done in March.

Propagation is effected by cuttings of shoots, about 3 in. long, inserted in sand, sand and peat moss, or vermiculite, in July; the cuttings are kept in a close frame and shaded from bright sunshine until roots have formed. They are then potted separately in small pots and later in larger pots. Seeds may also be sown under glass in spring.

The favorite kind is Swainsona galegifolia, a plant of climbing growth which will reach a height of 4 ft. or more; it bears flowers of reddish-purple color in summer; its variety coronillaefolia has pale rose-purple flowers, and the variety alba is white.

SWALLOW-WORT. See Chelidonium.

SWALLOW-WORT, BLACK. Cynanchum nigrum, which see.

SWAMP BAY. See Magnolia virginiana.

SWAMP HONEYSUCKLE. Rhododendron (Azalea) viscosum. See Azaleas.

SWAMP LILY. Crinum americanum, which see.

SWAMP LOCUST. Gleditsia aquatica, which see.

SWAMP PINK. Helonias, which see.

SWAN ORCHID. Cycnoches, which see.

SWAN RIVER DAISY. See Brachycome.

SWEDE OR SWEDISH TURNIP. These are other names for Rutabaga, which see.

SWEET ALYSSUM. Lobularia maritima, which see.

SWEET BAGS. These were popular from the sixteenth century until Victorian times. Old recipes are very elaborate, and the following is a typical and excellent recipe. "Take half a pound of Cypress roots, a pound of orris, three-quarters of a pound of rhodium, a pound of Calamus, three oranges stuck with cloves, two ounces of Benjamin, and an ounce of Storax and four pecks of Damask Rose leaves, a peck of dryed sweet Marjerum, a pretty stick of Juniper shaved very thin, some lemon pele dryedz let all these be powdered very grosely for the first year and immediately put into your bagge; the next year pound and work it and it will be very good again." Mary Doggett: *Her Book of Receipts* (1682).

Sweet bags in Victorian times were much simpler; they were commonly hung on the "wings" of the armchairs, or used for scenting linen. One of the best mixtures consists of equal parts of dried Lavender, Verbena and sweet Geranium leaves.

SWEET BASIL. See Basil and Ocimum.
SWEET BAY. Magnolia virginiana and Laurus nobilis, which see.
SWEETBELLS. Leucothoë racemosa, which see.
SWEETBRIER. Rosa Eglanteria, which see.
SWEET BUCKEYE. Aesculus octandra, which see.
SWEET CASSAVA. See Manihot.
SWEET CHERRY. See Cherry.
SWEET CICELY. Myrrhis odorata, which see.

SWEET FERN. Comptonia peregrina, which see.
SWEET FLAG. See Acorus.
SWEET GALE. Myrica Gale, which see.
SWEET GUM. Liquidambar Styraciflua, which see.
SWEETLEAF. Symplocos, which see.
SWEET MARJORAM. Majorana hortensis, which see.
SWEET OLIVE. Osmanthus fragrans, which see.

SWEET PEA: QUEEN OF ANNUALS
Full Details of Cultivation in Gardens and Greenhouses and for Exhibition

The Sweet Pea, because of its fragrance, its range of colors, its airy grace and its long-lasting qualities when used as a cut flower, has for a long time been a garden favorite. It is adaptable for growing outdoors during that part of the spring and summer when the weather is not excessively hot and is also extremely useful for winter cultivation in greenhouses.

Lathyrus odoratus, to give the Sweet Pea its botanical name, is a member of the Pea family, the Leguminosae. It is an annual which in its typical form climbs by means of tendrils, but dwarf, nonclimbing strains have been evolved under cultivation, and seeds of these are obtainable from seedsmen.

History of the Sweet Pea. The Sweet Pea is a native of Sicily, from where it was introduced into gardens in northern Europe about the year 1700. Since that time its development as a garden flower has been phenomenal; few other flowers have as interesting a history.

In the wild form the flowers of Lathyrus odoratus are normally purple and, so far as the records show, for the first 180 years after its introduction into the gardens of Europe only four or five other colors were developed.

In 1870 Henry Eckford, an English florist, began a program of plant breeding to develop the Sweet Pea. His success in "fixing" strains or varieties with new colors and larger and better-proportioned flowers that bred true from seeds was almost incredible. As a result of his great work the popularity of the Sweet Pea increased tremendously. Eckford's variety named Dorothy Eckford, which was introduced into cultivation in 1903, was his best.

On the West Coast, Sweet Peas grow vigorously and produce abundant flowers.

[12–12]
Sweet Peas

[12–12a]
Sweet Williams

[12–13]
Spiraea Bumalda Anthony Waterer

[12–13a]
Stokes' Aster
(Stokesia caerulea rosea)

[12–13b]
African Marigold
(Tagetes erecta variety)

[12–13c]
French Marigold
(Tagetes patula variety)

Sweet Peas grown for exhibition are usually trained as cordons. Here we see a row of bamboo stakes with a young Sweet Pea plant set at the base of each.

In 1912 a Sweet Pea variety having a new and distinct flower form was exhibited. It had a frilled or waved standard petal (the large, top petal) and was raised by Silas Cole who was gardener to Earl Spencer of Althorp Park, England. The variety was named Countess Spencer and was the forerunner of a race that has given the form and perhaps much of the vigor to modern Sweet Peas.

Interest in America in Sweet Peas was greatly stimulated about 1886 when the Eckford varieties were introduced. Not all of the new varieties were "fixed," and those that were not did not breed true to type, but from them many new varieties that did breed true were raised in America. It was soon found that California has a superior climate for growing Sweet Peas for the purpose of seed production, and an important seed-raising industry has arisen there.

Several new types of Sweet Peas have been developed in California. One of the most important is Lathyrus odoratus variety nanellus, known as the Cupid, Dwarf or Bedding Sweet Pea. It is a low, compact, nonclimbing plant and is available in a number of different flower colors.

Sweet Peas are classed in four main groups: the Giant Spencer or Ruffled varieties, which are most commonly used for garden purposes; the Multiflora varieties, which are remarkable for the number of flowers on each stem; the Cuthbertson varieties, which are a heat-resistant spring-flowering type; and the Early-flowering varieties, which are used for producing winter flowers in the greenhouse and for fall planting outdoors in regions of warm winters.

Ordinary Garden Culture

Soil Preparation. The Sweet Pea is primarily a cool-weather plant that requires an open, sunny location for its healthy growth. The best results are not easily obtainable except where the growing season is fairly cool. The soil should be deeply dug or plowed. A well-drained soil is most desirable, and it should be enriched with

Cordon-trained Sweet Peas, each neatly tied to its stake.

liberal quantities of thoroughly decayed organic matter, such as rotted manure or rich compost, and an application of superphosphate. Finely ground limestone or a dressing of lime should be forked into the surface if the soil tends to be acid.

The preparation of the soil may be done in early spring, but it is better to complete it in the fall before planting, to ensure that the seedbed will be thoroughly settled before the seeds begin to sprout. The Sweet Pea prefers a rather firm, moderately well-packed soil.

Seeding. For ordinary garden use, seeds should be sown at the earliest possible time in spring when the soil can be worked, because, as with culinary Peas, root growth is more rapid before the higher temperatures of late spring and summer prevail.

Where winters are not excessively severe, November sowing may be practiced with advantage; although the seeds may not germinate until spring, they will be ready to respond as early as it is possible for them to grow. As soon as November-sown seeds are planted, cover them with 3-4 in. of salt-marsh hay or straw; do not remove this until late winter or spring, when severe freezing weather is over. Fall seeding is

A modern Sweet Pea variety valued both for its fragrance and color.

recommended only for specially favored locations. In many localities mild spells of weather during winter may incite too-early growth and the covering may cause decay.

Before sowing in spring (but not in fall) it is advisable to chip the outer shells of the seeds of all varieties except those with white or cream-colored flowers, using a sharp pocket knife for the purpose. Chipping consists of removing a small piece of the seed coat so that moisture can enter more readily. The chip should be taken from the side away from the "eye" of the seed—that is, from the side away from where new growth develops.

In preparation for sowing, a trench or furrow 2-3 in. deep should be made; in the bottom of this the seeds are spaced 1-2 in. apart. Cover the seeds with a depth of soil equal to their own diameters. The soil that remains on each side of the trench after the seeds are covered will be filled in gradually by cultivation as the plants grow. When watering is done, the depression left at sowing time tends to keep water where it can soak down to the roots.

After the Plants Are Growing. As soon as the seedlings are above ground some form of support should be given. This may be done by inserting brushwood stakes or by erecting a fence of chicken wire, 5-6 ft. high, alongside the young plants.

The soil in which Sweet Peas grow must never become dry; weekly soakings with water are very essential in dry weather. One light dressing of a 5-10-5 or other regular, complete garden fertilizer (see Fertilizers), applied when the plants are half-grown, and immediately soaked in by watering heavily, is beneficial; but the best plan with Sweet Peas is to supply most of the plant food they need in organic form when the initial preparation of the soil is done. A 3-in.-thick layer of littery manure or other mulch placed along each side of the row in late spring tends to maintain an even and relatively cool soil temperature, which is essential to the well-being of Sweet Peas.

It is very important that all flowers are cut off before they go to seed. This will notably lengthen the time that long-stemmed, good flowers will be produced by the plants.

Sweet Peas for Exhibition

For the production of the finest-quality Sweet Peas for exhibition or other purposes the cordon system of training is recommended. This involves considerable detailed work, but, if carried out faithfully, the results are plants with flower stems 15-18 in. long or longer, each carrying 4 or 5 large and perfect blooms.

Under the cordon system each vine is allowed to develop one stem only; no branching is permitted. To achieve this, all side shoots or laterals are pinched out while they are quite small, just as soon as they can be removed with the finger and thumb without damaging the main stem. The vines are tied or otherwise secured to tall bamboo stakes and all tendrils are picked off.

Plants trained as cordons may be raised from seeds sown directly outdoors in early spring, or in mild localities in fall. When this is done the seeds are spaced 2 in. apart in a single row and later are thinned so that the plants stand 6-8 in. apart. A better plan is to sow in pots or flats in a greenhouse or cold frame in fall and set the plants out in the garden in early spring.

Preparations for raising a crop of exhibition Sweet Peas should begin the fall previous to the summer in which they are to bloom. Both the starting of the seeds in pots or flats indoors and the initial making ready of the soil where they are later to be planted outdoors should be done in October or November; just before severe frost sets in is the ideal time.

Soil Preparation Outdoors. Good soil and a sunny, well-drained location are required. Here, open a trench or ditch 2 ft. wide and 18 in. deep; place the good soil equally on each side of the trench. If the subsoil is of poor quality, remove it and replace it with good-quality loam to a depth of 2-3 ft. If the undersoil is good, fork over the bottom of the trench to correct any packing that may have been caused by treading on it and, if possible, mix in some coarse compost or other organic material.

Fill back all good soil to within 3 in. of the surface, at the same time mixing in rotted manure, rich compost or other decayed organic matter (2 parts soil, 1 part organic matter) and 3½ pounds of superphosphate to each 100 sq.

ft. of surface. Fill the upper 3 in. of the trench, and to within 3 in. above regular ground level, with good topsoil into which bonemeal has been mixed at the rate of a good handful to every 6 sq. ft. of surface. If lime is needed, as it will be if the soil is acid, a good sprinkling should be raked into the surface.

Seeds and Seed Sowing Indoors. Seeds of the finest named varieties should be purchased from a reputable seedsman. The soil in which they are sown should be carefully prepared. It may consist of 3 or 4 parts good garden soil (loam), 1 part peat moss and 1 part sharp sand. If the loam is a heavy clay, greater proportions of peat and sand will be necessary. All the ingredients should be sifted through a ½-in. mesh and thoroughly mixed together.

Flats or pots (the 5-in. size is suitable) may be used as containers in which to sow the seeds. Fill these almost to their rims but leave room for ½ in. of coarse sand to be spread over the surface. Water the filled containers thoroughly and leave them for an hour or so to allow surplus moisture to drain away.

In each pot, scatter 10-12 seeds and cover them with ¼ in. of sand. When sowing in flats, make drills ½ in. deep and 2½ in. apart in the soil surface (using the edge of a 6-in. wooden label or similar equipment to do this). Space the seeds in the drills 1 in. apart and cover them with sand. A cool greenhouse (40-50 degrees night temperature) or protected cold frame is an ideal place to keep the pots or flats after sowing.

When germination takes place, which occurs in 9-12 days, the seedlings must have all possible light and a cool, airy atmosphere. Watering must receive careful attention. As soon as the seedlings have formed their first leaves they may be transplanted singly to 2½-in. pots containing a soil similar to that used for sowing.

Keep the newly potted plants in a location in the greenhouse or cold frame where it is cool and airy and where there is good light. They should not, of course, be subjected to freezing but night temperatures of more than 50 degrees must be avoided. In 4 to 5 weeks they will be ready to repot into 4-in. pots. Use a soil similar to that used earlier but with a 6-in. potful of sheep manure and a 2-in. potful of superphosphate added to each bushel of the mixture and mixed in thoroughly.

After the last potting, the plants may be placed in a cold frame, except where winters are exceptionally severe. During mild weather the frame sash should be taken off. Retain all growth that develops until the pots are filled with roots, after which time most varieties may be pruned to two vines or stems to each plant. Orange-pink and orange-scarlet varieties are not such strong growers as the others and so should be pruned to one vine or stem to each plant. At this time they should be given supports of light brushwood.

Planting. This is done after the plants have been thoroughly hardened by exposure to the cold winds of spring. At that season they tolerate light frost. The time of planting is from the middle of March to the middle of April, depending on the locality; the important point is to plant as early as the ground is workable and danger of really severe frost has passed.

Make sure that the plants are watered well a few hours before planting. When planting, turn the pot upside down and give its edge a sharp tap with the planting trowel to release the plant from the pot. Dig a hole big enough for the roots to be spread out after shaking the old soil from them. Fill in fresh soil around the roots and pack it moderately firmly. If the plants need additional support, insert some brushwood stakes near them. This will protect the plants from wind, and new tendrils that develop will have something to which they can cling.

Staking. A substantial framework is necessary to hold the stakes for cordon-trained Sweet Peas. The strain on the supports during high winds will be enormous after the vines have grown tall. It is common to allow them to grow 8-9 ft. high. A strong post 10-12 ft. long should be inserted 3 ft. deep at each end of the row. Each of these should be strengthened by a guy wire attached to its top and to a strong stake driven into the ground beyond the end of the row. If the row is long it may be necessary to insert additional posts at intermediate points. When the posts are in position two wires are stretched from post to post, one 2 ft. from the ground, the other at a height of 5 ft. To these wires the

Greenhouse Sweet Peas in a solid bed.

stakes are tied 6-8 in. apart. While any straight stake is suitable, stout bamboo canes are most serviceable.

Pruning, Disbudding and Tying. Following planting, growth will be slow for two or three weeks and no pruning should be done until the plants are growing well again and are at least 18 in. high. When surplus side growth is left undisturbed, root growth develops more quickly than if all but the "cordon" or leading growth is pruned away. When fast growth is really obvious, all side growths, flower buds, and tendrils should be cut away and the leading growth tied to the stake. This must be done every 3-4 days.

Flowers should not be allowed to develop until the plants are 4-5 ft. high. This will be towards the end of May in most localities. Up to this time the surface soil should be kept loose and free from weeds with a hoe or cultivator. Periodic watering is likely to be necessary in most regions from the end of April onwards. Towards the end of May a mulch of litter, compost or other suitable material should be applied. Fresh manure should be used sparsely, if at all, because of danger of damage to the plants. The same caution should prevail in using chemical fertilizers. Slight overdoses may cause the flower buds to drop.

Shading. Although the Sweet Pea requires good light, some scarlet- and orange-flowered varieties retain their lustre better when the flowers are shaded from strong sunshine with cheesecloth.

Qualities for Exhibition. The judge of Sweet Peas looks for a straight stem that holds up the flowers. It should be 15-18 in. long but not excessively thick. There should be 4 or 5 flowers to a stem, evenly and pleasingly arranged, not separated too far from each other. The size of each should be approximately $3\frac{1}{2}$ in. across the standard (upper petal). They should be fresh, without blemish, of good clear color, and thickness of the petal should be ample to avoid an appearance of flimsiness. Flowers for exhibition should be cut late in the evening preceding the show, placed in containers filled with water and kept in a cool room overnight.

Greenhouse Culture

Seeds of Early Flowering or Cuthbertson varieties of Sweet Peas may be sown late in August to produce flowers at Christmas and on into late winter. The best plan is to sow them where they are to grow and bloom rather than to transplant them. A solid bed (one that is not elevated) may be used for sowing, or boxes 1 ft. wide, 1 ft. deep and of any convenient length, or 8-10-in. pots. Rich well-drained soil gives best results. The greenhouse roof must not be shaded, because Sweet Peas require all possible sunshine. A fall and winter night temperature of 50 degrees F. is ideal. During the daytime a 5- or 10-degree rise is permitted or even a few degrees more on very sunny days.

Giant Spencer or Ruffled varieties of Sweet Peas are good for producing spring flowers if they are sown in September. Potting, planting, disbudding, etc., is similar to that recommended for outdoor exhibition culture. The plants should be set in the beds, boxes or pots in which they are to bloom in November. This crop may be used to follow Chrysanthemums.

For greenhouse-grown Sweet Peas it is best to use new soil for each crop. Supports usually consist of thin wires nailed 8 in. apart to one end of the bench, and stretched along the top of the soil, tightened and nailed to the opposite end of the bench. A framework of metal or wood 6 ft. high is erected at each end of the bench. To the top of this wires parallel to the rows of wire at the bottom are stretched. Strings attached to the bottom wires at 8-in. intervals are stretched tautly and tied to the top wire immediately above. As the plants grow they are twisted around these strings and this gives sufficient support. These cordon Sweet Peas grow quickly and, when they reach the tops of the strings, the strings may be cut, the vines laid along the ground and twisted around a new string 4 ft. away. They will then start to climb up the new string and will supply good flowers until late in April.

SWEET PEPPER BUSH. See Clethra alnifolia.

SWEET POTATO. This favorite American vegetable is really a kind of Morning Glory, botanically Ipomoea Batatas, but in cultivation in the United States it rarely produces flowers. Its wild progenitor is a native of tropical America, which accounts for the fact that the Sweet Potato is a crop that thrives best where summers are warm and comparatively long. Sweet Potatoes may be cultivated without difficulty in southern New Jersey and southwards, and home garden crops can be produced on Long Island, New York, and even further north provided they are planted in sheltered locations and in light, well-drained soils.

Certain varieties of Sweet Potato, particularly the moist-fleshed ones, are often called Yams, but there is no strict agreement as to which varieties are properly so called. The use of the word Yam for varieties of Sweet Potato is confusing because a completely different plant, Dioscorea, is correctly known by this name.

Unlike the common Potato, or Irish Potato as it is often called, the Sweet Potato is not propagated by planting tubers or pieces of tubers. Instead, rooted sprouts (young shoots) are taken from tubers started in hotbeds and are planted in the garden after both soil and weather are really warm. These sprouts or "draws" are produced commercially in vast quantities by specialists and, because in their young stages they are tricky to handle, the home gardener is wise to buy the draws he needs for planting, rather than to attempt to raise his own.

Soil and Cultivation. Sweet Potatoes thrive best in very sandy soils; they are unsuitable for

Sweet Potatoes are the tuberous roots of a plant which belongs to the Morning Glory family.

planting in clay soils or in mucks. In preparation for planting, the soil should be plowed or spaded and, if fertilizer is needed, the application of one low in nitrogen should be made. Excessive nitrogen results in vigorous vine growth at the expense of tuber development. Because of this it is often considered better not to fertilize at all before planting Sweet Potatoes but to set them in ground that was well fertilized for a previous crop.

Planting and Varieties. Planting should not be done too early. In southern New Jersey the last week in June is time enough; further south, earlier dates are appropriate, as early as the first week in March in Louisiana, and in early April in southern California. In the South, Sweet Potatoes should be planted in rows 4-5 ft. apart with distances of 20-24 in. allowed between plants in the row. In the North they may be set considerably closer, a spacing of 2½ ft. between the rows and 15 in. between the plants in the rows being sufficient. The plants may be planted on the flat or the soil may be hilled up to form ridges and the plants set in these.

Varieties suitable for northern gardens are the drier-fleshed ones, of which Yellow Jersey and Big-stem Jersey are among the best; for southern gardens the moist-fleshed varieties are preferred. These include Nancy Hall, Porto Rico, Pumpkin and Yellow Belmont.

Cultivation and Harvesting. Once Sweet Potatoes are planted they need little attention. In their early stages frequent shallow surface cultivation to destroy weeds and promote growth is necessary, but once the vines cover the ground this can no longer be done. It is advisable to move the vines occasionally during their early growth to prevent them from rooting into the ground.

Harvesting should be done at the end of the growing season or as soon as the vines are touched by frost. At the first indication of frost damage, immediately cut off all the vines to prevent the tubers from being spoiled by juices that run back from the frost-killed vines, and then proceed to dig the tubers. A fork is a suitable tool to use for this work. Great care must be taken not to damage the potatoes when digging or during subsequent handling. Cuts and bruises not only mar the appearance of the tubers but encourage the development of rots caused by fungi.

After they are lifted, the potatoes are left on the ground surface until they are dry, which, on a bright day, will not take more than an hour or two, then they are sorted and carefully placed in bushel baskets or boxes.

Storage. Sweet Potatoes are not an easy crop to store. To ensure good results the crop must be thoroughly mature at the time of digging and must be handled in such a manner that the tubers are not cut or bruised. In addition the tubers must be well "cured" soon after digging and must then be stored in a uniform temperature of 45-55 degrees.

Curing is effected by keeping the tubers in

Then place it in a glass partially filled with water, letting the pegs rest on the rim of the glass.

If the Sweet Potato is placed in a warm room in a light location, both shoots and roots soon develop.

To grow a Sweet Potato as a house plant, first stick two or three wooden pegs into it.

The Sweet Potato grown in water indoors produces vigorous running shoots. They bear heart-shaped green leaves.

a temperature of 80-90 degrees (usually maintained by the use of artificial heat) in a well-ventilated storage house. The length of time required to complete curing depends upon the variety and upon weather conditions. Experienced persons can judge by the "feel" of the potato when the curing process is completed. The inexperienced may be guided by the appearance of young shoots on the tubers in the warmer part of the storage place; when these are seen, the temperature should be lowered gradually to 50-55 degrees.

Where only a few bushels of Sweet Potatoes are to be stored they may be placed in bushel baskets or crates, cured near the cellar furnace and then kept in a dry place where the temperature remains fairly constant, 45-60 degrees.

As House Plants. Sweet Potatoes make attractive and interesting house plants. The usual method is to obtain a mature tuber (one that has not been heat-treated before marketing to the extent that it will not sprout) and stick three toothpicks or similar slivers of wood in a circle around its sides in such a way that they protrude at right angles. The tuber is then lowered into a glass jar or other container of water (it is well to add a few pieces of charcoal to the water) until the toothpicks rest on the rim of the container and support the Sweet Potato. The water should be maintained at such a level that it always touches the bottom of the tuber. It is advisable to change the water occasionally.

If the jar and Sweet Potato are kept in a sunny window in a warm room green, leafy, vinelike shoots will soon develop from the tuber. These may be trained to stakes, strings or wires or the jar may be suspended and the shoots allowed to trail downward. Similar results may be had by planting a Sweet Potato tuber in a pot of soil and keeping the soil moist.

SWEET POTATO VINE, WILD. Ipomoea pandurata, which see.

SWEET ROCKET. Hesperis matronalis, which see.

SWEET SCABIOUS. See Scabiosa.

SWEET-SCENTED SHRUB. Calycanthus, which see.

SWEET SHRUB. Calycanthus, which see.

SWEETSOP. Annona squamosa, which see.

SWEET SPIRE. Itea virginica, which see.

SWEET SULTAN. Centaurea moschata, which see.

SWEET WILLIAM. This favorite early summer flower is descended from Dianthus barbatus, a native of the mountain meadows of southern and eastern Europe. Today, in its numerous shades of rich colors, it is one of the most popular of biennial plants.

Seeds provide the easiest and best means of propagating Sweet Williams. The seeds are sown thinly, in drills 12 in. apart, in a nursery bed or cold frame in May or June. When about 2 in. high, the seedlings are transplanted, 6 in. apart, in rows about 12 in. apart in nursery beds or, where winters are severe, in cold frames.

In mild climates the plants may be transplanted in September or October from the nursery rows to the locations where they are required to bloom the following summer. In severe climates, however, they should remain in the cold frames all winter, well protected with mats or other suitable covering on cold nights and well ventilated on mild days, and should be transferred to their flowering places in early spring.

The plants should be lifted carefully with plenty of soil around the roots and be planted 10-15 in. apart. Sweet Williams thrive in a sunny position and ordinary well-cultivated garden ground.

Sweet Williams produce flowers of various colors.

In cold climates Sweet William plants should be wintered in cold frames. Here fine specimens are ready for planting where they are to flower.

Most of the present-day strains of Sweet William come true to color or type when raised from seeds. While mixed colors may suffice for some gardeners, the full beauty of Sweet Williams is only realized when the plants are massed in a bed or grouped in a flower border in separate colors.

Though perennial, the Sweet William is best treated as a biennial and raised from seed each year.

Most seedsmen list good strains of seeds in distinct colors.

SWEET WILLIAM, WILD. Phlox divaricata, which see.

SWEET WIVELSFIELD. The name of a hardy annual or biennial plant, raised by cross-breeding between the perpetual-flowering Allwoodii Pinks and the Sweet William. It is described under Dianthus.

SWEET WOODRUFF. See Asperula odorata.

SWERTIA—*Felwort* (Swer′tia). A group of plants belonging to the Gentian family, Gentianaceae, natives of Europe, Asia and North America. The name commemorates Iman Swert, a bulb fancier of Holland. Swertias are found in wet or boggy ground in mountainous places and are usually somewhat dull and drab in their coloring, though not without a certain quaint charm.

Swertia perennis is native of bogs in the Alps of Europe and Asia and also occurs in North America from Colorado and Utah northward. It has narrow leaves and erect spikes of star-shaped flowers of a dull, slaty blue in summer. A damp spot in a wild garden or bog garden will suit it best. There are a great many Asiatic species of Swertia, some of which have been sent to European and American gardens by various plant-collecting expeditions, but none has proved worthy of garden room. Propagation is by seeds sown in a pan of loam, leaf mold, and sand in a cold frame in spring.

SWISS CHARD. This vigorous, somewhat coarse-leaved vegetable is also called Spinach Beet. It is of considerable value as a substitute for Spinach and is cooked and eaten in the same

Swiss Chard is an easy-to-grow vegetable and a welcome substitute for Spinach.

way. By making two sowings it is possible to ensure a long continuous supply of leaves suitable for harvesting. It is usual to sow the seeds in early spring and again in July; the first sowing will provide leaves for picking in summer and the second will continue the supply during fall and, in mild climates, in winter and early spring. The plants remain productive for a long time and should not be destroyed after the first gathering of leaves, for a fresh supply will develop.

This plant needs rich soil that does not dry out quickly. The seeds are sown in drills 18 in. apart and, as the plants are of vigorous growth, the seedlings must be thinned out until they are about 9 in. from each other.

SWORD LILY. Gladiolus, which see.

SYAGRUS (Syag'rus). Tropical American, feather-leaved Palms, mostly with short trunks, belonging to the botanical family Palmaceae. With the exception of one species, S. Weddelliana (often grown as Cocos Weddelliana), few kinds are known to be in cultivation in North America. They are adapted for outdoor cultivation only in the very warmest, frost-free parts of the United States, and require the same general cultivation as Cocos, which see. The name Syagrus is from the Greek *syagros,* a wild boar, an ancient name in use for a Date Palm long before South American Palms were discovered.

Indoor Cultivation. Syagrus Weddelliana is a handsome pot plant for house decoration and it is raised commercially for this purpose. It is comparatively easy to grow in a greenhouse having a minimum temperature of 60 degrees F., the atmosphere being kept moist during the hot summer months by damping down and syringing.

Repotting is done in March, when necessary, using a compost of equal parts of loam and peat, with a sprinkling of sand. Plenty of water is needed in summer, but rather less in winter.

Young plants can be raised from seed sown in pots of light compost and germinated in a propagating case with bottom heat in a warm greenhouse.

The chief kind is S. Weddelliana, which has a rather slender stem or trunk. It grows to an eventual height of 6-7 ft. and is topped by a crown of graceful, slender, arching leaves. This slow-growing Palm is a native of Rio de Janeiro. Other kinds are S. insignis, 3-8 ft. tall; S. macrocarpa, 15 ft. or more high; and S. petraea, an almost trunkless kind.

SYCAMORE. This name most properly belongs to Ficus Sycamorus, which see. In North America it is often applied to Platanus, especially Platanus occidentalis. In Great Britain the Sycamore Maple, Acer Pseudo-Platanus, is called the Sycamore.

SYCAMORE MAPLE. Acer Pseudo-Platanus, which see.

SYMBOLISM. Plant symbolism is conspicuous in the art of all the great Eastern civilizations, and in the art of Western Europe it was also an important feature until the seventeenth century. A comprehensive study of Eastern or Western flower symbolism would fill volumes.

Lotus. The most ancient flower symbolism appears to be that of the Lotus flowers. In Vedic symbolism, Asia was a four-petaled Lotus, the mighty peaks of the Himalayas being the inner circle or upturned petals, the center the home of the gods, China the eastern petal, Persia the western, Turkestan the northern, and the plains of India the southern. In Indian art, Buddha's throne is nearly always represented with the outer fringe of petals turned downwards.

Cypress and Fruit Trees. Designs in which these figure are common in Indian art. The trees symbolize life (fruit trees), and death (Cypress).

Medieval Plant Symbolism. With the exception of Leonardo da Vinci and Albert Dürer, all the great masters made use of flower, leaf and fruit symbolism in sacred pictures.

Rose. This flower was long excluded from sacred works of art, for it was the flower of Venus. But so beloved a flower could not be ignored, and gradually it was introduced. In early Christian symbolism the Rose signified the blood of the martyrs. Later the flower signified Divine Love. For instance, in Botticelli's "Coronation of the Virgin," the Rose symbolizes the Love of God. In Botticelli's "Adoration," in the Pitti Palace, angels sprinkle Rose petals over the Holy Child, who lies in a garden surrounded with Roses.

Garlands of Roses signify the joys of Heaven, and they are usually depicted worn by angels and the souls of the blessed. The Rose is also associated with the Virgin Mary, but not to such an extent as the Lily. In Velasquez' "Coronation of the Virgin," God the Father crowns her with a wreath of Roses.

Lily. As early as the eighth century the Venerable Bede, an English monk and historian, wrote of the Lily as the emblem of the Virgin. In still earlier times the white Lily signified the happiness of Heaven, but subsequently it was used to symbolize purity, and particularly the purity of the Virgin. The early Siennese artists, however, retained the older meaning of the Lily as the flower of Paradise. In pictures of the Annunciation, Gabriel the Archangel is frequently depicted holding a Lily.

Carnation. This flower had much the same meaning as the Rose. In the "Mary Garden," by an unknown master of the Middle Rhine of the fifteenth century, Carnations are depicted growing to the right of the Virgin. In Hugo van der Goes' "Adoration" in the Uffizi, three Carnations are placed in a transparent vase.

Iris. In early Flemish pictures this flower is frequently depicted in sacred subjects. It invariably signifies the royal ancestry of the Holy Child. The use of the Iris with the same symbolism is also conspicuous in the works of the early Spanish masters.

Columbine. The name Columbine is derived from the Latin word for dove; the petals of the wild Columbine resemble a group of doves in shape and hence the popular name of the flower. In sacred pictures the Columbine symbolizes the seven gifts of the Holy Spirit. In Hugo van der Goes' "Adoration" (Uffizi Gallery) a seven-flowered Columbine is depicted in a vase before the Holy Child. In Hubert van Eyck's "Queen of Heaven," seven dark blue Columbines are set on the golden crown, in which Roses and Lilies are also depicted.

The Wild Strawberry. This plant signifies the fruits of righteousness. In the well-known "Madonna of the Strawberries," painted by a fifteenth-century Rhenish master, the Madonna is shown seated on a raised bed planted with Strawberries. Botticelli depicted wild Strawberries among Violets and Daisies in several of his pictures.

Violet. This flower was the symbol of the humility of the Son of God in deigning to visit the earth in human form. In Stephen Lochnar's altar piece in Cologne Cathedral, the Holy Child takes a Violet from His Mother's hand.

Daisy. First used by Botticelli, the flower symbolizes the innocence of the Holy Child.

Lily of the Valley symbolizes humility. In "A Mary Garden," by a fifteenth-century Rhenish master, Lilies of the Valley are shown.

Acanthus Leaves. These were commonly used by medieval artists as a symbol of Paradise.

Palm Leaves. They symbolized the martyrs' triumphs. In early paintings of the saints, they are frequently depicted with Palms and the instruments whereby they were put to death.

Olive. A twig or branch of this tree in early sculpture and paintings symbolizes peace. In Botticelli's "Nativity" the olive-crowned angels hold branches of Olive.

Apple. The fruit symbolizes the fall of man, and in sacred pictures refers to the sins for which Christ died.

Cherries signify the joys of Heaven. In Memling's picture of the Holy Child and His Mother in the Uffizi, the Holy Child holds Cherries in one hand and the other is held out to take an Apple from the attendant angel's hand.

Pomegranate. This is generally believed to be the symbol of immortality. According to Gregory the Great, the fruit was the emblem of the Church, the numerous seeds being united in one fruit. In Old Testament times the High Priest's robes were adorned with golden bells and embroidered Pomegranates.

Grape Vine. This is one of the most sacred of Christian symbols, hallowed by Christ's words: "I am the Vine." It has been used from the earliest times as the symbol of Christ.

SYMPHILID. See Pests and Diseases.

SYMPHORICARPOS—*Snowberry* (Symphoricar'pos). Leaf-losing shrubs of variable habit of growth, bearing small white or pinkish flowers in rather dense clusters during late spring or early summer; the flowers are followed by attractive berries (see Berried Trees and Shrubs), in some instances white, in others reddish. The berries are not very attractive to birds; therefore

Symphoricarpos albus laevigatus, the best of the Snowberries, has large white fruits in winter.

they remain in good condition for several months. Some of these shrubs are of erect growth, others are more or less trailing. Most of the cultivated kinds are natives of North America, where they occur from the colder regions into Mexico, but one is found wild in China.

This shrub belongs to the Honeysuckle family, Caprifoliaceae, and its name is taken from the Greek *symphoreo,* to bear together, and *karpos,* fruit, an allusion to the clustered fruits.

Planting and Pruning. The Symphoricarpos is not difficult to cultivate. It thrives in a variety of soils and gives good results on light or heavy land. No regular pruning is required, but a little thinning of the older branches every two or three years is useful. One kind, S. albus (S. racemosus), is often grown because it succeeds well in semi-shade as well as in full sun. Other kinds should be planted in more open locations. They can be planted in spring or fall.

Propagation. Division forms an easy means of propagation of some kinds, particularly of the common S. albus, but seeds may also be sown in light soil in a greenhouse in February. Cuttings or short side shoots will form roots in a cold frame in July.

The Common Snowberry. S. albus, the Snowberry or Waxberry, better known as S. racemosus, is widely distributed in North America, from Quebec southwards. It grows about 3-5 ft. high, and is recognized by its dense clusters of rose-flushed flowers in June and July, and by its round white fruits, which ripen in autumn and remain in good condition throughout the winter unless injured by severe frost. Some forms or varieties are more free-fruiting than others; the best should be selected for the garden, others being relegated to the woodland. One of the best is named laevigatus, which has large, handsome fruits and grows to a height of 6 ft.

S. mollis is a low bush, sometimes almost, if not wholly, prostrate. It is a native of western North America, with small, rounded leaves and small clusters of white or pinkish flowers, which are succeeded by white fruits.

The Indian Currant or Coralberry. S. orbiculatus, the Indian Currant, or Coralberry, is a spreading bush 4-6 ft. high, with elliptic leaves, green above and whitish beneath. The small, dull white flowers are borne in dense clusters from July to September, and are followed by purplish-red fruits. There is a variety with golden-variegated leaves named variegatus. The Indian Currant occurs natively from New Jersey to Georgia and Texas.

Other Kinds. S. sinensis, the only Chinese kind, was introduced into cultivation in 1907. It is a bush, 3-4½ ft. high, with white flowers and blue-black fruits. Other kinds occasionally planted are S. occidentalis, the Wolfberry; S. oreophilus; and S. microphyllus, a Mexican kind. S. Chenaultii, a hybrid between S. microphyllus and S. orbiculatus, has berries that are red with whitish markings.

SYMPHYANDRA (Symphyand'ra). Hardy perennial or biennial plants suitable for the rock garden or flower border. They are found wild chiefly in eastern countries and belong to the Bellflower family, Campanulaceae. The name is derived from *symphuo,* to grow together, and *andros,* an anther.

These plants need well-drained soil and thrive in a sunny or slightly shady place. Clayey soil must be made suitable by adding leaf mold, compost or peat moss and sand freely. The plants are not, as a rule, very long-lived and in many gardens they are treated as biennials, a fresh stock of plants being raised from seeds every year. The seeds are sown in a flat of sifted sandy soil placed in a frame or greenhouse in April or May; the seedlings, when large enough to be handled, are potted separately in small pots and are grown in a cold

The blue, bell-flowered Symphyandra Wanneri, an attractive rock-garden plant.

frame during the summer months. When well established, they may be planted in the rock garden or towards the front of the flower border in a sunny or slightly shaded position.

Few kinds are in cultivation. The favorite is Symphyandra pendula, which grows 10-12 in. high and bears cream-colored flowers. S. Wanneri grows only about 6 in. high and bears blue flowers. Another kind is S. Hofmannii, 18 in., which has white flowers. All bloom in summer. Their flowers are bell-shaped.

SYMPHYTUM — *Comfrey* (Sym'phytum). A small group of hardy herbaceous perennial plants, which includes the common Comfrey (S. officinale), found wild in Europe and Asia and escaped from cultivation in North America. They belong to the Borage family, Boraginaceae, and are natives of the Caucasus and other countries of eastern Europe. The name is an old Greek one.

These plants are scarcely suited to cultivation in the formal garden; they are useful, however, for the wild garden and for planting by the side of a garden pool or in other places where the soil is moist. They need little or no attention and can be increased by lifting and separating the old plants into rooted pieces in autumn. Planting may be done in autumn or spring.

The chief kinds for garden cultivation are S. asperum (asperrimum), 3-4 ft., pink and blue flowers; S. caucasicum, 2 ft., blue; and S. tauricum, 3 ft., cream-white. One called the Scarlet Comfrey is S. officinale coccineum (bohemicum); it grows 2 ft. high and bears red flowers. All bloom in early summer. There are several varieties with variegated leaves.

SYMPLOCOS — *Sweetleaf* (Sym'plocos; Symplo'cos). A large group of trees and shrubs that have a wide natural distribution, mostly in the warmer parts of Asia, Australia and America. Few are cultivated and only one, S. paniculata, is hardy in the North. They belong to the Symplocos or Sweetleaf family, the Symplocaceae.

Symplocos paniculata, the Sweetleaf, bears clusters of small, fragrant white flowers in early summer.

The name is derived from *symploke,* a connection, and refers to the fact that the bases of the stamens are united.

The Sweetleafs thrive in any reasonably good soil; S. tinctoria needs one that is decidedly moist. Light shade or full sun suits S. paniculata; S. tinctoria needs partial shade.

These shrubs may be propagated by cuttings of half-ripe wood inserted in a bed of sand, or sand and peat moss, in a moist, shaded greenhouse or cold frame in summer, by layering and by seeds. The seeds usually do not germinate until the second spring after sowing. Self-sown seedlings often spring up freely under fruiting bushes and these are easily dug up, transplanted to a nursery bed for a year or two, and finally transferred to their permanent places when they are two to four years old.

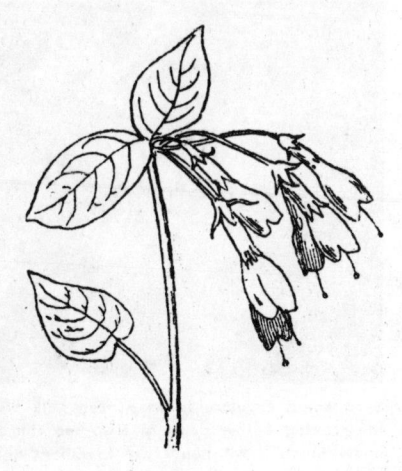

The cream-white flowers of the Comfrey named Symphytum tauricum.

The bright turquoise-blue berries of Symplocos paniculata.

Fragrant Flowers and Beautiful Fruits. The flowers of Symplocos are small but they are aggregated in dense clusters that are borne with great freedom. Those of S. paniculata, a native of China, Japan and the Himalayas, are white, those of S. tinctoria, native from Delaware to Florida and Louisiana, are yellowish. Both species have fragrant flowers.

But the flowers do not provide the most attractive feature of S. paniculata; it is most remarkable for its beautiful berries, which are produced in abundance and are bright turquoise blue. Unfortunately these berries are much liked by birds and the bushes are likely to be stripped of their fruits soon after they ripen in late summer or fall.

S. paniculata is a deciduous shrub or small tree which, under favorable circumstances, attains a height of 25-40 ft. but often is lower. S. tinctoria is evergreen or partially evergreen, grows to a height of 15-30 ft. and has orange or brown berries. This latter species is the source of a yellow dye.

SYNADENIUM (Synaden'ium). Three or four African shrubs belonging to the Spurge family, the Euphorbiaceae. The name is derived from *syn,* united, and *aden,* a gland, and refers to a technical character of the glands of the involucre. S. Grantii, the African Milkbush, is the most commonly cultivated kind. S. Grantii variety rubra has red foliage. A rarer kind that is sometimes cultivated is S. cupulare.

Synadenium Grantii is an erect, succulent shrub that attains a height of 10-12 ft. and has rounded, fleshy stems which become woody with age. It contains an abundance of white, milky sap which is reported to be poisonous. Its narrow, obovate leaves are dark green above and paler beneath and are often tinged with red or purple. Their veins are darker green than the remainder of the leaf surface. The leaves attain a maximum length of about 4 in. The flowers are dark red, small and are in branched cymes (flattish clusters).

Synadenium cupulare differs from S. Grantii in having broadly obovate leaves and small greenish flowers. It attains a height of 3-5 ft. Its milky sap is said to be poisonous.

Culture. The African Milkbush is hardy only in frost-free climates, such as that of southern Florida, but it is fairly commonly grown in greenhouses and even in sunny window gardens by fanciers of succulent plants. It requires essentially the same conditions that suit most Cacti but its soil should never be allowed to dry entirely. A well-drained soil is essential because stagnant moisture is likely to cause the roots to rot. Sandy loam, enriched with bone

Synadenium cupulare is an African Milk Bush that is suitable for growing out of doors in frost-free climates and also as a house plant. It withstands dry conditions quite well.

meal and a little dried cow manure, makes a good potting soil. S. cupulare responds to the same culture as S. Grantii.

When these shrubs are grown in greenhouses, a night temperature of from 50-60 degrees is satisfactory, with a daytime rise of 10-15 degrees permitted. Full exposure to sun is preferred but partial shade is tolerated. Specimens that have filled their pots or tubs with healthy roots benefit from occasional applications of dilute liquid fertilizers.

Propagation is easily effected by cuttings planted in a pot or well-firmed bed of coarse sand which should be kept just barely moist (neither wet nor dry) until they are well rooted, when they may be potted individually in containers just large enough to hold the roots without crowding. The cuttings, after they have been taken from the parent plant and have been prepared by removing their lower leaves and cutting across their bases with a sharp knife, should be allowed to lie in the shade for a day or two so that the cuts may heal, before they are planted in the sand.

SYNGONIUM (Syngon'ium). Tropical climbers, natives of the warmer parts of the West Indies, South and Central America and Mexico. They belong to the Arum family, the Araceae, and some kinds are in favor as decorative foliage plants for cultivating in pots in greenhouses and houses. When grown for these purposes, the specimens are usually small and may show foliage characters which differ from those of mature plants of the same kinds. The name Syngonium is derived from *syn,* united, and *gone,* womb, and refers to the fact that the ovaries are united.

Most commonly grown Syngoniums are S. podophyllum and its varieties. S. podophyllum is often misnamed African evergreen and Nephthytis Afzelii. This last name properly belongs to a quite different plant that is a native of Africa. S. podophyllum is a native of Mexico.

The cultivation of Syngoniums presents no difficulties. They are good plants for locations where light is poor. The soil in which they are planted should be loose and coarse and contain an abundance of organic matter. It should be kept always evenly moist but not constantly saturated. Spraying the foliage with clear water on all favorable occasions is beneficial. The plants should be staked when they need this attention or be provided with other suitable supports. Propagation is very easily effected by means of cuttings, inserted in a mixture of peat moss and sand. The cuttings root satisfactorily in a temperature of about 70 degrees. They should be kept where the atmosphere is humid and be shaded from direct sun.

Syngonium podophyllum is a popular house plant.

Kinds. S. auritum, Five Fingers, has bright green leaves that are usually divided into three but sometimes into five leaflets. It is a native of Jamaica.

S. podophyllum has rich green, long-stalked leaves which on young plants are arrow-shaped but on more mature specimens are divided into five or seven leaflets or fingers. It is a native of Mexico. Syngonium podophyllum variety albolineatum has silver midribs and veins. S. podophyllum variety albovirens has ivory-colored or greenish-white leaves edged with deep green. S. podophyllum variety Emerald Gem has a crinkled green leaf and the plant remains compact.

Other species of Syngonium that may be found in the collections of fanciers are: S. Hoffmannii from Central America, with grayish-green leaves with silver veins and center; S.

macrophyllum, from Central America, with fine emerald-green leaves which have a velvety appearance; S. xanthophyllum (sometimes misnamed S. podophyllum variety Green Gold), a native of Mexico which has smooth green leaves with ivory-colored centers; S. xanthophyllum variety tricolor, from Costa Rica, with narrow leaflets that are light green or ivory-colored and have a dark green border; and S. Ysidro, a native of Costa Rica, with green leaves and silver along the midribs.

SYNONYM. A name that has been superseded by another. To avoid confusion, synonyms are often placed in parentheses after the correct botanical names of plants.

SYNTHYRIS (Syn'thyris; Synthy'ris). A small group of hardy dwarf plants, native to western North America, belonging to the Figwort family, Scrophulariaceae. The name is derived from *syn*, united, and *thyris*, a little door, and refers to the closed valves of the seed capsule. They are delightful for cool positions in rock gardens and wild gardens, where they should be given a soil rich in leaf mold or other decayed organic matter. They begin to flower in earliest spring, and continue to bloom for a long time. They may be increased by careful division of the roots in spring or after flowering, and also by seeds sown in a pan of loam, leaf mold and sand in a cold frame in spring or early autumn.

Plants for the Rock Garden. Synthyris rotundifolia, 4-5 in. tall, has rounded, slightly hairy or rough leaves, toothed at their margins. The little white or pale blue, bell-shaped flowers are in short spikes. This plant is native from Oregon to California. There is a larger-leaved variety with darker blue flowers and taller stems called S. rotundifolia Sweetseri.

Synthyris reniformis grows to about 9 in. tall and has long-stalked, rounded or kidney-shaped leaves that are deeply toothed and are smooth. Its flowers are blue or blue-purple. It occurs as a native from Washington to California.

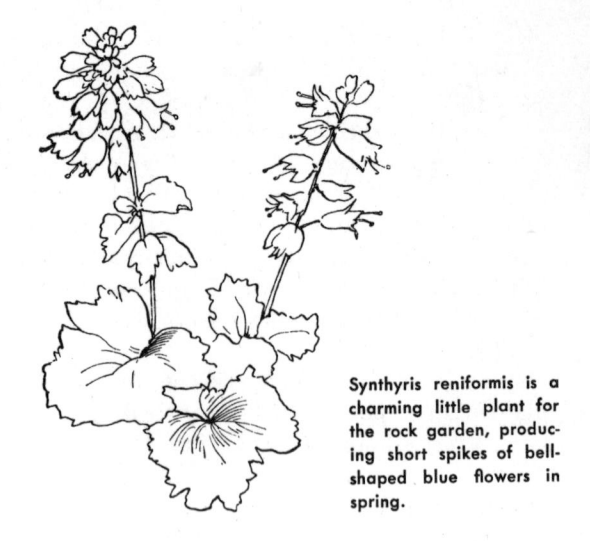

Synthyris reniformis is a charming little plant for the rock garden, producing short spikes of bell-shaped blue flowers in spring.

Synthyris major grows to about 8 in. high, has shining, lobed leaves and purple flowers. It is sometimes designated as a variety of S. reniformis. It is a native of Washington, Oregon and Idaho.

Synthyris rubra is a curiosity sometimes cultivated but scarcely worth garden space. The flower spikes are without petals, forming a poor bottle brush of reddish anthers. S. pinnatifida has feathery leaves and 8 in. spikes of soft blue, pink or whitish flowers. It is native of the mountains of Utah and Idaho. S. alpina, from Wyoming and Colorado, has ovate or oval, scalloped leaves and fine spikes of blue or purple-blue flowers. S. plantaginea has lilac-blue or pink flowers on spikes 8-12 in. tall, and is later than the others, flowering in May. It is native from Wyoming to New Mexico.

SYRIAN JUNIPER. Juniperus drupacea, which see.

SYRINGA or LILAC
Beautiful and Fragrant Spring-flowering Shrubs

Syringa (Syrin'ga). Leaf-losing shrubs or small trees, most of which are perfectly hardy in the North. They are distinguished by their opposite, often heart-shaped leaves, and by their large clusters of lilac, blue, reddish, white or cream flowers, which in some kinds are very fragrant.

[12–14]
Tabebuia serratifolia

[12–14a]
Japanese Yew
(Taxus cuspidata nana)

[12–14c]
Bald Cypress
(Taxodium distichum)

[12–14b]
Tagetes tenuifolia pumila

[12—15]
African Marigolds
(Tagetes)

[12—15a]
Taxus baccata aurea

Lilacs are among the most popular of flowering shrubs. They may be had in a variety of flower colors. Most are fragrant.

The commoner kinds of Lilac are among the most popular of flowering shrubs, and the appearance of the flowers heralds the change of the season from spring to summer. They are wild in southeastern Europe and Asia, and upwards of twenty species are known, in addition to hundreds of hybrids and named varieties.

The word Syringa is sometimes used as a common name for the Mock Oranges or Philadelphus, but its correct use as a botanical name is for Lilac. Syringa belongs to the Olive family, Oleaceae, and the name is from the Greek, *syrinx,* a tube, possibly because the name was first applied to Philadelphus.

The wood of Lilacs is hard, close-grained, yellowish with brown and reddish marks. It is attractive and suitable for turnery, though rarely used for the purpose.

Lilacs lend themselves to many forms of garden decoration; very charming results are often obtained when they are planted at the foot of an old wall so that the flowering branches appear well above the top. They are also excellent for large and small groups, isolated specimens, masses in the shrubbery and for informal hedges. They are exceedingly popular with almost everybody, and few gardens of any size in temperate climates are without one or more.

Propagation by Seeds and Cuttings. The species or wild types can be increased by means of seeds sown in light soil in greenhouse or frame, as soon as ripe or the following spring. Cuttings of the leafy shoots of many varieties that cannot be grown true from seed, may be made 3-4 in. long in June and inserted in sand in a cold frame. Or cuttings 9 in. long may be made of ripened wood in late autumn and winter and buried in sand in a cold frame over winter, to be planted in nursery rows in the garden in spring. But all the named varieties are more satisfactory if raised from layers.

The Lilac bushes at the left add greatly to the attractiveness of these flower borders and serve as a screen for the summer house.

Layering. When only a few plants are required, it is enough to layer the lower branches, but when large numbers are wanted it is better to keep plants in a nursery bed purposely for providing layers. Some people graft named varieties on stocks of the common Lilac, Syringa vulgaris, but it is not a good practice, for S. vulgaris is so liable to produce suckers; if these are not pulled up, they will in time take over and smother the named variety. Privet has also been used as a stock for Lilacs, but it has not proved very satisfactory.

Hints on Cultivation. Loamy soil is best for Lilacs, although they thrive in light and in clayey land. Good results over a long period can only be expected where the soil is of good quality. If the soil is poor, growth becomes thin and weak, and flowering suffers. Lilacs are not

Pruning Lilacs. (Left) Correct—old growth should be cut away near the root. (Right) Incorrect—topping or dehorning disfigures the shrub.

difficult to transplant and the work can be carried out at any time in fall or spring. A surface dressing of decayed manure or rich compost placed above the roots every second year is beneficial, and several applications of liquid fertilizer applied during May and early June will materially assist growth.

Pruning should take the form of the removal of suckers from the base, and of weak shoots, especially those inside or towards the center of the tree. This should be done as soon as the flowers have faded, and the old flower heads should be cut off at the same time. Severe annual pruning, other than the removal of suckers, is not advised. But when the plants are becoming weak and few flower heads are formed, the removal of weak inside wood, supplemented by applications of fertilizer, often results in vigorous growth and more flowers. This is the case with the garden varieties rather than the species or wild kinds. A little occasional thinning is usually all that the latter require. Overgrown bushes may be pruned back into old wood, with the result that new shoots will be formed from dormant buds. In extreme cases, when the bushes have become excessively tall and leggy they may be cut down in early spring to within about 1 ft. of the ground. Following this severe operation they should be fertilized and kept well watered in dry weather. Under this treatment they will form shapely bushes and may be expected to begin blooming in 2-3 years.

Lilacs for Forcing. Lilacs for forcing in the greenhouse are often grown specially for the purpose and are usually restricted to a few branches. Weak shoots are removed in order that the full vigor of the plants can be concentrated on the production of a few strong growths with well-developed buds. During the growing season they are fertilized liberally, and about August each plant is chopped around with a spade, and the ground opened a little to check growth and assist in ripening the wood.

Forcing begins soon after the leaves have fallen, and the forced plants, after the flowers have been gathered, are cut back, hardened off and replanted out of doors to be forced again in about two years time.

The Common Lilac, S. vulgaris, is a large shrub or small tree sometimes 20 ft. high, with a trunk 9-12 in. in diameter. It is a native of southeastern Europe and has been grown in European gardens since the latter part of the sixteenth century and in American gardens since early colonial times. References are made to it in both the diaries of George Washington and of Thomas Jefferson.

The most attractive of the old, original forms or varieties bear large, dense clusters of very fragrant flowers. There are several varieties, including alba, with white flowers; caerulea, with rather slender clusters of small pale blue-lilac flowers; and purpurea, which is reddish-purple. But the typical kind and its early varieties have been superseded by the newer named varieties having superior forms and richer coloring. Because the early hybridization was carried out by the great French horticulturists the Lemoines (father and son) of Nancy, these hybrids are often called "French Lilacs." American hybridizers have raised a few varieties but even today the majority of the improved varieties of the Common Lilac, S. vulgaris, in cultivation were raised by the Lemoines.

More recently S. vulgaris has been hybridized with varieties of S. oblata. These are described below under S. oblata in the discussion of Chinese Lilacs.

The long tube and narrow petals of the flowers of this Lilac give a unique fleecy effect. John Dunbar, Superintendent of the Rochester, New York, Parks, named the plant for his granddaughter, Joan Dunbar.

French Hybrid Lilacs.

Best Varieties of Common Lilac. *Single-flowered:* Vestale, white; Mont Blanc, white; De Mirabel, violet; Cacour, violet; President Lincoln, blue; Decaisne, blue; Maurice Barres, blue; Firmament, blue; Jacques Callot, lilac; Lucie Baltet, pink; Congo, reddish-purple; Mme. F. Morel, reddish-purple; Reaumur, reddish-purple; Ludwig Spaeth, deep purple; Monge, deep purple; Mrs. W. E. Marshall, deep purple.

Double-flowered: Ellen Willmott, white; Edith Cavell, white; Mme. Lemoine, white; Marechal Lannes, violet; Violetta, violet; Olivier de Serres, blue; President Grevy, blue; Victor Lemoine, lilac; Leon Gambetta, lilac; Henri

Martin, lilac; Katherine Havemeyer, pink; Mme. A. Buchner, pink; Paul Thirion, reddish-purple; Mrs. Edward Harding, reddish-purple; Adelaide Dunbar, deep purple; Paul Hariot, deep purple.

The Hungarian Lilac. S. Josikaea, the Hungarian Lilac, forms a bushy shrub 10-12 ft. tall and bears slender clusters of slightly fragrant, deep lilac to violet-colored flowers in June. It is not particularly handsome in bloom; its chief value lies in the lateness of its flowering period. The variety of S. Josikaea named eximia has large clusters of rose-colored flowers. S. Josikaea has been hybridized in Canada with S. reflexa to produce the Josiflexa hybrids.

The Persian Lilac. S. persica, the Persian Lilac, is a singularly beautiful shrub when in flower. Forming a shapely bush of slender branches, it usually grows 4-5 ft. high, bears large numbers of small, graceful clusters of lilac-colored, sweetly scented flowers. It requires little or no pruning and always blooms well. The variety alba has white flowers, and in laciniata the margins of the leaves are divided into fine segments. Some botanists regard the variety laciniata to be a distinct species and name it S. laciniata, and believe S. persica to be of hybrid origin. S. persica is widely distributed from Iran to western China and has been known in European gardens since 1640.

S. persica, crossed with S. vulgaris, produced a very beautiful fragrant-flowered Lilac called S. chinensis. It is intermediate in habit between the two parents, forms a shapely bush 8-12 ft. high, and bears its clusters of fragrant, purplish-lilac flowers freely. The variety alba has white flowers. The variety duplex has double purplish-lilac flowers. S. chinensis is sometimes called the Rouen Lilac.

The Himalayan Lilac. S. emodi, the Himalayan Lilac, is another vigorous and attractive shrub; unfortunately it is not hardy far north. It may grow 15-18 ft. high, has large leaves, which are green above and silvery beneath, and bears dense heads of whitish-pink or lilac-tinged flowers in June and July that have a privet-like odor. It has been grown in gardens since 1840. There is a variety, aureo-variegata, with golden-variegated leaves, and another, aurea, with yellowish leaves. S. hybrida is a hybrid between S. emodi and S. vulgaris, with characteristics most like those of the former.

Chinese Lilacs. S. pekinensis is a shrub or small tree of the same type; it has smaller leaves but very similar heads of flowers: its variety, pendula, is a very graceful shrub with drooping branches. It is a native of China.

S. Julianae is one of the best of the newer Chinese kinds. It was received from western China in 1900 and is a graceful, early-flowering bush 5-6 ft. high. The lilac-purple, fragrant flowers are in medium-sized clusters and open in early spring. There is a variety with white flowers. S. velutina (Palibiniana) is a vigorous bush, up to 10 ft. high, which was introduced from Korea in 1917; it bears long, slender branched clusters of pale lilac flowers. This kind is found wild in China and Korea.

One of the most conspicuous of the native Chinese Lilacs is S. reflexa, a vigorous shrub 10-12 ft. high, from central China, with large handsome leaves, and dense, nodding clusters of reddish flowers which open about the end of May. The leaves are often 5-5½ in. long and 2-2½ in. wide. Crossed with S. villosa it has become the parent of the very fine group of Canadian-raised hybrid Lilacs that are collectively called Prestoniae hybrids. Among the best of these varieties are Isabella, Jessica and Nerissa. Hybridized with S. Josikaea, S. reflexa has given rise to a group of Lilacs called Josiflexa hybrids. These also were raised in Canada.

Syringa Julianae is one of the most pleasing species of Chinese Lilacs. Its flowers are lilac purple.

S. villosa is a large bush, 10-12 ft. high, native to northern China, and belonging to the same group as S. emodi. It flowers from short shoots produced on the previous year's wood, and on the tips of vigorous shoots of the current year, the latter bearing the finer clusters. The flowering time extends from the end of May to July. The flowers are usually rosy-lilac and freely produced. Owing to its vigorous and shapely habit and prolonged flowering, it is a shrub that deserves more attention from gardeners.

S. Komarowii is a large shrub, 16 ft. high, native to western China and closely related to S. reflexa; the flowers are reddish-purple and produced in dense nodding clusters in June.

S. microphylla is a graceful bush of slender growth with small leaves, scarcely more than an inch long, and branched clusters 4-5 in. long of small, tubular, lilac-colored flowers in June. It is a native of northern China.

S. pinnatifolia differs from the other Lilac species by bearing pinnate leaves, a characteristic only found elsewhere among Lilacs in the laciniate-leaved variety of S. persica. S. pinnatifolia is a native of western China, where it forms an erect bush about 10 ft. high. Its leaves are $1\frac{1}{2}$-3 in. long and are made up of seven to eleven small leaflets. The flowers are white, or white tinged with lilac, and are in small clusters up to $3\frac{1}{2}$ in. long. The plant is more curious than beautiful and must be regarded as one of the least decorative kinds.

S. oblata, from China, has the distinction of being one of the earliest of Lilacs to flower. It grows to a height of 12 ft. or thereabouts, and bears dense clusters of pale lilac-colored blooms in late April or early May. S. oblata variety alba has white flowers. Hybridized with the Common Lilac, S. vulgaris, S. oblata variety Giraldii has given rise to early-flowering hybrids which bloom a week or ten days before the Common Lilac. The best of these are Lamartine, pinkish-lilac; Louvois, dark lilac; and Montesquieu, dark lilac. S. oblata variety dilatata, hybridized with the Common Lilac, S. vulgaris, has given rise to the excellent hybrids Assessippi, lilac, and Pocahontas, purple, which bloom about ten days earlier than the Common Lilac.

S. Sweginzowii, a native of northern China, is an upright-growing shrub that attains a maximum height of about 10 ft. It has fragrant, lilac or reddish lilac-colored flowers in June. Its chief value rests in the lateness of its season of bloom. S. Sweginzowii variety superba is said to bloom more profusely but otherwise is similar.

S. tomentella (Adamiana), a vigorous bush from western China, has flower clusters rather like those of S. emodi, produced in June.

The Japanese Lilac, Syringa amurensis japonica, forms a small tree that bears huge panicles of creamy-white flowers in early summer. The flowers have a rather disagreeable odor.

S. amurensis, from Manchuria and China, is a late-flowering kind that grows about 12 ft. tall and has creamy white flowers somewhat resembling those of a large-flowered Privet (Ligustrum).

The Japanese Lilac. S. amurensis variety japonica, the Japanese Lilac, is especially worthy of note; it is a small tree up to 30 ft. high and is remarkable for its huge bunches of small white or pale cream-colored flowers which open in June and July. At first sight they look more like flowers of giant-flowered Privet than Lilac. This kind is a native of Japan.

SYRINGING. Syringing is a term used by gardeners to describe the spraying of plants with a forceful stream of water broken into a fine spray in such a way that the lower as well as the upper leaf surfaces are thoroughly wetted and washed. It is done, especially in greenhouses, to forcibly dislodge insects and other

Using a hose to syringe plants in a greenhouse.

pests, such as mealy bugs and red spider mites, to remove dust and grime and to promote humid atmospheric conditions.

The term syringing had its origin in the fact that gardeners at one time used, and sometimes still do, a hand-pumping instrument called a syringe for this purpose; today it is a more common practice to make use of the hose for syringing, and special syringing nozzles are made that produce a fine, forceful spray.

Syringing Must Be Done with Judgment. Certain plants, notably very hairy-leaved kinds such as African Violets and Gynuras, react badly to having their leaves wetted. Syringing may spread bacterial diseases and the spores of fungus diseases as well as leaf (foliar) nematodes and some other pests. It should never be done if leaf nematodes are present; nor so late in the day that the foliage will not dry before nightfall; nor on dull days when the leaves are apt to lie wet more than about an hour.

Carried out with good judgment, syringing is a most beneficial practice, for it not only helps greatly in keeping plants clean but also does much to promote healthy growth.

House plants may be syringed outdoors during favorable weather; or you can stand them in a sink or bathtub, if this is more convenient. Syringing should never be so heavy that the soil is saturated in the process, because if this is done repeatedly the good accomplished by syringing the foliage will be more than offset by the harm done to the roots by overwatering.

T

TABEBUIA (Tabebu'ia). A group of evergreen trees and shrubs, all natives of tropical America and the West Indies; a few are suitable for planting in the far South. They are included in the Bignonia family, the Bignoniaceae. The name is a native Brazilian one.

Tabebuias need rich soil for their best development and may be propagated by seeds, cuttings and air layering. Kinds likely to be cultivated are T. argentea, 25 ft., flowers yellow; T. pallida, 50 ft., flowers white with colored veins or pink; T. serratifolia, 30 ft., flowers yellow. The first-named kind is a native of Paraguay. T. pallida occurs wild in tropical South and Central America and the West Indies, T. serratifolia is a West Indian native.

TABERNAEMONTANA (Tabernaemonta'na). Free-flowering, evergreen trees and shrubs belonging to the Dogbane family, Apocynaceae, and resembling Gardenia. They are natives of tropical countries. The name commemorates J. T. Tabernaemontanus, a German botanist of the sixteenth century. Although there are a large number of species, widely distributed throughout the tropics, only two or three kinds are cultivated in North America.

The cultural care of Tabernaemontana is the same as that of Ervatamia, which see. Kinds likely to be grown include T. citrifolia, 6 ft. tall, flowers white, fragrant; T. grandiflora, 6 ft., flowers yellow, fragrant. The plant often called T. coronaria is now named Ervatamia coronaria, and the plant cultivated as T. grandifolia is apparently a form of this.

TABLE MOUNTAIN ORCHID. Disa, which see.

TACAMAHAC. Populus Tacamahaca, which see.

TACCA (Tac'ca). Curious evergreen, perennial, herbaceous plants that are natives of many tropical regions and are suitable for cultivation in moist tropical greenhouses. They belong to the Tacca family, Taccaceae and are sometimes known under the name of Attaccia. Tacca is the Malayan name. T. pinnatifida (leontopetaloides) contains much starch in its rhizomes, which, when extracted and prepared for food, is called East Indian Arrowroot or South Sea Arrowroot.

The kinds cultivated have creeping rhizomes or rootstocks; large, oval, wrinkled leaves; and umbels or bunches of curious purplish-brown flowers furnished with whisker-like growths which hang downwards. The flower clusters are borne on top of stout stems 18-24 in. high.

Tacca Chantrieri, the curious Devil Flower, a native of Malaya.

Summer and Winter Treatment. During the winter the plants are at rest and comparatively little moisture is required, but as soon as growth commences in spring, they should be shaken free of the old soil and repotted in a mixture of peat moss, sand and loam. The pots must be well drained and during active growth an abundance of water is required. Specimens that have filled their pots with roots benefit greatly from regular applications of dilute liquid fertilizer. A suitable minimum winter temperature is 55 degrees; during the season of active growth (spring to fall) a minimum of 60-65 degrees should be maintained.

Propagation is effected by dividing the rhizomes at repotting time in spring.

Kinds most likely to be cultivated are T. Chantrieri, the Devil Flower, a native of Malaya; T. cristata (aspera), a native of Malaya; T. pinnatifida (leontopetaloides), a native of tropical Asia, Africa and Australia.

TAGETES: AFRICAN AND FRENCH MARIGOLDS
Useful and Easily Grown Flowers for Garden and Greenhouse

Tagetes (Tage'tes) are annuals of great decorative value during the summer and autumn months. They are natives of Mexico and South America and belong to the Daisy family, Compositae. The name is said to have been derived from a mythological deity, Tages. These Marigolds are quite distinct from the Pot Marigold or Calendula. See Calendula.

The two chief types of Tagetes are the African Marigold, Tagetes erecta, and the French Marigold, Tagetes patula. The former reaches a height of 2-4 ft. and bears large, single or

Flowers of two distinct varieties of African Marigolds.

double flowers of orange or yellow coloring; the latter grows from 9 in. to 2 ft. high and the flowers are yellow, or yellow marked with reddish-brown. In recent years hybrids between the African and French varieties have been developed. In addition, two other species of Tagetes are grown in gardens, T. lucida, the Sweet-scented Marigold, and T. tenuifolia (signata).

The African Marigolds are represented by numerous handsome double varieties which bear large, rounded flowers in orange and various shades of yellow, on strong stems. They are extremely useful in garden beds and borders during the summer months. Much effort has been spent in attempting to develop a white-flowered variety and while not yet successful some modern varieties have pale creamy yellow flowers.

In height of plants and form of flowers their is considerable variation and groups of varieties are designated in seedsmens' catalogs as Carnation Flowered and Chrysanthemum Flowered. There are many other varieties with flowers in a great number of distinct shapes and forms, and some, even, with odorless foliage. If the plants are well grown they will last in bloom until cut down by frost, and provide brilliant masses of color in the garden in autumn. They are useful as cut flowers.

When to Sow Seeds. The African Marigolds may be raised from seeds sown about 6 weeks before the plants are to be planted outdoors, in a greenhouse in which a temperature of 50-55 degrees is maintained. The seeds are sown in pots or flats filled with sifted sandy soil; they are lightly covered with similar soil and the containers are covered with glass and shaded from sunshine. If kept moist, the seeds will germinate in a few days.

When the seedlings are 1-2 in. high, they should be transplanted to flats, 3-4 in. deep, filled with a sandy, loamy compost; they are

A single-flowered French Marigold.

Spading over a border in preparation for planting Marigolds.

After spading, the surface of the ground is raked smooth.

Young plants are set out from flats. Care is taken to preserve as many roots as possible.

A thorough watering with a fine spray follows planting.

placed 3 in. apart. They should remain in the flats until it is time to plant them out of doors after danger of frost has passed and the weather is warm and settled. For two or three weeks after transplanting to flats the seedlings should be kept in the greenhouse to assist them to become established quickly. Subsequently, they are grown in a cold frame and, as the time for planting draws near, they are hardened off by ventilating the frame more freely, and finally are fully exposed to the air.

It is also quite practicable to grow African Marigolds by sowing the seeds in the locations where the plants are to remain, but the plants obtained by this method will not bloom quite so early as those raised under glass. The seeds are scattered thinly in a well-prepared seedbed outdoors as soon as danger from frost has passed, and the seedlings are thinned out until they are not less than 10 in. apart.

A location fully exposed to the sunshine must be chosen for the African Marigolds; they are not a success in shady places. It is a mistake to set them in very rich soil, or they will make rank, luxuriant growth at the expense of flower production. They should be planted 12-15 in. apart.

The French Marigolds. The varieties of these vary in height from 6-24 inches. The taller ones are useful for grouping towards the front of flower borders and for the production of cut flowers; the very dwarf ones are commonly used for edging flower beds. There are both double-flowered and single-flowered varieties.

Among the dwarfer varieties Naughty Marietta is popular. It has rich golden-yellow flowers attractively marked with brownish-red. The single flowers of Red Head have a crested center of yellow and maroon and surrounding petals of mahogany, bronze and gold. Sunny has single, bright yellow flowers marked with cerise at the bases of the petals. Ruffled Red has mahogany-red flowers edged with yellow. All these are single-flowered varieties. Of the dwarf double French Marigolds, some of the best are Spry, maroon with bright golden centers; Tangerine, bright tangerine-orange; Lemon Drop, clear lemon-yellow; and Yellow Pygmy, with tiny, light yellow chrysanthemum-like flowers. There are single forms of the tall French Marigolds, but these are not so popular as the dwarf varieties.

French Marigolds require the same general cultural care as that detailed for African Marigolds. They may be started in a greenhouse or raised from seeds sown directly outdoors. If sown directly outdoors the seedlings germinate quickly, provided they are kept moist. They must be thinned out in good time to give them every chance to develop sturdily.

It is a mistake to grow these plants in too rich a soil, for they will make vigorous growth

In a very few weeks the border is a blaze of color. These are French Marigolds.

but will not bloom very freely. Neither is it wise to plant them anywhere except in full sunshine, for in shade or partial shade they become very leafy, and their blossoming is disappointing.

African-French Hybrid Marigolds. A race of hybrids between the African and French Marigolds, raised in America in recent years, are named Burpee's Red and Gold Hybrids. As yet the strain is not fixed and the plants vary in the color of the flowers they produce. Some are solid red, some solid yellow, others various combinations of red and golden-yellow. Flower colors vary on the same plants at different periods during the season. The flowers are double, 2-3 in. in diameter; the plants are bushy and grow about 18 in. tall.

These African-French Hybrid Marigolds require the same culture as their parent types. They bloom throughout the summer and fall and are good cut flowers. Because the strain is not fixed a few true African Marigolds usually appear among the seedlings. Even while they are very small it is easy to segregate these from the hybrids because the African type has green stems whereas those of the hybrids are red. The African Marigolds normally grow taller than the hybrids and should be planted separately.

Other Kind of Tagetes. A Tagetes of very distinct appearance and of great charm and usefulness is T. tenuifolia (signata) pumila. In recent years this has been listed under the name of Dwarf Signet Marigold. It is a native of Mexico and forms a broad, bushy plant 1 ft. or less tall. It has finely divided foliage and bears a multitude of single, golden-orange flowers about 1 in. in diameter, each with but few ray florets.

Tagetes tenuifolia variety pumila requires the same cultural care as the dwarf French Marigolds and, like them, is a splendid subject for planting in groups at the fronts of borders, for bedding and for setting out as edgings to flower beds.

The Sweet-scented Marigold, Tagetes lucida, is an attractive species from Mexico that does not appear to be very much cultivated. It grows about 1 ft. tall, has fragrant foliage and carries its golden or orange-yellow flowers in dense terminal clusters. It requires the same cultural care as the other kinds.

In Greenhouses. All kinds of Tagetes are useful plants for growing in greenhouses for winter and spring display. They are elegant pot plants and are also useful as cut flowers. Some seedsmen offer special winter-flowering varieties which bloom freely even when days are short and light less intense than in the summer.

African Marigolds grown three plants together in a 6-in. pot.

One plant of a dwarf French Marigold grown in a 5-in. pot.

One of the best of these is called Lieb's Winter Flowering.

For winter bloom, the seeds should be sown in August or September; for spring bloom, sow them in January. The seedlings should be transplanted to flats, or individually to small pots, and later potted in larger receptacles as needed. Pots measuring 5-7 in. in diameter are satisfactory sizes in which to let the plants flower. Good results may be had by growing either one or three plants in each pot.

The soil for Tagetes grown in greenhouses should not be overrich but it should be well drained. When the plants have filled their final pots with roots, weekly applications of dilute liquid fertilizer will be of great benefit.

At all times these plants must be exposed to full sun and should be provided with airy, rather cool conditions. A night temperature of 50 degrees is ample; on dull days the temperature may rise about 5 degrees and on sunny days 10 or even 15 degrees.

By supplementing daylight with artificial light (either of the fluorescent or incandescent kind) earlier and more flowers can be obtained from Tagetes grown in greenhouses in winter.

TAIL GRAPE. Artabotrys, which see.

TAINIA (Tain'ia). Terrestrial Orchids with somewhat flask-shaped pseudobulbs, each of which terminates in a single tall leaf. The flowers are in erect spikes near the base of the bulbs, and have narrow segments. Most kinds bloom in spring and summer. The plants are found wild from Ceylon to Malaya. The name Tainia means a band, and alludes to the shape of the lip.

A suitable compost consists of fibrous loam, two thirds, and one third of osmunda fiber, sphagnum moss and a little sand. A greenhouse with a warm, moist atmosphere is required in summer, and water may then be given freely, provided drainage is good. In winter, the plants should be kept in a temperature of about 60 degrees, and water withheld, unless the pseudobulbs begin to shrivel. Shading is required in summer. If necessary, the plants should be repotted early in the year when fresh growth begins.

T. latifolia, from India, has spikes 2 ft. high and greenish-brown flowers. T. Hookeriana, from Burma, is very similar, but larger.

TAIWANIA CRYPTOMERIOIDES (Taiwa'nia). A very interesting evergreen tree which grows up to 200 ft. high with a trunk 20 ft. or more in girth, in Formosa and western China. It is allied to Cryptomeria, from which it differs chiefly in its more spiny leaves and the shape of its cones. It was introduced to western gardens in 1920 but is not generally hardy; in fact, it can only be expected to thrive in the warmest parts of the United States.

Cuttings of young shoots, planted in a propagating bench in a close and warm propagating frame in early summer, root freely and form leading shoots better than plants of many kinds of Conifers raised from cuttings. Taiwania has been found to succeed in ordinary loamy soil where the climatic conditions are suitable.

The tree grows naturally at elevations of 6,000-8,000 ft. on Mount Morrison, in Formosa, and was first discovered in 1904. It belongs to the Taxodium family, Taxodiaceae, and the name is taken from Taiwan (Formosa). This interesting Conifer is suitable for planting in Florida and California and other warm regions.

TAKE. This term is used by growers of Chrysanthemums to indicate the method of disbudding or removing superfluous flower buds. When a flower bud first forms on a Chrysanthemum plant, other and smaller buds develop beneath it; these are removed a few at a time to allow the chief bud to make uninterrupted progress. The removal of these buds is called "taking the bud."

The gardener uses the word "take" in other senses. He speaks of taking cuttings when he refers to removing the shoots from the parent plant. When grafting or budding, the scion or bud is said to have "taken" when it has formed a successful union with the understock.

TALINUM—*Fameflower* (Talin'um). More or less succulent (fleshy), perennial, herbaceous plants with pretty flowers that last only a few hours but follow each other in order of opening and provide a display over a long period. They belong to the Purslane family, the Portulacaceae. The name is of uncertain origin; possibly it is derived from a native African appellation.

About 15 kinds of Talinum are known to botanists and they are found as natives in many of the warmer regions of the world but most notably in the Americas. Only a few kinds are cultivated, and of these only one, T. teretifolium, is hardy in the North.

Talinums Are Sun Lovers. These plants need a soil that is on the dryish side and is very well-drained. Apart from that, they require no special cultural care. They are readily increased by means of seeds and by cuttings and leaf cuttings. The tender ones may be grown as pot plants in greenhouses or window gardens and in mild climates in rock gardens. The hardy T. teretifolium is a good rock-garden plant.

Kinds. T. calycinum, 8 in. tall, flowers pink, native from Arkansas to Mexico; T. okanoganense, 1 in. tall, flowers white, a native of Washington; T. paniculatum, 2 ft. tall, flowers red to yellowish, a native of the southeastern United States and southwards (a variety of this species that has its leaves edged with white is cultivated); T. patens, 2 ft. tall, flowers carmine-red, a native of the West Indies and eastern South America; T. patens variety variegatum, similar to the last, but with leaves attractively variegated with white or pale pink; T. teretifolium, 4-10 in., flowers pink, a native from Pennsylvania to Georgia and Texas; T. triangulare, 2 ft. tall, flowers red, white or yellowish, a native of tropical America.

TAMARACK. Larix laricina, which see.

TAMARIND. Tamarindus indica, which see.

TAMARINDUS INDICA—*Tamarind* (Tamarind'us). A genus consisting of only one species. It is a tropical tree which produces fruits of considerable economic value. This tree, which is found wild in tropical Asia and Africa, belongs to the Pea family, Leguminoseae. The name Tamarindus is derived from *tamar,* date, and *Hindi,* Indian, the plant being sometimes called the Indian Date. It grows up to 80 ft. in height, has pinnate (feather-like) leaves and small racemes of pale yellow flowers, which are succeeded by seed pods containing several seeds embedded in a brown, pulpy substance. This pulp is acid in flavor and is extensively used in making cooling drinks.

TAMARISK. Tamarix, which see.

TAMARIX—*Tamarisk* (Tam′arix). Leaf-losing trees or shrubs with very slender branchlets clothed with tiny, scalelike green or grayish leaves, the finer branchlets falling in autumn with the leaves. The flowers are small, usually pale or bright pink, sometimes almost white, numerous flowers being produced together in clusters of varying size.

Shrubs for Seaside Gardens. Tamarisks are resistant to sea air, and are among the best of all shrubs and trees for planting in exposed places near the coast. They also thrive in inland gardens. Numerous kinds are known, but a few only are in cultivation in North America. The cultivated kinds are mostly of European and Mediterranean region origin. Tamarix gives its name to the family Tamaricaceae, and the name is the ancient Latin name for the plant.

Planting and Propagation. Cuttings of ripened shoots, 9-12 in. long, made in summer or fall and inserted in a cold frame, are the usual means of propagation; in mild climates the cuttings may be inserted in the places where the plants are to grow. These shrubs thrive in light and heavy soils, and they will grow in sea sand. There are, however, one or two kinds, more particularly T. pentandra and T. odessana, that give satisfactory results only when planted in loamy garden soil. Some kinds need no regular pruning, but T. pentandra and T. odessana should be cut hard back in spring to within two or three buds of the base of the previous year's wood, to encourage them to flower satisfactorily.

Tamarisks as Hedge Plants. These plants can be used as hedge plants. If planted densely, they may either be allowed to develop without much pruning into an informal hedge, or kept within definite bounds by clipping in summer. As a rule, clipped hedges are 2-4 ft. high.

The branches of Tamarisks are tough and are often used in parts of Europe for weaving into lobster pots for fishing purposes.

The English Tamarisk. This is T. anglica, a tree or bush, sometimes 15-20 ft. high with a trunk 12 in. or more in diameter. It is wild throughout the maritime regions of western Europe. The flowers are pale pink or whitish and they are produced in summer. The English

Tamarisk is suitable for planting in the central and southern United States.

The French Tamarisk. T. gallica, the French Tamarisk, is a closely allied and very similar tree or shrub. It also is used in gardens near the sea, and is the common Tamarisk of the Mediterranean region. It is hardy in the central United States.

Pink Flowers in May. T. tetrandra is one of the most decorative of the early-flowering kinds. A native of southeastern Europe and western Asia, it usually develops as a widely spreading loose bush, 10-12 ft. high. The flowers are pink and borne in slender clusters, 1½-2 in. long, in May. As the flowers are produced freely, a well-grown bush is very attractive. This kind is hardy in the central and southern states. A closely allied kind is T. parviflora, also from southeastern Europe. It grows 12-15 ft. high and bears pale pink flowers in spring. This kind is hardy in southern New England.

T. aphylla, Athel Tamarisk, is a native of western Asia that grows to a height of 30 ft. It has been planted as a windbreak in desert and alkali soil regions in western North America. It is not hardy in the North.

Beautiful Shrubs. T. pentandra is a very beautiful shrub found in southeastern Europe and Asia. It may grow 10-12 ft. high, but is often cultivated as a low shrub. If cut back each spring, it forms plumose (feathery) branches during summer, 2½-3 ft. long, clothed with bright green leaves among which short cylindrical clusters of pink flowers appear in July, throughout the greater part of the shoot. It must be given really good soil and, as soon as plants show signs of deterioration, they should be replaced. T. pentandra is hardy in southern New England. T. odessana, from the Caspian region, is a rather similar shrub with pink flowers, requiring the same treatment. It is somewhat hardier than T. pentandra.

T. hispida, the Kashgar Tamarisk, is a shrub, 6 ft. high, with slender branchlets clothed with blue-green leaves. The flowers are pink and freely produced in summer. It is not always very amenable to cultivation. It comes from the Caspian Sea region, and is hardy in the central and southern United States.

T. chinensis, Chinese Tamarisk, is a Chinese tree or large shrub, 15 ft. or more high. It bears pink flowers and is hardy in the far South only. T. juniperina, from China and Japan, is doubtfully hardy in the North. It grows 15 ft. tall and has pink flowers in spring.

TAMPALA. A vegetable of comparatively little importance that is used in the same manner as Spinach and Swiss Chard. It is a horticultural variety of Amaranthus tricolor.

Tampala is distinctly a warm-weather crop. Seeds should be sown in well-drained, fertile soil in a sunny location after the ground has warmed and the weather settled. The seed may be sown directly outdoors and should be covered with soil to a depth of about ¼ in. The rows should be 18-24 in. apart and the plants in the rows thinned to stand 15-18 in. apart. The leaves may be cut and used when they are about half-grown and while they are yet tender.

TANACETUM—*Tansy* (Tanace'tum). Hardy, herbaceous perennials of moderate value in gardens. T. vulgare (Common Tansy) is the principal kind; it is widely distributed as a wild plant in Europe and occurs as an escape from cultivation in North America. At one time it was held in high esteem as a tonic, febrifuge (for dispelling fever), and vermifuge (to remove worms from animal bodies). This plant grows 2-3 ft. in height, has finely divided feathery

Tanacetum vulgare variety crispum has ornamental foliage and clusters of buttonlike yellow flowers.

leaves and bears terminal clusters of small yellow flowers in summer. The variety crispum is more dwarf, has more finely divided leaves, and is worth while growing in gardens for the ornamental appearance of its foliage. T. Herderi, from Turkestan, is a rare, dwarf kind with silvery leaves and small, bright yellow flowers, suitable for the rock garden.

Tanacetum is easy to cultivate. The plants flourish in ordinary garden soil in a sunny or semishaded position. Propagation is by dividing the clumps into small portions at planting time in autumn or spring, the rooted pieces being planted directly in their permanent positions. Tanacetum belongs to the Daisy family, Compositae. The name is of uncertain derivation.

TANAKAEA RADICANS (Tana'kaea). This is a pretty Japanese woodland plant suitable for a cool, half-shady location in the rock garden. It requires peaty soil, or loam with a large proportion of well-decayed leaf mold added. It has creeping wiry stems, clothed with elliptic, pointed, leathery leaves, deep green and toothedged, and spikes of feathery creamy-white flowers on 6-in. stems in May. It is increased by careful division or by cuttings of the running shoots, taken when soft and rooted in sand in a cold frame in early summer.

Tanakaea is a choice and uncommon plant, but one of very great charm, and deserves to be grown more often than it is. It belongs to the Saxifrage family, Saxifragaceae, and is named after a Japanese botanist, Yoshio Tanaka.

TANGELO. A hybrid between the Tangerine (Citrus nobilis variety deliciosa) and the Grapefruit (Citrus paradisi). See Citrus.

TANGERINE. Citrus nobilis variety deliciosa, which see.

TANS AND DYES. Various vegetable substances are rich in tannin, a chemical which has the property of changing various substances, that are easily subject to decay, into decay-resistant material. This property is taken advantage of in transforming hides into leather.

Tannin and dyeing properties often go together, and some substances are used for the dual purpose. However, natural dyes have been very largely displaced by coal-tar dyes.

With tanning substances it is different, for there is an increasing demand for the best kinds. Tannin is found in many parts of plants but is often most highly developed in definite parts of particular species. Thus the tannin contents may be highest in bark, heartwood, husks of fruits, leaves and young shoots, roots or even in galls caused by insect pests.

Oak Bark. At one period this bark was in considerable demand for its tannin. In these days, however, extracts from other countries are imported more cheaply than Oak bark can be produced, or are more easily manipulated; thus there is not much demand for Oak bark.

Wattle bark is a popular tanning material. It is produced extensively in Natal and other parts of South Africa. The chief kinds grown for this purpose are Acacia decurrens, A. decurrens varieties dealbata and mollis and A. pycnantha. The richest bark is taken from trees 10-12 years old. The bark of A. pycnantha contains 40-50 per cent of tannin, that of other kinds 36-39 per cent.

Tannin Is Obtained from the Sumac. Rhus coriaria is widely grown in Sicily and is also cultivated in Cyprus for its leaves and shoots, which are very popular for tanning light-colored good-quality leathers. Leaves of Rhus Cotinus are also collected for tanning purposes in southern Europe, and galls are collected from Rhus succedanea in China and Japan for similar use. Roots of Rhus pentaphylla contain about 25 per cent of tannin; they are collected from the dry hillsides of Morocco, and other parts of North Africa.

The tanning material known as Divi-divi is the dried husks of the seed pods of Caesalpinia coriaria. The supply is largely from Central America, but some quantity is obtained from Java, India and Australia. Quebracho is the heartwood of a tree from the Argentine Republic, Schinopsis Lorentzii. It contains about 20 per cent of tannin and its use results in a firm, good-quality leather.

Canaigre or Tanner's Dock (Rumex hymenosepalus) is grown in Mexico and the United States for its tuberous roots, which contain 26-30 per cent of tannin. It is very useful in tanning yellow leathers.

Myrobalans, the fruits of Terminalia Chebula

and T. belerica, are collected in an unripe state in India, and nearly 25,000 tons are marketed annually for tanning purposes. Gambier is a tanning substance obtained by boiling leaves and shoots of a climbing shrub, Uncaria gambier, and evaporating the moisture until a hard extract is obtained. The plant is a native of the East Indies.

Tannin from Acorn Cups. Valonia tannin is obtained from acorn cups of the Valonia Oak, Quercus Aegilops, from Asia Minor and the Balkan Peninsula. The bark of various American Oaks, in addition to that of European kinds, is rich in tannin, and the galls of several kinds are regularly collected for their tanning properties. European Chestnut wood contains a percentage of tannin; the wood is cut into chips and an extract prepared from it. Pine and Larch bark are used in some countries for tanning purposes, as is also Willow bark. High-class leathers are prepared with the use of Pomegranate bark.

Cutch is a black, coal-like tanning extract obtained by boiling chips of the wood of Acacia Catechu, evaporating the water and drying the extract. This is largely prepared in India and Burma and is in great demand.

Indigo. Most of the tanning substances have also dyeing properties, but few vegetable dyes are of great consequence in the present day. A dye that is still useful is Indigo. It is prepared from the stems and leaves of a few kinds of Indigofera, such as I. suffruticosa (Anil.), I. tinctoria, I. arrecta and I. sumatrana. The dye is largely prepared in India and to some extent in Java. The stems are soaked in water, during which time they are constantly agitated. Fermentation is set up and, after a period of 10-15 hours, the water is drained off and the residue sundried. It is then cut into cakes for export for dyeing purposes.

Chinese, Korean, and Japanese Indigo are obtained from the shoots and leaves of Polygonum tinctorium, and West African Indigo from leaves and shoots of Lonchocarpus cyanescens.

Woad, the dyeing product at one time much used in blue dyes, was produced from leaves of Isatis tinctoria.

Annatto is an orange-red dye obtained from the seeds and the surrounding pulp of the fruit of a South American and West Indian plant, Bixa Orellana. Its great use at the present time is in coloring cheese, butter, and other foodstuffs.

Safflower is a dye obtained from the yellow flowers of Carthamus tinctorius. Mixed with starch or talc, this dye is much used in cosmetics.

Saffron, used for coloring various articles of confectionery, and also used for flavoring, consists of the dried stigmas of flowers of Crocus sativus.

Henna is a dye produced from the powdered leaves of Lawsonia inermis, a shrub wild in various parts of northern and eastern tropical Africa, Madagascar, tropical Asia and Australia. It is much used in hair dyes, often in conjunction with Camomile.

Old Fustic is a dye obtained from the wood of a South American tree, Chlorophora tinctoria. It is most important in dyeing woollen goods, particularly for olive-yellow and old gold colors. In mixture with other substances it produces various brown and drab shades.

Other Sources of Dyes. The wood of Osage Orange, Maclura pomifera, can be used for yellowish dyes; Brazil Wood and Peach Wood, kinds of Caesalpinia, produce red, pink and chocolate shades; Madder, Rubia tinctoria, can be used in dyeing the yellower-toned reds, pinks and grayish lilacs; the Walnut for browns; Genista tinctoria for yellows; Persian Berries, the fruits of various kinds of Rhamnus, produce yellow, orange and green shades; Heather, Calluna vulgaris, produces brownish-yellow; Logwood, Haematoxylun campechianum, can be used for blacks, and Quebracho for yellows.

TANSY. See Tanacetum.

TAPE GRASS. See Vallisneria.

TAPIOCA. A starchy foodstuff prepared from the tuberous roots of the Cassava plants, Manihot esculenta (utilissima) and M. dulcis variety Aipi, the former producing Bitter Cassava, the latter, Sweet Cassava. In a raw state the former is not wholesome, but after the roots have been ground and repeatedly washed, the deleterious substances are mostly washed away and any that are left are dissipated by heating. See Cassava.

TAPROOT. A term used in describing the principal root of a tree or plant, from which the main stem is a direct development.

Sometimes, in the cultivation of trees and plants with pronounced taproots, it is necessary to shorten these for the purpose of ensuring the development of bushy specimens. A tree or plant with a strong downward-growing taproot generally makes vigorous growth, and has a limited number of strong, straight branches. Shortening the taproots checks the growth of those branches and, as a result, other and less luxuriant shoots are produced. It is frequently necessary to shorten the taproots of dwarf fruit trees. See Root Pruning.

TARA VINE. Actinidia arguta, which see.

TARAXACUM. This is the botanical name of the Dandelion. The cultivation of this plant as a salad is dealt with under the heading of Dandelion, which see.

TARO ROOT. See Colocasia.

TARRAGON. This is the common name of Artemisia Dracunculus, a shrubby plant which is grown for its leaves, which are used in salads and seasoning, and in the manufacture of Tarragon vinegar. The woody stems grow 3 ft. in height, and are clothed with entire (undivided), lanceolate, narrow green leaves, 2 in. in length. The flowers are inconspicuous.

Tarragon is cultivated in the herb garden and its leaves are used both fresh or dried.

Details of Cultivation. Light, well-drained soil and a sunny position are necessary. The roots are planted in April, 18 in. apart, and the soil is watered in dry weather. As the flower buds appear they are pinched out in order to throw all the energies of the plant into leaf production. The leaves may be gathered at any time during the summer for immediate use.

To provide a supply for the winter, the shoots are cut off just as the flower buds commence to form, for the essential oils are most abundant at that period. The shoots are tied in bundles and hung in a dry, airy shed or room. In a few weeks the leaves are stripped off and packed into bottles.

To provide fresh green shoots for winter use, a few plants may be lifted, cut back to 6 in. and planted in a deep box filled with ordinary garden soil. If the box is placed in a warm greenhouse young growths will continue to form throughout the winter.

Needs Winter Protection. In cold districts Tarragon plants need protecting with ashes, which should be heaped up around the roots in autumn. To maintain a vigorous stock it is necessary to raise a few plants annually. These are obtained by inserting cuttings in a sand propagating bed in a cold frame or greenhouse in spring or summer. French Tarragon, the most esteemed variety, rarely, if ever, produces seeds. Seeds of Tarragon offered commercially give rise to plants of an inferior kind.

TARWEED. Madia, which see.

TASMANIAN LAUREL. Coprosma and Anopterus, which see.

TASSEL FLOWER. Emilia, which see; also Amaranthus caudatus.

TAXODIUM (Taxo'dium). Leaf-losing and evergreen cone-bearing trees of great interest. They are attractive throughout summer by reason of their bright green leaves; moreover, the foliage of the leaf-losing (deciduous) kinds is particularly beautiful in spring because of its delicate color, and again in autumn, when it turns to yellow and rich brown before falling.

Taxodium belongs to the Taxodium family, Taxodiaceae, and the name is taken from Taxus, Yew, and the Greek *eidos*, like, a reference to the shape of the leaves.

These trees succeed in cultivation both in swampy and in drier ground. They even thrive when entirely surrounded by water. In a state of nature, T. ascendens, the Pond Cypress, and T. distichum, the Bald Cypress, cover large areas of swampy ground in the southeastern United States.

When growing in wet land, the trunk of T. distichum becomes swollen at the base, and from the main roots woody structures are produced which grow upwards and above the surrounding water or wet ground, sometimes to a height of several feet. These growths, which are called "knees," are sometimes 10 ft. high. Their function appears to be to carry air to the submerged roots.

Bald Cypress or Southern Cypress. Taxodium distichum, the Bald Cypress or Southern Cypress, grows into a very large tree, 100-150 ft. tall in the South, with a trunk of considerable girth. Although it is hardy in the North, it does not grow so big there.

A Tree for Moist or Swampy Ground. Bald Cypresses may be set out in permanent places when they are about 2 ft. high. They can be planted in very moist and even swampy ground, but thrive best where the surface is dry and the water table 12 or 15 in. beneath the surface. Young trees are usually dense and fastigiate (narrow-erect) in habit, rather like a Lombardy Poplar, but the heads gradually widen out as the trees approach maturity. There may be some difficulty in establishing a definite leading shoot, and thinning of the upper branches may be necessary during the earlier years. Later, a definite central lead is more easily maintained.

The Bald Cypress is an excellent tree for planting on the sides of lakes or streams, on islands or in other places subject to flooding, as well as in naturally moist ground. It is also a useful tree for places away from water. Where the ground is naturally on the dry side, its growth is slow. Several varieties of T. distichum are recognized, including fastigiatum, pendens and pyramidalis.

Pond Cypress. This is the common name of T. ascendens, a kind closely related to the Bald Cypress, T. distichum. The Pond Cypress is usually a smaller and narrower tree than the typical T. distichum, has less spreading leaves and the "knees" are usually less numerous and prominent. It is native from Virginia to Florida and Alabama but is hardy much further north. It requires the same cultural conditions as the Bald Cypress.

The Montezuma Cypress. This Mexican native, T. mucronatum, in its natural home is evergreen, but it is reported to be deciduous (leaf-losing) when planted towards the northern limit of the area in which it will grow. It is suitable for planting in California, Florida and other mild climates.

The Montezuma Cypress is extremely long-lived and with age becomes enormous in diameter and girth. It does not grow so tall as the Bald Cypress. One of the most famous trees in the world is the specimen of this species growing in the churchyard at El Tule. This enormous specimen must have been a large tree at the time of the conquest of Mexico. Some authorities believe it to be older than the oldest Big Tree (Sequoiadendron).

Propagation. Seeds form the best means of propagation. They should be sown in flats in a greenhouse or broadcast in a bed of soil in a cold frame in spring. The young trees should be planted in moist soil in a nursery and given some protection during the first winter, if very cold weather is experienced. The ends of the shoots are likely to be killed while the trees are young, but with age the tree is hardier.

Economic Uses. The timber, though light in weight and not strong, is of considerable importance by reason of its ability to withstand wet conditions without undue decay. It is much used for water pipes, vats, cooperage, lining vats and tanks such as are used in the chemical trade, general carpentry, ventilators, greenhouse construction and many other purposes for which this quality is essential.

TAXUS: THE YEWS

Splendid Evergreens for Many Landscape Uses

Taxus (Tax'us) are beautiful evergreen trees and shrubs that are natives of North America, Europe and Asia. They belong to the Yew family, Taxaceae. The name is an old Latin one for Taxus baccata, the European Yew.

The leaves are small and, in most cases, are dark green on wild trees, but they are variable in color on cultivated forms. Male and female flowers are usually produced on different trees in early spring. The male flowers are yellow and produced in small catkins; the female flowers are greenish, very small, and difficult to find. The fruit is a small, hard, dark green or brownish seed surrounded, except at the apex, by a

The spreading form of the Japanese Yew, Taxus cuspidata, is here used effectively as a screen. It is planted in a soil bank supported by a wall.

fleshy envelope that is red and juicy when ripe.

Shoots, leaves and seeds contain poisonous properties, and have proved fatal to both human beings and cattle. This is especially true of the English Yew. The flesh surrounding the seeds, however, is not toxic, and it is interesting to note that deer eat the foliage of Taxus cuspidata with relish and without apparent harm.

The Japanese Yew, Taxus cuspidata, has been sheared well and forms a magnificent hedge.

It is generally understood that shoots and leaves are in their most dangerous state when partly withered.

Valuable for Landscaping. Yews are among the finest evergreens for landscaping uses. In addition to the wild kinds, there are numerous garden varieties and hybrids which show great variation in height, habit of growth and other important characteristics and this makes it possible for the planter to select from among them those that suit his purposes best.

Yews, allowed to grow without clipping or shearing, develop into magnificent specimen plants, but they stand pruning well and are among the finest of all evergreens for planting as formal hedges and for topiary work. (See Topiary Work.) The prostrate and spreading kinds are effective ground covers.

Yews may be transplanted without undue difficulty even when quite large. Should they outgrow their allotted space, they may be pruned back severely and will "break" (put forth new shoots) even from thick old branches that have been cut back. In this respect they differ from many other evergreens.

Yews Thrive in Most Soils. Very fine old trees are often found growing naturally on limestone soils, but they also grow on sandy loam, heavy

Taxus cuspidata espaliered against a brick wall.

loam and on peat. They do not succeed where the subsoil is waterlogged, and even old trees may be killed by the sudden raising of the natural water level, as is brought about by flooding or by the silting up of ditches or open drains, obstructions in drainpipes or by grading operations.

Mulching the soil surface with old, rotted manure, rich compost, leaf mold or other suitable organic material is of great benefit. An application of a complete fertilizer each spring is beneficial.

When to Plant Yew Trees. When the trees are moved with a mass of soil attached to the roots, transplanting may be carried out in early autumn or early spring or, in mild climates, in winter; however, when there is considerable root disturbance, September and April are the best months for the work. Whether specimen or hedge plants are planted, the ground should be prepared beforehand and, if there is any danger of waterlogging, arrangements must be made for draining the ground. If, when the trees are received, the roots appear to be dry, soak them with water before planting, and give them a good watering as soon as the work is completed. If the weather is hot and dry the trees should be shaded from hot sun for a week or two, and sprayed twice a day with water. The removal of the ends of some of the branches will assist in re-establishing the trees by lessening the strain on the roots.

Should the leaves fall, there need be no cause for alarm; it is one of Nature's means of assisting recovery. If, however, the leaves shrivel or turn brown and remain on the branches, root action is not proceeding in a satisfactory way. In such a case, cut the branches back, spray the trees several times a day, and shade from sun until new shoots appear. Severe pruning, when required by old trees, should be done in March or April.

Pruning. Yews required for trees must be carefully pruned from early life; it is important that the growth of the lower branches should not interfere with the leading shoots. Those Yews which have a tendency to produce several shoots from the base are the best to select for hedges or for topiary work. Pruning may be done at any time from spring to fall.

Hedges and clipped specimens should be sheared in spring, just before new growth begins, and again about midsummer if necessary.

Raising Yew Trees from Seeds. Yew trees can be raised by sowing seeds as soon as ripe in a frame, or out of doors in spring. Seeds to be sown out of doors may be kept in sand from

The dense, dark green Taxus cuspidata nana makes a magnificent specimen when trained as an espalier.

Young plants of Taxus propagated from cuttings.

the time of collection to sowing. When quantities of Yew seeds are required, they should be collected as soon as the flesh of the fruit begins to turn red, for the ripe fruits are eagerly eaten by birds. The seeds can be freed from the flesh by washing.

Taking Cuttings. Cuttings of all kinds of Yew can also be rooted by placing them in a bed of sand, or sand and peat moss, in a cold frame in July or August and leaving them there all winter, or by inserting them in a greenhouse propagating bench in October or November. This is one of the methods adopted for increasing varieties which cannot be reared true from seed. Grafting is also practiced on stocks of common types previously established in pots. This work must be carried out in a warm greenhouse in spring. Yew can also be increased by layering and air layering.

The Japanese Yew. In most parts of North America the Japanese Yew, Taxus cuspidata, and its varieties and hybrids are the most valuable kinds.

When Taxus cuspidata is raised from seeds

The bright red berrylike fruits of Yews contrast well with their dark green foliage.

Taxus cuspidata, when raised from seeds, develops an upright habit of growth. It is one of the finest hardy evergreens.

it develops into symmetrical, broad-conical, upright-growing specimens, each with a well-defined central trunk or leader. Such plants are generally offered for sale by nurseries under the name T. cuspidata capitata. If plants are propagated by means of cuttings taken from side branches of these capitate specimens, they do not develop into tall, conical plants with well-defined central leaders, but, instead, form broad-spreading specimens without any definite central trunk or leader. Such plants are sold by nurseries as Taxus cuspidata. Botanically, both

When propagated from cuttings of side shoots, Taxus cuspidata develops as a broad-spreading, bushy specimen.

types are Taxus cuspidata; they are precisely the same species; the difference in appearance is due only to the method of propagation employed.

The Japanese Yew is hardier than the English Yew and grows more quickly. It withstands the winters of New England and under the most favorable conditions will develop into a tree 50 ft. tall but in cultivation is usually considerably smaller than this. It is a native of Japan, Korea and Manchuria.

Among the best-defined varieties of the Japanese Yew are T. cuspidata aurea, with leaves slightly variegated with yellow (this variety is likely to appear brownish and unattractive in winter); T. cuspidata aurescens, a low-growing variety in which the young leaves are bright yellow (this variety is more tender than most; it requires a sheltered location); T. cuspidata densa, a very compact, slow-growing variety with deep green foliage; and T. cuspidata fastigiata, a dwarf, erect columnar kind.

T. cuspidata nana, a dark green, dense, bushy form of moderately fast growth, is one of the best evergreens for low hedges, foundation plantings and similar uses. This is the plant frequently offered in nurseries as T. cuspidata brevifolia and T. brevifolia; it should not be confused with the T. brevifolia of botanists, which is a native of the Pacific Northwest and is much more tender.

Other well-defined varieties include T. cuspidata nigra, with very dark green foliage; T. cuspidata ovata, a kind with leaves that are broader than normal; T. cuspidata pyramidalis, a variety of distinct pyramidal growth habit; T. cuspidata Thayerae, a wide-spreading variety with more or less horizontal branches with foliage of a type that gives them a somewhat feathery appearance.

The Media Hybrids. Between the Japanese Yew, T. cuspidata, and the English Yew, T.

The spreading type of Taxus cuspidata used effectively as a foundation planting.

baccata, a series of very valuable hybrids have been raised. These are classed together under the group name of Taxus media. They are somewhat less hardy than the Japanese Yew but they may be depended upon as far north as Massachusetts and perhaps further north. They include a most interesting selection of plant forms and habits.

Among the best of these hybrids are T. media Andersonii, an erect, freely branching variety; T. media Brownii, erect and conical and growing to an ultimate height of about 8 ft.; T. media Hatfieldii, a shrubby, conical variety with spreading branches; T. media Hicksii, a dark green, bushy kind with many very erect branches; T. media Kelseyi, a dense, upright plant that is said to fruit heavily; T. media pyramidalis, erect and of loose-branching habit; T. media Wardii, an erect, compact variety; T. media Wellesleyi, a broad, erect-growing variety.

The English Yew. This magnificent evergreen, Taxus baccata, is generally less reliable and less useful in most parts of the United States than it is in Europe. It is well adapted for growing in the Pacific Northwest. In the East it is hardy as far north as southern New York and parts of New England, but it is generally not so satisfactory for those areas as the Japanese Yew and the media hybrids between the Japanese Yew and the English Yew. Some varieties of the English Yew, notably the low T. baccata repandens, are much hardier than the typical form of T. baccata. The English Yew grows more slowly than the Japanese Yew and the hybrid kinds.

A closely sheared specimen of the English Yew, Taxus baccata.

Taxus media variety Hicksii is an erect-growing Yew that makes a splendid solitary specimen and is useful for planting as hedges.

Taxus baccata is a densely branched tree when growing in the open; when growing closely together, the trees may become branchless for a considerable height, and then have a head of moderate size. Under favorable conditions the English Yew grows 30-60 feet high with a trunk 9-20 ft. in girth. Very large and old trees are often found in churchyards in Great Britain; the Yew has been associated with churches and churchyards for hundreds of years. The spirally arranged, narrow leaves are dark green, $\frac{1}{2}$-$1\frac{1}{4}$ in. long, and each of the solitary hard seeds is enclosed in a red fleshy aril or cup.

There are many well-marked varieties which differ from the type in habit, size and color of leaves, and in one instance in the color of the aril of the fruit.

Trees 1,000 Years Old. It is suggested that some of the oldest trees of Taxus baccata in the British Isles exceed the age of 1,000 years, and this may well be correct. Some of these trees are

The Dovaston Yew, Taxus baccata Dovastonii, has distinctly drooping branchlets.

mere shells bearing living branches, and have probably remained in much the same state for many generations.

The English Yew has the peculiarity of producing young erect stems from near its base; growing close to the trunk, they sometimes become enclosed by wood of the old tree. In these cases a transverse section cut from a trunk may show several enclosed stems. It is possible that some old trees may even have been rejuvenated by one of these secondary stems, and that the original trunk has disappeared.

Varieties of English Yew. There are numerous varieties of the English Yew. One of the most useful and hardiest is T. baccata repandens, which is of neatly prostrate habit with arching, lax branches and bluish-green leaves.

T. baccata Dovastonii is a very distinct and handsome variety with horizontal branches and pendent branchlets; the leaves are dark green and larger than those of the type. It is sometimes called the Westfelton Yew.

T. baccata lutea (fructu-luteo) is exactly like the common English Yew and grows as large, but the fleshy covering of the seed is golden instead of the familiar red. T. baccata gracilis pendula is a very graceful Yew with weeping side branchlets.

The varieties epacrioides and ericoides are of low, compact habit, with small leaves, and are suitable for planting in the rock garden. T. baccata expansa is a wide-spreading kind of low stature suitable for covering banks. T. baccata Foxii is another dwarf variety suitable for the rock garden.

Golden-leaved Yews. A very attractive variety of T. baccata is named adpressa. It is of compact, bushy habit, growing 10-12 ft. high, with short, dark green leaves, $\frac{1}{4}$-$\frac{1}{2}$ in. long. There are several subvarieties of it, including adpressa aurea, a very handsome shrub with golden leaves; and argentea, with white and green leaves, a less attractive shrub than aurea.

Other varieties of the English Yew with golden leaves are T. baccata aurea, Barronii, Dovastonii aureo-variegata, elegantissima and semperaurea. T. baccata Barronii is of specially good color, and Dovastonii aureo-variegata and elegantissima quickly grow into large bushes.

The Irish Yew, T. baccata stricta (fastigiata),

The Irish Yew, Taxus baccata variety stricta, is of very formal appearance. Without shearing, it develops into a narrow, erect specimen.

is well known by reason of its stiff and erect habit. It is useful for planting as formal avenues and is much used in churchyards in Great Britain. There are several varieties with colored leaves—for example, fastigiata aurea, the Golden Irish Yew; fastigiata grandis and Standishii, also with golden leaves, and argentea, a less useful form with silver-variegated leaves. The Irish Yew is sometimes called the Florence Court Yew, because the two original specimens were found near Florence Court in Ireland.

The Ground Hemlock or Canadian Yew, T. canadensis, is a native of eastern North America as far north as Newfoundland. It attains a maximum height of about 6 ft. but is usually lower and forms a more or less straggling or nearly prostrate shrub. Its foliage does not possess the rich, dark green coloring of other Yews but tends to be yellowish; for these reasons it is less useful as a garden plant. Nevertheless the Ground Hemlock can be used to good effect as a ground covering under trees and in woodlands where sheltered conditions can be provided. It is not suitable for planting in exposed wind-swept locations. It is an especially good plant for setting beneath evergreens.

Other Yews. The Western Yew is native from Montana to California and British Columbia. This is the true Taxus brevifolia and must be clearly distinguished from the plant commonly sold in nurseries as T. brevifolia, which is really T. cuspidata nana. In its native home the Western Yew makes a tree 45 ft. or more tall but it is not a common plant in cultivation. The Chinese Yew is Taxus chinensis, a kind which, as its name suggests, is a native of China. It is hardy in the North but is not common. In its native home it forms a tree about 50 ft. tall.

TEA. Tea of commerce is the dried young leaves of an evergreen shrub, Thea sinensis. The bush is a native of China, but has long been cultivated in India, Ceylon, Japan, Java, Natal and other countries; more recently it has become an important agricultural crop in Nyasaland.

The best-quality Teas, known as pekoe, are produced from the tips of the shoots and the very young, partly developed leaves. From larger leaves, second-rate qualities, known as souchongs, are produced, and inferior qualities are known under the term of congoes. Dust and bits of broken stem are also disposed of as poor-grade Teas. See Thea.

TEABERRY. Gaultheria procumbens, which see.

TEA, NEW JERSEY. Ceanothus americanus, which see.

TEAK. The wood of a tropical tree, Tectona grandis, a native of India, Burma, Siam and other parts of the Far East. It grows 120-150 ft. high with a long trunk, free from branches for a good part of its length, sometimes 90-100 ft.

Teakwood is very popular for many kinds of work, particularly for shipbuilding, paneling, and furniture. It is also widely used for carving in Far Eastern countries.

The wood is oily in character, very durable, does not split easily after seasoning, and keeps its shape well after working. When green, it is very heavy and sinks in water; therefore it is usual to girdle and kill the trees two years before they are felled, in order that, with drying, they may become light enough to float. After cutting, they are hauled to the nearest river by elephants and floated down to the mouth on flood water.

As Teak is one of the most useful and valuable timbers in use, very great care is taken of the forests. Felling is by selection, and only a percentage of the trees over a certain diameter are allowed to be felled at one time. By this means the forests are kept fully stocked with good timber.

TEA, LABRADOR. Ledum groenlandicum, which see.

TEA, OSWEGO. Monarda didyma, which see.

TEASEL. See Dipsacus.

TEA TREE, AUSTRALIAN. Leptospermum laevigatum, which see.

TECOMA (Te'coma; Teco'ma). Tender shrubs that occur naturally from the southern United States to Argentina, and may be cultivated outdoors in the far South. Many of the plants previously known by this name are now included in other genera such as Bignonia, Campsis, Doxantha, Pandorea, Podranea, Stenolobium and Tabebuia, which see. Tecoma belongs to the Bignonia family, the Bignoniaceae.

The name is derived from the Mexican name Tecomaxochitl.

Tecomas grow well in any fairly good soil and in full sun. They may be propagated by seeds, cuttings and by air layering. The one most likely to be cultivated is T. Garrocha, a native of the Argentine that grows about 5 ft. tall and has yellow or salmon-yellow flowers. A plant named T. Smithii is thought to be a hybrid between Stenolobium stans and Tecomaria capensis; it breeds true from seeds.

TECOMARIA CAPENSIS — *Cape Honeysuckle* (Tecomar'ia). An evergreen vine or shrub, native to South Africa, that grows well in the far South. This species belongs in the Bignonia family, the Bignoniaceae, and is sometimes known in gardens as Tecoma capensis. The name Tecomaria is derived from Tecoma, a genus of plants which it closely resembles.

Tecomaria capensis is a very handsome plant and, if clipped or pruned, it can be used with good effect as a hedge. Its flowers are orange-red to scarlet and very decorative. They are borne for a long season.

Tecomaria capensis thrives in any fairly good soil, prefers full sun and is easily propagated by seeds, cuttings and by air layering. A few other species of Tecomaria are known to botanists but do not appear to be in cultivation. As wild plants, they occur in South Africa and South America.

TECOPHILAEA—*Chilean Crocus* (Tecophilae'a; Tecophil'aea). There are but two kinds; both are small bulb plants, natives of Chile. The name Tecophilaea commemorates Tecofila, the daughter of Billotti, a botanist. They belong to the Bloodwort family, the Haemodoraceae.

A Lovely Blue Flower. Tecophilaea cyanocrocus, known as the Chilean Crocus, is a small flower. The narrow, glossy green leaves, 2-3 in. high, are followed in spring by flower stems, 3-4 in. high, each with a flower bearing a superficial resemblance to a Crocus, with broad, obovate perianth segments. Each flower is about 1½ in. long, and is of an intense blue, like that of the finest Gentian, shading to a white center. There are in cultivation varieties of pale blue and lilac shades, but these are not nearly so beautiful and desirable as the pure blue type.

This exquisite plant, which was discovered at La Dehesa in the foothills of the Andes, near Santiago, in Chile, in 1872, and then introduced to cultivation, has always remained very rare in gardens.

Not Easy to Manage. In cultivation Tecophilaea is not easy to manage. It requires light, well-drained loam and a sunny location; protection

The beautiful but difficult-to-grow blue Chilean Crocus, Tecophilaea cyanocrocus.

from wet during its dormant season is an advantage. It is safest perhaps in an alpine house (cool greenhouse), where the watering can be regulated at will. Tecophilaea is not hardy in the North. T. cyanocrocus is a flower of the very greatest brilliance and beauty, and a treasure which every lover of choice bulbs and rare alpine plants would enjoy possessing.

TECTARIA (Tectar'ia; Tect'aria). A large genus of cool greenhouse and hothouse ferns of wide distribution throughout the tropics. Many of its members were previously included in the genus Aspidium and some other genera. They belong to the family Polypodiaceae. The name is derived from *tectum,* roof, and refers to the coverings of the spore bodies.

Tectarias are comparatively easy to grow successfully in a minimum temperature of 60 degrees F. They are best potted in spring, as new growth is starting, in a mixture of 3 parts sandy peat and 1 part loam. Rather loose potting is recommended. They need plenty of water in summer, and appreciate light shade and a moist atmosphere maintained by frequent syringing. The supply of water should, of course, be reduced considerably in winter. New plants are best raised from spores (see Ferns).

Handsome kinds include: T. crenata, fronds 2 ft. or more long by 18 in. across, from the Philippines; T. decurrens, 2-4 ft., Moluccas; T. latifolia, 2-3 ft., Polynesia; T. Lawrenceana, 2 ft., Madagascar; T. polymorpha, 2-4 ft., Malaya; T. Ridleyanum, 1-1½ ft., West Indies; and T. varians, 3-4 ft., West Africa.

TECTONA GRANDIS—*Teak* (Tec'tona). A very large tree, native to Malaya, India, Burma and adjacent regions, and sometimes planted for ornament in the far South. It is of great economic importance as the source of teakwood (see Teak). Tectona belongs in the Vervain family, the Verbenaceae. Its name is derived from the Indian name for this tree.

Tectona grandis thrives in tropical regions and may be propagated by seeds, air layering and cuttings. It is reported to thrive best on calcareous (limy) soils.

TELANTHERA. Alternanthera, which see.

TELEGRAPH PLANT. Desmodium motorium (gyrans), which see.

TELLIMA—*Fringe Cup* (Telli'ma; Tell'ima). A small group of some five or six species of hardy plants native to western North America and belonging to the Saxifrage family, Saxifragaceae. The name Tellima is an anagram of Mitella, in which genus Tellima was formerly included.

Tellima grandiflora is the only kind of any garden worth. In effect it is like a strong-growing Heuchera with rather lush foliage, and simple spikes of greenish-white flowers, 12-18 in. tall. In spite of a lack of color the flowers have grace and a certain quaint charm.

This is a useful plant for filling cool, dampish corners on the outskirts of the rock garden and the shrubbery, or for ground cover in the wild or woodland garden. It is increased easily by division of the roots, and blooms in April and May.

TELOPEA (Telo'pea; Telop'ea). Very beautiful evergreen trees and shrubs, embracing two species from Australia and one from Tasmania, which bear showy heads of crimson flowers. They were previously included in the genus Embothrium, and belong to the family Proteaceae. The name is from *telopas,* seen at a distance, and refers to the brilliant flowers.

Tender Shrubs. The Telopeas are suitable for growing in California. They thrive best in light, peaty, loamy soil. Propagation is by layering.

The Waratah, T. speciosissima, is a shrub up to 8 ft. tall, with glossy leaves 9 in. long and dense heads of coral-pink flowers with crimson bracts. T. oreades will grow to 40 ft. tall, bearing terminal heads of crimson flowers. T. truncata, from Tasmania, has rich crimson flower heads.

TEMPERATURE. Both atmospheric and soil temperatures are important factors in gardening. If these are either too high or too low the rate of growth of plants is reduced or stopped. Temperatures within critical ranges often determine, in part at least, the functioning of such physiological processes as seed germination, the instigation of flower buds and whether a plant remains dormant or grows actively.

Out of doors the gardener can do comparatively little to modify temperatures, but what modest results he can accomplish are often

This Chinese Evergreen, Aglaonema modestum, has suffered from being exposed to excessively low temperatures, causing its leaves to wilt. Tropical plants like this require a minimum temperature of 55 to 60 degrees.

important. By selecting sheltered planting locations, such as nooks against buildings, he can often succeed in growing plants that elsewhere in his garden would be killed by winter cold. Mulches placed on the soil around plants keep the roots cooler in summer and warmer in winter. In some parts of North America smudge pots are used to produce a smoke that blankets the garden and prevents too rapid loss of heat from the soil at night.

Indoor Temperatures. The maintenance of suitable temperatures is an essential detail in the cultivation of plants in greenhouses. The temperature can be maintained by careful ventilation and the regulation of the warmth provided by hot-water pipes, or other means used for heating purposes. The temperature ought to be as regular as possible; there should be a fixed minimum temperature at night, the minimum varying according to the kinds of plants being grown.

When, in the morning, owing to the increased warmth out of doors, the temperature indoors has risen 10 degrees above the minimum, the greenhouse must be ventilated, and the ventilation should be increased later when outdoor weather conditions permit. In the afternoon, as the warmth of the sun declines, the ventilation should be reduced, and finally the ventilators should be closed before the sun has ceased to shine on the roof of the greenhouse.

The ventilation of hotbeds and cold frames follows the same principles as those outlined for greenhouses. See also Ventilation.

TEMPLETONIA RETUSA — *Coralbush* (Templeton'ia). A winter-flowering Australian shrub of the Pea family, Leguminosae, named in honor of John Templeton, an Irish botanist.

This shrub is sometimes cultivated outdoors

Ventilating a cold frame by propping up the sash. This is done to prevent the temperature inside the frame from rising too high for the plants it contains.

in warm regions such as California and Florida and may also be grown as a greenhouse plant. When grown indoors, it requires the same culture as Acacia, which see. It attains a height of about 6 ft. and may be propagated by seeds and cuttings. Its flowers are pea-shaped and red.

TENDER. A term used by gardeners to indicate those plants which are not sufficiently hardy to be grown out of doors permanently in a particular region or locality because of their inability to withstand winter cold. As used in this Encyclopedia, the term, unqualified, means that the plants to which it is applied are not generally hardy in the Northeastern and North Central United States and adjacent Canada.

TENDRIL. Slender or threadlike organs, possessed by some plants. The tendrils twist themselves around supports with which they come in contact, and thus enable the plant to climb. Tendrils may represent modifications of stems or leaves or even of inflorescences (flower clusters). They are conspicuously present in Peas, Sweet Peas, Cucumbers, Grapes, Passion Flowers.

TEN-WEEKS STOCK. See Stock.

TEPHROSIA (Tephros'ia). A group of shrubs and herbaceous plants of little horticultural importance. They belong to the Pea family, the Leguminosae. The name is derived from *tephros,* ash-colored, and refers to the appearance of the foliage.

In southern Florida, T. candida, a shrub about 10 ft. tall and a native of India, is sometimes planted as a windbreak. Its flowers are white. T. virginiana, a perennial 2 ft. tall, occurs as a native from Maine to Florida and New Mexico and is rather pretty and worth growing in a wild garden. Its flowers are yellowish-purple. Tephrosias are propagated by seeds. They need dryish soils and open locations.

TERMINALIA (Terminal'ia). A group of trees and shrubs belonging to the Combretum family, the Combretaceae, and mostly natives of tropical Asia. The name is derived from *terminus,* end, and alludes to the fact that the leaves are frequently in clusters at the ends of the shoots. Several kinds of Terminalia produce valuable timber in their native countries and some are used as sources of dyes and tannin. Some kinds are planted for ornament in the warm regions, including southern Florida. The fruits are edible.

Terminalias thrive in a variety of soils. They are propagated by seeds. The most common kind in Florida is T. Catappa, the Indian Almond, Tropical Almond or Myrobalan. This is an excellent street tree. It attains a maximum height of about 80 ft. and casts dense shade. The leaves assume handsome red coloring before they fall, which happens twice each year. T. Catappa is a native of Malaya.

Other species that are likely to be grown in Florida are T. Arjuna, 80 ft., a native of India; T. australis, 10 ft., a native of Brazil; T. Muelleri, a small tree, a native of Australia; T. Saffordii, a native of Guam.

TERMINAL SHOOT. A term used by gardeners to indicate the shoot which forms the end of the main stem or of a main branch of a tree or plant. All other shoots are called side shoots or laterals.

TERNSTROEMIA (Ternstroe'mia). Evergreen trees and shrubs, related to Camellia and belonging to the Tea family, Theaceae. The name honors the Swedish naturalist, Christopher Ternstroem.

The only kind cultivated is Ternstroemia japonica (Cleyera japonica), which forms a bush up to 12 ft. tall, with glossy green leaves, and white or pale yellow flowers produced from the axils of the leaves early in the year. It is a native of Japan.

Small plants make decorative specimens when grown in pots in a cool greenhouse. They are potted in a compost of equal parts of loam and leaf mold, with coarse sand added. In March or April the plants are transferred to slightly larger pots. The pots must be well drained and water given in moderation, or the tips of the leaves will turn brown. Very little pruning is necessary; it is sufficient to shorten the extra-vigorous shoots to maintain the symmetry of the plants. In the warmer parts of the United States this plant may be grown outdoors.

Propagation is by inserting pieces of young shoots in a propagating bench in spring or summer. They are set under a bell jar or in a close propagating case in the greenhouse and, when rooted, are potted singly in 3-in. pots.

TERRARIUMS: ATTRACTIVE DECORATIONS FOR THE HOME
Their Construction, Planting and Care

A terrarium is a transparent box or other container in which plants are cultivated indoors. Its chief purpose is to ensure that the plants it contains are surrounded by a more humid atmosphere than that of the room in which the terrarium is placed; for this reason it is usually fitted with a top, also transparent. To prevent too much humidity inside the terrarium, means of ventilation should be provided; for this purpose an adjustable top is often used.

Glass, supported in a metal or wooden frame or fitted together with clamps, is most commonly used for the construction of terrariums but transparent plastics are also employed.

The base of a terrarium normally consists of a metal or metal-lined tray. This contains soil, in which plants are set directly, or a layer of gravel, peat moss or other moisture-holding material on which potted plants are stood.

Terrariums may be elaborate or simple. An old aquarium, with holes drilled in its bottom for drainage purposes and a sheet of glass as a cover, serves excellently; other containers that are sometimes used are fish bowls, brandy glasses, and large bottles. Because some of these have no holes in their bottoms, free drainage is not possible, and great care must be taken in watering.

Terrariums may be used as decorative furnishings, as plant hospitals in which specimens which have suffered from poor treatment are

In rooms where the atmosphere is too dry to grow African Violets (and other plants) terrariums are recommended. This transparent plastic terrarium accommodates one plant. It is very decorative.

nursed back to health, and as propagating cases. Many cuttings that will not root successfully in an open room will do so in the moister atmosphere of a terrarium. A terrarium makes it possible to grow successfully in the average house many plants that are unlikely to thrive in an open room—many kinds of Orchids, for example.

What to Plant. If the plants are to be set directly in soil rather than kept in pots, they should be arranged in such fashion that a delightful miniature landscape or decorative effect is secured. It is important that all the plants used in any one terrarium be of kinds that succeed under the same general conditions; it is folly to plant, for example, desert Cacti and moisture-loving tropical Ferns together, or native

Even a terrarium that is not covered offers shelter from drafts and retains more atmospheric moisture than the surrounding air. Plants grown in such a terrarium usually thrive better than those in an open room.

Even Cacti may benefit from the protection afforded by a terrarium. This plastic terrarium is made in the form of a miniature greenhouse.

plants gathered from northern woods with tropical foliage plants. There is a vast variety of plants from which to make selections. The following are suggestions.

For a terrarium located in a warm room with good light but little direct sunshine: African Violets, Aglaonemas (such as A. modestum, the Chinese Evergreen), Begonias of low-growing kinds, Blood Leaf (Iresine), Calatheas, Crotons, Cryptanthus, Dracaenas. Ferns (small-growing, tropical kinds), Fatshederas, Ficus pumila, Fittonias, Palms in small sizes, Peperomias, Pileas, Prayer Plant (Maranta leuconeura variety Kerchoveana), Scindapsus and Syngoniums.

For a terrarium located in a cool room in good light but little direct sunshine: Acorus gramineus, Boxwood (Buxus sempervirens variety suffruticosa), Coprosma, Daphne odora, evergreen Euonymus, Fatshedera, Ficus pumila, English Ivy (small-leaved varieties), seedling Mahonias, Lysimachia Nummularia, Pachysandra, Pittosporums, Primroses, Strawberry Begonia, seedling Yews.

For a terrarium located in a warm room and in sun: All kinds of Cacti as well as other kinds of succulent plants.

Woodland plants for a terrarium located in a cool room with good light but not direct sunshine: Antennarias, Bleeding Hearts, small Ferns including Christmas Fern, Holly Fern and Maidenhair Fern, Hepatica, Partridgeberry, Pipsissewa, Rattlesnake Plantain, Synthyris, Violets, Wintergreen, and seedlings of many trees such as Cedars, Hemlocks, Hollies, Junipers and Pines.

Planting the Terrarium. When the plants in a terrarium are grown in individual pots, their arrangement is a simple matter and adjustments can be made as the plants grow. A somewhat different situation exists when the plants are set directly in a soil mixture in the base of the terrarium.

Glass vessels of many types are used as modern terrariums.